Elijah Pierce

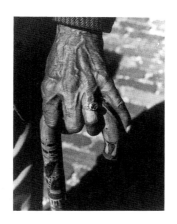

Woodcarver

ELIJAH PIERCE

WOODCARVER

COLUMBUS MUSEUM OF ART

OHIO

1992

DISTRIBUTED BY

UNIVERSITY OF WASHINGTON PRESS

SEATTLE AND LONDON

This volume has been published in conjunction with the exhibition *Elijah Pierce, Woodcarver*, organized by the Columbus Museum of Art, Curator of European Art E. Jane Connell in association with Curator of American Art Nannette V. Maciejunes.

Principal funding for the exhibition and publication has been provided by The Henry Luce Foundation, Inc. Additional funding for the publication and educational programs has been provided by the National Endowment for the Arts and the Ohio Humanities Council.

Editor: Norma Roberts
Copy editors: Carolee Belkin Walker and Martha Morss
Publications Assistants: Cheryl Wipert and Andrew Male

Library of Congress Cataloging in Publication Data
Elijah Pierce, woodcarver / [editor Norma Roberts].
        p.   cm.
     Published in conjunction with the exhibition of same name,
  organized by the Columbus Museum of Art, curators : E. Jane Connell
  and Nannette V. Maciejunes.
     ISBN 0-295-97252-1 (University of Washington Press : pbk. : alk.
  paper) : $35.00
     1. Pierce, Elijah—Exhibitions. 2. Afro-American wood-carving—
  —Exhibitions. 3. Folk art—United States—Exhibitions.
  I. Roberts, Norma J. II. Columbus Museum of Art.
  NK9798.P44A4   1992
  730'.92–dc20   91-78320

Cover: Detail of *Crucifixion*, cat. no. 99
Back cover: *The Place of My Birth*, cat. no. 1

Photography Credits
Photographs of works of art reproduced in this catalogue have been supplied by the owners or custodians of the works. Exceptions and additional credits follow. The numbers are catalogue numbers unless otherwise specified.

Gavin Ashworth: 78; Dirk Bakker: 121; Jeff Bates: 1–4, 6–14, 16, 18–25, 28, 30, 33, 36–40, 42–43, 46–48, 52–57, 60–62, 66, 70–73, 79, 84, 86–88, 90–91, 93, 96, 98–101, 103–104, 106, 109, 115, 122, 124, 129, 131–139, 142, 144, 147–149, 154, 157, 160, 164–165, 167–169, 171–172; Charles F. Bechtold: 67, 141, 143, 146, 166; Steven Benson: 108, 130, 151, 153, 159, 173; Joel Breger: figs. 3, 8, 9, 12; Chester Brummel: 5; Geoffrey Kerrigan: 77; Frank C. Lewis: 126; Fredrik Marsh: 83; Bernard Mehl: half-title page; Owen Murphy: 15; Charles Nairn: 92, 116, 119, 123; Edward Owen: 140; Ted Spiegel: p. 195; William P. Steele: 128; Michael Tropea: 45, 58, 75–76; Jeffrey Wolf: p. 233

Design and production by Scott Hudson, Marquand Books, Seattle, Washington
Type output by The Type Gallery, Seattle, Washington, in Palatino, Martin Gothic, and Biltmore.
Printed and bound in Japan by Toppan Printing Co., Ltd. on 128 gsm New Age

CONTENTS

PREFACE

In 1974, the Columbus Museum of Art acquired four carvings by Elijah Pierce. This important acquisition took place soon after the museum had organized *Elijah Pierce, Wood Carver* in November–December 1973—one of the first exhibitions of Pierce's work to be held in a major public institution. For the next ten years, the museum and the Columbus community watched as Pierce gained international recognition as a prominent African American artist.

After Pierce's death in May 1984, the future disposition of the large personal collection of his work became a serious concern to his family, the community at large, and the museum. Budd Harris Bishop, director of the museum at that time, felt strongly that the museum would be the logical and appropriate repository for the Pierce collection, as it was for the paintings of George Bellows, another twentieth-century American artist who made his home in Columbus. When informed that Estelle Pierce, the artist's widow, wished to relinquish the collection to a worthy home, the museum took immediate action to acquire it. On May 24, 1985, the carvings, study objects, and archival materials—together numbering about two hundred items—were purchased from the Pierce estate. The largest collection of works by a single artist in the museum's permanent holdings and the most comprehensive group of Pierce works to be maintained by a public institution was thereby established. Thus began an exciting and fruitful period of research, documentation, exhibition, and programming of the Pierce collec-tion, which continues to this day. From the beginning, it was the museum's intention to develop a definitive retrospective exhibition of the art of Elijah Pierce. Recalling the museum's formal recognition of the artist in a modest exhibition nearly twenty years ago, we chose to name this exhibition the same as the first: *Elijah Pierce, Woodcarver.*

Extensive research by the curatorial staff in association with art historians, folklorists, artists, collectors, and Columbus community and Pierce family members led to many new discoveries and challenged old interpretations about Pierce and his art. The exhibition and this publication present a more comprehensive and interdisciplinary study of Pierce than has been accomplished to date. What better time to celebrate a man such as Elijah Pierce, for the year 1992 marks the one hundredth anniversary of his birth. And—given the many issues that divide us as a nation in this closing decade of the twentieth century—this is a fitting time to commemorate an artist who speaks in surprising ways to contemporary needs in the remarkable body of works that constitute this exhibition.

The museum is especially grateful to Estelle Pierce, whose decision to transfer her husband's carvings from the Long Street barbershop and art gallery to the Columbus Museum of Art has provided scholars and public alike with a rich trove of African American art. We also owe a debt of gratitude to those members of the Pierce family who provided important information to help document the artist's life.

Our most profound thanks are due The Henry Luce Foundation, Inc., which believed in the merits of the project and provided generous support for its realization. We are also deeply indebted to the National Endowment for the Arts and the Ohio Humanities Council for providing additional funding for the publication and educational programs.

In planning the exhibition and the accompanying publication the museum has enjoyed the privilege of working with an especially fine group of scholars, most of whom have studied the artist's works over a period of many years. Gerald L. Davis, Michael D. Hall, John F. Moe, Regenia A. Perry, and Aminah Robinson contributed enlightening essays, and Margaret Armbrust Seibert provided an exhaustive chronology and bibliography. Each has earned our respect and admiration.

In gratitude we also remember the late Robert Bishop, who provided the introduction to this volume and who, in championing the cause of American folk art, became over the years a friend and supporter of the Columbus Museum of Art.

Most important, it is the staff of the Columbus Museum of Art which breathes life into a major undertaking such as this by attending to a host of organizational details. While I am grateful to each and every one, a few deserve special commendation. Curator of European Art E. Jane Connell in association with Curator of American Art Nannette V. Maciejunes assumed the massive tasks of organizing the exhibition and providing the catalogue notes in the annotated checklist of the exhibition. Editor Norma Roberts expertly managed the editing of contributions and the many aspects of production to provide a cohesive and inviting publication. Director of Collections Roger Clisby, Director of Education Sharon Kokot, Director of Development James Weidman, and their staffs made essential contributions to the implementation of the project.

We are, in addition, deeply grateful to the many individuals and institutions that lent works to the exhibition to supplement those in the museum's collection, thereby enhancing the presentation in wonderful ways.

Elijah Pierce wished for himself and his work to be remembered. He wanted his carvings to be readily accessible and their meanings to be relevant to all in the years to come. "I think as long as you live and after you have died your work will live on," Pierce said. "That's one thing I have to believe. I've made some history, and after I've passed off this old sinful world, I live on." The exhibition *Elijah Pierce, Woodcarver* is this museum's affirmation of Pierce's artistic legacy, offered with the hope that many will profit from the human as well as the aesthetic dimensions of this undertaking.

MERRIBELL PARSONS
Executive Director

7

CURATORS' STATEMENT

Elijah Pierce was a savvy observer of contemporary life and very much a product of his time. His upbringing in Mississippi was rooted in the historical, religious, and aesthetic values of the African American community. His life encompassed post-slavery times, the great migrations north, segregation, the civil rights movement, two world wars, and the wars in Korea and Vietnam.

Pierce was encouraged since childhood to believe that he had a special calling. He wanted to make history, to have his carvings live on after his death. He believed God charged him to preach through the vehicle of wood carving. His "pulpit" was the Long Street barbershop—the social center of the African American community in Columbus and the secular counterpart to the church.

Pierce's wood carvings are connected not only to a personal religious calling but also to identifiable traditions and values within the complex and multi-layered culture of which he was a part: black and white, folk and popular, religious and Masonic, neighborhood and national. The carvings reflect a wide variety of vernacular sources: newspapers, comics, book and magazine illustrations, oral history, popular songs and hymns, current events, and folktales. To this extensive list we can add such means of communication as toasts, jokes, blues songs, and photographs of cultural heroes such as Joe Louis, Booker T. Washington, and Martin Luther King, Jr.

From sources such as these, Pierce created a rich visual vocabulary, constantly evaluating and interpreting the world in terms of his own experiences. He navigated a very personal course through the secular and spiritual worlds, and the medium of wood provided the essential vehicle for the subjects he chose to communicate through his art. The relatively small scale and portability of the carvings allowed for their easy dissemination into the community at large. Unquestionably, Pierce made very calculated use of imagery, iconography, and technique to affirm and perpetuate his own history and beliefs and to capture a local and national audience.

As an artist Pierce can no longer be characterized as a simple creator working solely under divine inspiration, or as an outsider who survived in a complex urban world. As this exhibition takes a closer look at Pierce, it also participates in the reconsideration of a long held popular understanding of folk art. For more than two decades, in many writings and at such gatherings as the Winterthur Conference on American Folk Art of 1977 and the Washington (D.C.) Meeting on Folk Art of 1983, the nature of folk art has been avidly debated in terms of both its aesthetic and cultural meanings. Its sophistication as an art form and importance as a social document have been recognized. In our consideration of the life and art of Pierce, we have sought to illuminate both the aesthetic and social meanings of the artist's life and work and thus to affirm the connections between folk and art, between cultural and personal artistic expression.

Many books and exhibitions on American folk art have been produced by art museums in the past decade. Few, however, have successfully addressed the contributions of a single artist. Most exhibitions have been group shows. Those that have focused on only one artist have seldom succeeded in integrating biographical, social, and aesthetic issues, which are particularly relevant for African American folk artists. The goal of this exhibition is to provide an in-depth look at Elijah Pierce and by extension to encourage ongoing scholarship in the fields of both African American art and American folk art.

To accomplish this formidable task, we selected 173 works to reflect Pierce's roles as carver, barber, minister, Mason, and community historian. The core of the exhibition is drawn from the museum's permanent collections. Other extremely important works from major public and private collections have been added to round out the full chronological, thematic, and stylistic range of Pierce's oeuvre. Works essential to the study of Pierce are included: religious subjects, such as his masterpieces, the *Book of Wood* and *Crucifixion*; autobiographical works; moralizing tales; political subjects; sports subjects; and a sampling of lively animal and figure carvings. While the religious reliefs constitute the largest number of carvings, many secular subjects are featured to provide a necessary balance and more realistic view of Pierce's oeuvre.

The book that accompanies the exhibition is a compilation of the research and documentation of Pierce which has been undertaken at the museum since 1985. Prefaced with comments by the late Robert Bishop, former director of the Museum of American Folk Art, five essays consider Pierce in terms of a variety of major philosophical and disciplinary approaches to folk art. The essayists are Gerald L. Davis, a folklorist; John F. Moe, a historian; Michael D. Hall, a sculptor; Regenia A. Perry, an art historian; and Aminah Robinson, a Columbus artist to whom Pierce was a friend and mentor. Through the diverse yet interconnected perspectives of these scholars and artists, Pierce's life and art are examined and celebrated.

Cutting against the stereotype of the anonymous folk artist, the publication includes a chronology of Pierce's life, compiled by art historian Margaret Armbrust Seibert, professor of art history, Columbus College of Art and Design, who con-

ducted fieldwork on the artist during his lifetime. One of the first in-depth chronologies written for a folk artist, this includes all presently available information on Pierce's life, exhibitions, awards, and honors. The book also features an exhaustive bibliography on Pierce, prepared by Seibert. The array of references found in both the chronology and the bibliography reflects the widespread recognition that Pierce experienced in his lifetime and that continues today.

We are especially grateful to the many scholars, friends of Pierce, and Pierce family members who joined us in putting together a rich tapestry detailing the artist's life and art for presentation in this exhibition and publication. In particular, we wish to thank Susan James-Gadzinsky, Pennsylvania Academy of the Fine Arts; Erskine Peters, University of Notre Dame; Ivana Spalatin, East Texas State University; John Vlach, George Washington University; and William H. Wiggins, Jr., Indiana University. In addition, three colleagues served as constant beacons of support, providing sound guidance in all our endeavors: Lynda Hartigan, National Museum of American Art; Henry Glassie, Indiana University; and Eugene Metcalf, Miami University.

We also wish to thank members of Elijah Pierce's family, who helped document the artist's life: Nellie Brookins, Carrie Pierce Curton, Adeline Gilbert, Alexis Pierce, Dana Pierce, Dorothy Pierce, and Zetta Pierce. Pierce's friends and associates, as well as our own, also provided much needed information and assistance: Lonnie Cumberlander, Dewell Davis, Lisa Greenberg, Isiah Holoman, Kojo Kamau, Annette Oren, John Owens, Mike Sweeney, the late James M. Vicars, and the late Mary Ann Williams.

Finally, we sincerely acknowledge our colleagues on the Columbus Museum of Art staff. Their constant enthusiasm and support make all things seem possible.

E. JANE CONNELL
Curator of European Art

NANNETTE V. MACIEJUNES
Curator of American Art

INTRODUCTION

Elijah Pierce was one of the greatest men I have ever met. This self-taught carver was also a great American sculptor.

Elijah came from humble beginnings. Born in 1892 in rural Baldwyn, Mississippi, he lived with his family in a log cabin believed to have been partially built by his father, a former slave. Tilling the soil was not to Elijah's liking. By the time he reached sixteen years of age, he had set up as a barber. When Zetta, Elijah's first wife, died around 1915, he took to the road. He survived by working odd jobs as they occurred and eventually established himself as a barber in Danville, Illinois.

In 1923, Elijah moved again, this time to Columbus, Ohio, where Cornelia, his second wife, resided. After working in several barbershops, including one owned by John Dixon, he built his own shop on Long Street in 1954. This barbershop was unlike any other I ever went to. There were two rooms—one for cutting hair and the other for carving when business was slow.

My first visit with Elijah Pierce was in 1974. I had become aware of the artist because Michael and Julie Hall, at Cranbrook Academy of Art in Bloomfield Hills, Michigan, were visiting him frequently and returning to the Detroit area with wonderful pieces for their collection. I was struck by the rich poetry, expressive detail, and obvious religious fervor of his bas-relief sculpture. The latent patriotism he expressed so vigorously in some of his carvings appealed to my own sensibilities. Even so, I had simply not been adequately prepared to visit with this incredible man face to face or to walk through his barbershop.

When I arrived on my first visit, there was a young boy in the barber chair and another customer waiting. I took my place in line and got a fine haircut, during which time I talked with the barber about the weather, world affairs, and other pleasantries. In a short time, our conversation shifted to religion, a favorite topic with the artist. Even before I revealed my interest in his art, he told me of his great masterpiece, *Book of Wood,* which he had completed many years before, in 1932. After finishing my cut, Elijah invited me into the carving room, and with the zeal of a preacher he explained in great detail the thirty-three large wood reliefs mounted on cardboard and fastened together with string. Each page in the book revealed a year in the life of Jesus, who was depicted as a black.

Elijah's reading of his book to me was one of the thrilling experiences of my life. This very tall, very thin, frail man became transfixed as he hunched over the book, telling me about the carvings while I became as enchanted by their vivid, forceful, and rich details as I was by their creator and his profound understanding of the Bible.

Elijah came to religion naturally. He was from an intensely religious family, and his father served as a deacon of the Mt. Zion Baptist Church in Baldwyn. The artist was himself ordained in 1920.

I visited Elijah Pierce many times in the years prior to his death on May 8, 1984. I met his third wife, Estelle, and marveled at their warm relation-

Elijah and Cornelia Pierce

ship. As often happens in an artist's family, his wife came to make art as well. Even today I have a small American flag painting that she finished while I was in Columbus on one of my visits.

As Elijah Pierce became well known in art circles around the world, it became increasingly difficult for him to tend to his barbering. After the late 1970s, most of his time was devoted to making remarkable carvings and whittlings in wood and to receiving endless streams of visitors who came to meet and admire him and experience, first hand, the woodcarver extraordinaire.

The Columbus Museum of Art acquired more than one hundred pieces by Elijah Pierce in 1985 from his estate. The museum is a fitting home for these works—his barbershop was located just behind the institution. Elijah enjoyed extensive attention from critics, museum directors, and curators during his lifetime, and his works continue to draw enthusiastic response to this day. Thankfully, this exhibition and publication will offer many more people the opportunity to see and understand the true genius of Elijah Pierce.

ROBERT BISHOP

Elijah Pierce, Woodcarver

Doves and Pain in Life Fulfilled[1]

Gerald L. Davis

Whether art imitates life or life mirrors art is a discussion which has little applicability to most African American traditional communities. In such communities life and art are inseparable, being so inextricably fused that the absence of expressive structures and forms would relegate daily living to hollow, uninteresting, textureless, marginal status. Life is exuberant, cautious, communal, patterned, brilliant, ordinary, necessary everyday stuff; art is aesthetic, sensate, dynamic, structured, textured, pragmatic. Whether it is a Sunday-go-to-meeting milliner's creation worn at an improbable jaunty angle with a regal grace, or an apparently idiosyncratic signature strut that seems to defy all laws of body mechanics; whether it is a system of language and argot virtually incomprehensible to the "outside" world but enormously seductive, evocative, powerfully compelling and empowering to the practitioners, or a household quilt apparently haphazardly pieced by a community member in which are imbedded the most complex of philosophical judgments and which bears unmistakable linkages to utilitarian and decorative fabrics constructed in African communities many hundreds of years earlier;[2] whether it is a sermon preached or performed by a master in a church to a congregation that seems to the uninitiated on the verge of anarchy because the testimonies to faith and truth uttered concurrently by tens and hundreds of voices are so dense and expressive, or a reduction of the narrative units and symbols of the performed African American sermon to the hallowed, reverential medium of wood, which inherently bears the elements of life and the enormous potentiality of expressive creativity and invention, African Americans are surrounded by intentional constructions informed of daily existence and given sentient breath and sensual form through a generously endowed creative necessity.

The traditional African American folk artist does not create, work, or invent in isolation. Standards of excellence for a chosen form are learned both formally and indirectly from family members and neighbors. That is, one can be formally selected as a master's apprentice in her or his community, or one can learn, *seemingly* indirectly, by observation and trial and error in the context of a native aesthetic.[3] One learns the technologies of craftsmanship, along with the more esoteric notions that complete one's mastery of a medium, to the satisfaction of established masters and through the recognition of the general community.

One of the more interesting and academically useful notions is that of *equivalences*. While a folk artist may excel in one expressive structure—quilt tops, split oak baskets, taletelling, etc.—certain selected structural elements of one form or mode may be applied to other forms. These shared "expressive equivalences" provide to any community a sense of continuity and cultural unity that crosses genre boundaries, and their common occurrence among African Americans may help to explain why a fine blues singer can be a reasonably accomplished folk sculptor, or a jazz performer can be a quite magnificent poet in formal and folk idioms, or a male fife player can be a wonderful quilt-top piecer and a glorious taleteller and a passable basketmaker—all, of course, identifiable in the contexts of traditional African American aesthetics. By definition the folk artist is known to segments of his or her community. And whatever the quality of the affection, or disaffection, with the artist's product, the community recognizes its form and may embrace its effect.

While the self-conscious creation of formal, literary poetry should not in any way be equated with the constructive processes of forms of traditional expressive systems, excerpts of a poem written by master wordsmith Gwendolyn Brooks, in which she intentionally approximates both the sound and structure of the African American urban narrative idiom, may serve to illustrate in gross terms the workings of a "community aesthetic." In her poem "The Sundays of Satin-Legs Smith"[4] Brooks lovingly illustrates the complex expressive behaviors of an urban lover/hero and identifies something of the heady aesthetic of everyday living so many African Americans manifest:

> Inamoratas, with an approbation,
> Bestowed his title. Blessed his inclination
> . . .
> He sheds, with his pajamas, shabby days.
> And his desertedness, his intricate fear, the
> Postponed resentments and the prim precautions.
> . . .
> Now, at his bath, would you deny him lavender
> Or take away the power of his pine?
> What smelly substitute, heady as wine,
> Would you provide? life must be aromatic,
> There must be scent, somehow there must be some.
> Would you have flowers in his life? suggest
> Asters? a Really Good geranium?
> A white carnation? would you prescribe a Show
> With the cold lilies, formal chrysanthemum
> Magnificence, poinsettias, and emphatic
> Red of prize roses? might his happiest
> Alternative (you muse) be, after all,
> A bit of gentle garden in the best
> Of taste and straight tradition? Maybe so.

> But you forget, or did you ever know,
> His heritage of cabbage and pigtails,
> Old intimacy with alleys, garbage pails,
> Down in the deep (but always beautiful) South
> Where roses blush their blithest (it is said)
> And sweet magnolias put Chanel to shame.[5]

Perhaps the poet will forgive a paraphrasing of her elegant lines, but for African Americans who live parts of their lives "in the tradition" (most African Americans participate at some level in the maintenance of traditional cultural forms, although those who are active, dynamic participants or who are artists are, of course, proportionately few). But "life must be [artistic]. There must be [aesthetic form], somehow there must be some." Even Mr. Smith's most mundane and gritty Monday-to-Saturday existence can be mediated by an aesthetic sensibility that flowers magnificently on Sunday and that is best interpreted in the context of African American community history and social life.

From Monday to Saturday Mr. Smith, *Mr. Smith,* is an ordinary, common African American man. Little distinguishes him, perhaps, from millions of other men jailed in America's cities by social and economic circumstance. Certainly his is a life without fragrance during those six days when the expressive impulse rests, seemingly dormant. But on Sundays, "He wakes, unwinds, elaborately: a cat . . . / . . . he designs his reign . . . /He sheds, with his pajamas, shabby days . . . /Postponed resentments and the prim precautions." And should the point be missed that this is no mere "pretty" collection of phrases and words but a sociopolitical essay in verse that encompasses a whole, entire people and a sociohistoric migration, Brooks challenges her readers, "Now, at his bath, would you deny him lavender/Or take away the power of his pine?/. . . But you forget, or did you ever know,/His heritage of cabbage and pigtails,/Old intimacy with alleys, garbage pails,/Down in the deep . . . South/Where roses blush their blithest (it is said)/And sweet magnolias put Chanel to shame." "Life must be aromatic [artistic]."

Finally, Brooks offers her readers a motivation for the Sunday transformation of a commoner to a king preparing to meet his adoring public, *his* community, "His inamoratas . . ./Bestowed his title. Blessed his inclination." Brooks's narrative representation of a community aesthetic is best understood, or perhaps can only be fully appreciated, in the context of African American sensate systems. Mr. Smith's lovers, *his* Sunday community, his intimate congregation, in recognition of his talents and product and his genius, bestowed upon him the wholly sensual, delicious title "Satin Legs" he is entitled to bear for twenty-four hours every seven days until breath leaves him.

It may be disturbing to some readers that a commemorative essay on Columbus's internationally renowned and celebrated woodcarver Elijah Pierce should begin in such a manner. The notion that brackets this prologue of sorts is the nettlesome business of discovery intended here to mean the initial identification of a craftsperson or artist by an outsider and the attempt to bestow upon the discovered artist an "original" validation that derives from external and perhaps competing cultural sensibilities. The *sotto voce* supposition, of course, is that the "discovered" artist has no previous validating recognition. A folk artist's aesthetic community is rarely given credibility by collectors/discoverers. So for purposes of this essay, the operative query becomes: By which evaluative set of standards and perspectives do we recognize the genius of traditional folk artists? This writer's handle on the query, weighted in favor of native aesthetics, is phrased thusly: Are there identifiable systems of artistic judgment and aesthetic structures vested in the peculiar and unique histories of communities that permit those communities to recognize and evaluate—pass artistic judgment on and maintain standards of excellence for—native expressive forms?

Pierce was born in 1892. By age eight, or approximately by the year 1900, he was already carving. Pierce the "folk artist" was discovered quite unexpectedly around 1970.[6] Discovery by the world of museums and collectors can have a salutary effect on the traditional artist, of course. Travel, honors, enhanced income, and documentation of the artist's life and thoughts are certainly some of the benefits of discovery. And from all reports, Pierce enjoyed the exposure to the world of collectors and the benefits that came to him very late in his life, and he took them all in stride. Pierce did not set aside his church, his community, or his beloved Masons.[7] These were his foundation, his lifelong base, the source of his artistic, moral, and spiritual sustenance and knowledge. He was nurtured and loved by his people, and in his turn Pierce embraced them and their corporeality with a gentle, abiding love and a towering, commanding sense of compassionate mission. Pierce was no stranger to the transient, seductive riches promised by the world, nor was he unaware of the vicissitudinous pathways traveled by others. But it was to his moral, physical, spiritual, and aesthetic community that his allegiances were anchored.

Perhaps it was providential that external acclaim came so relatively late in Pierce's life. From his earliest years, this man of God-inspired talent and steely determination negotiated a pathway between his terribly onerous religious calling, prophesied by the terms of his birth, and his single-minded passion to avoid the imprisonment of his venturesome soul and spirit by social and political circumstance. His art, his chosen interactive expressive form, became the mediator in this internal war. His community, easily recognizing the terms of his struggle and the quality of his gift, became his balm, his guardian, his lover, his mirror, his anchor as he moved inexorably toward the inner peace and resolution that finally came to him. His wood became the vessel for his sermons, his *exempla*, his medium of discourse, and served as his pulpit. The carvings were not generally the elements of Pierce's worldly persona. Rather, these were his several voices that resonated most fully within the intimacies of African American life and history and his own very private soul. "With the knife and wood," wrote Mark Ellis in a *Columbus*

Dispatch piece on Pierce's funeral, "Pierce achieved a simple eloquence. He expressed visions inspired by the Bible and interpreted a world that revolved around his barbershop, home, and church."[8] It is easy to feel comfortable with Ellis's summation; at least one can feel warmly immersed in its quality. But the scale in his journalistic reduction of Pierce's life misses the grand, almost cosmic proportions of Pierce's place in the lives of *his* people.

During an interview with Aminah Robinson, a close friend and protégée of Pierce's and an acclaimed artist in her own right, I was cautioned against being too academic in examining facets of Pierce's life.[9] Yet I am both an African American and an academic, and therefore doubly committed to fully understanding certain phenomena through means that may be more oppositional than complementary, since each arises from quite different cultural assumptions. And it is because of this that I am so drawn to this man Pierce and his very human contradictions and complexity. And it may explain why I am so compelled by the notion that Pierce's biography and his works called "sermons in wood"[10] are mutually illuminating. In all of this Aminah Robinson's caution is a methodological beacon. The logic or illogic of academic analysis is insufficient to probe the variety of queries that arise from even a cursory examination of the weft and warp of Pierce's life. One must also repair to the untidy environs of African American religious faith and belief and social practice and custom to understand the compacted parallels between Pierce's reverential knifestrokes in his wood and his reflections on his own pathways and the human condition of his community in Columbus, where he lived for over sixty years.

At first glance there would appear to be little relationship between Pierce's vocation as a barber, his avocation as a carver of wood, and his profound sense of calling as a religious. In several of his interviews in the years since his discovery by Boris Gruenwald, Pierce himself connects the tripartite elements suggested above, as in the following quotations attributed to him: "I've been barbering and carving so long they both come natural."[11] And "I've been running from preaching for twenty years . . . and my second wife used to say I had to carve every sermon I never preached. I guess the good Lord put me on the woodpile."[12] And "When I was about eight or nine, I would work all day for a pocketknife. Then my dog and I would go down to the creek bank and fish and whittle. I'd pick a tree that had soft bark, maybe a beech, and carve anything I could think of. Horses, dogs and cows, anything that came to mind. And if I got sleepy, I'd just lie down in the woods and my dog wouldn't let nothing come near me."[13]

It is difficult to know how to enter the universe of ideas represented above and reordered to suggest an implied and unified psychic continuity in Pierce. Certainly the first correspondence, between barbering and wood, is recognizable to many African American religious traditionalists as fundamentally spiritual, although the term as we know it would rarely be employed in the sense that it appears here. "Mystical" may be a closer approximation of the attachment African Americans form to the person who regularly does their hair and to their physical places of business.

More than a mere ornamental surface, hair and hair preparation are elements of an essential body of emic material referred to as African American hairlore, and it can be a near metaphysical index to one's very soul, being, psychology, personal history, and in the aggregate a group's social history. To the person to whom one entrusts the "doing" of one's hair, sometimes discovered after a lengthy search and exhaustive conversations with friends and acquaintances, is yielded significant power. That power frequently transcends the relatively few moments a customer spends in a barber's or hairdresser's place of business. If the church is the focus of a community's sacred or religious energies, the beauty parlor and the barbershop are the secure environs of its secular, or worldly, rituals. The attributes shared by the personalities central to the healthy functioning of both environments, the preacher and the barber/hairdresser, can be interchangeable and can involve healing mechanisms perceived as spiritual, deep and intimate trust, and a sort of sustaining power in the social and political affairs of the community.

For many African American traditionalist Christians, there can be a direct linear relationship between the persona of Jesus Christ the carpenter and those male African American members of any community who are utilitarian carpenters or decorative or expressive woodcarvers. While all talent is perceived as God-given, those master carvers or workers of wood who are recognized as especially talented can be thought of as divinely inspired, a superordination of sorts of the "God-given" categorization. To push this concept a bit further, one can be fairly passive in the development of one's God-given talent, but to possess a divinely inspired talent means that one cannot run away from one's destiny. A person is under a deep and abiding obligation to realize such a gift in concrete terms and specific behaviors.

Whether Pierce recognized his early interest in fashioning aesthetically expressive objects from wood as divinely inspired, and therefore inescapable, is unclear. What is clear is that Pierce found respite from the demands of the outside world and his father's Baldwyn, Mississippi, farm in the ancient, solitary woods near his home, where he would carve initials, the names of family members, and representational figures in standing trees or would whittle animals and other small figurines from scraps he would find on the forest floor.[14] And though Pierce described himself as "the black sheep, a little oddball who didn't play much with the other kids,"[15] in his youth he began a practice that he continued throughout his life: giving carved pieces to people who admired his work or persons with whom he wanted to share a bit of himself. Apparently the sharing of this extension of the self was as important as the reverential fashioning of objects from the wood he both admired and needed. "I'd give the things I whittled to the kids in school. I just got a real joy out of whittling."[16]

Reports of woodcarvers' and carpenters' com-

pelling love and compulsive, at times obsessive, attachment to wood abound in a variety of academic literatures. Some carvers ascribe to the wood anthropomorphic qualities, regarding the products they fashion as their "children." Frequently, carvers will tell interviewers that a piece of wood will sit in a corner for years until an appropriate image emerges, as in a privileged communication between two intelligences. Pierce was no stranger to this manner of transcendent relationship with his wood and his carvings. As late as 1974, he reported to an interviewer, "Most of the carvings are from a vision I see. I *see* a picture in the wood or *hear* a sermon [in the wood]. . . ."[17] And in 1971, Pierce reported, "I usually pray over a piece of wood before I ever put a knife in it. I pray to him for inspiration."[18]

While it would be foolish to conclude that all workers of wood feel this way about their medium, this peculiar deep respect for the "personalities" of woods lends to the woodcarver a quality that borders on the mystical. While working with Tennessee African American woodcarver Alvin Jarrett, folklorist William Wiggins recorded this comment: "Jarrett sees 'an account of ancient days' etched in the growth rings of cedar trees—King Solomon, the settling of Tennessee, and his forefathers' slavery are all wrapped up in this wood that he carves."[19]

In his later years, after he settled in Columbus with his second wife, Pierce's practice of giving his carvings to members of the Gay Tabernacle Baptist Church (formerly Gay Street Baptist Church), of which he was an associate pastor, seemed to be connected to a sort of divination process. According to several members of the church, Pierce would deliver a sermonette during the Sunday service; at the conclusion, he would present to some unsuspecting member of the church a recently completed woodcarving, frequently of a religious subject, or a Masonic theme, if appropriate to the receiver.[20] How or by what special dispensation Pierce would arrive at a theme appropriate to a receiver does not appear to be explained anywhere in the sizable body of Pierce materials, but reportedly many of those who received his carvings in this way were surprised at the aptness of the carving and its relationship to the receiver. It may very well be that Pierce's vocation as a highly respected barber in the community gave him access to some of this information, which was perceived as personal by recipients of his carvings. But, no matter, by his middle years it was clear that the Gay Street congregation had accepted as legitimate Pierce's prophetic sensibilities.

Even if one were inclined to regard with some skepticism the traditional bases of these readings or the powerful confluence of symbols that marked Pierce as profoundly exceptional and spiritually gifted, one would find it difficult to dismiss the extraordinary circumstances of Pierce's birth and the particular character of the formation of his personality in the context of his deeply religious family, two factors that have a direct application to the nature of Pierce's "sermons in wood" carvings. There is a sense in all of this that Pierce understood the inevitability of his assumption of his personal destiny as a public religious and quite intentionally used his aesthetic expressive form, his carving, as an instrument of negotiation between his religious destiny, which he regarded as onerous and vigorously attempted to deny for a time, and his embrace of a fully evolved secular lifestyle, replete with a love of dancing, an appreciation for elegant and splendid haberdashery, and the companionship of women. If this reading seems a bit expansive and perhaps wide of the mark, one has only to return to a quotation offered earlier, "I've been running from preaching for twenty years. . . . I guess the good Lord put me on the woodpile." The "woodpile" in African American Christian parlance means trials and tribulations and holds the promise of the sweetness of salvation after the bitterness and disappointment of "worldly" travails.[21]

The following excerpt taken from an interview with Pierce[22] might well serve to illustrate metaphorically Pierce's time on the "woodpile" on his way to full acceptance of his destiny. Without apol-

ogy for the length of the excerpt, this may also be one of the few examples of the type of sermonette Pierce delivered preceding the bestowal of a carving. Clearly a Pierce sermonette had an expressly didactic function. Reflecting on his carved relief *The Man That Was Born Blind Restored to Sight* (Fig. 1), Pierce said:

> And when I get a picture in mind I want to carve it. And as I carve it sometimes I get so lifted up in the spirit of God that I stop. These things haven't been cut with the sharp instruments that I use because he's helping me to do that work. I just wish that you or others could see how he will use you when you give up and put him first in all your undertakings. He said "The greater work that we could do if you only obey him." Lot of people don't put enough trust in God, they try to do too much themselves. Well the world today, brother, wouldn't be in the condition it's in if we had love one for another as we should, as brothers. To me, my religion, I love you as though you were my own dear brother. Not only you, all people. I don't carry no hate in my heart against nobody. If I can do you any good, I'll do it. But I wouldn't lay one straw in your way. Anything I could do to help. My greatest joy is to make others happy. I believe that's my work that was assigned to my hands by the Heavenly Father above.
>
> So that picture, I love it. It's a part of *me*. And as I've so often said when I sell a picture, I ask God's blessing upon that picture. Let it be a blessing in the home because it is a part of me. Trying to instill or leave a message in that home, representing my Heavenly Father.
>
> He saw that man. He was born blind in his mother's womb. And he was crying. He was by the wayside and Jesus stopped and went out and takin' time out to heal him and give him sight. He made a drug out of spittle in the clay and anointed his eyes and told him to go to the pools alone and wash [that] he may see.
>
> Being obedient, he did what he was told to do and he received his sight. He had been beggin' and had been seen by lots of people from his youth up. And after he was received of sight, he went rejoicing in the streets and the people was amazed because they knew he was a blind man

Fig. 1.   Elijah Pierce, *The Man That Was Born Blind Restored to Sight*, 1930, carved and painted wood relief, 32 x 12 in. (81.3 x 30.5 cm), Milwaukee Art Museum: Michael and Julie Hall Collection of American Folk Art

and now he sees. And they asked him who healed him? "Who gave sight to the blind?" He said, "A man came along"—he didn't even know his name —but "a man came along and told me what to do. Made spittle, stooped down and made spittle in the clay and anointed my eyes."

"Ain't you the one that was born blind? Why and how?" They went to his parents and asked about him. They told 'em "yes, he was born blind." "But how is it now that he see?" They said, "he is of age, ask him." One thing he said, "I was blind but now I see." [Pierce laughs, rejoicing.] You know that's wonderful! I *was* blind but now I see! He went on his way rejoicing. It ain't no secret what God can do.[23]

Pierce's rejoicing near the conclusion of this segment of his interview with Hall indicated his regard for the profundity of the parable and its relationship to his own life, complementing Pierce's more generalized celebratory testimony to the power and the glory of God. The dynamism inherent in this reification of the sacred example illustrated by a secular application is at the heart of Pierce's translation of the biblical parable of the blind man into striking relief in his carving. This essential dynamism as a structural signature is apparent in most, if not all, of those works by Pierce now referred to as his "sermons in wood." It is a dynamism reflected as well in the unique structure of the performed African American sermon, which requires that a preacher heavily weigh her or his message in the context of the secular world within an ontological framework of abstracted religious principles. Indeed, Pierce's own life embodies this tension, which, coupled with his gift and his inescapable sense of mission, is realized in the magnificent body of religious work for which he is principally known. It is no wonder that Pierce's personal rejoicing in the interview comes as a transition between the end of the sacred example and what would appear to be Pierce's own reflective commentary, "You know, that's wonderful! I *was* blind but now I see. He went on his way rejoicing. It ain't no secret what God can do."

Born to deeply religious Christian parents on March 5, 1892, Pierce was reportedly named Elijah by his mother, Nellie, in recognition of his blessed birth. Elijah Pierce was born "with a veil,"[24] a thin membrane that sometimes covers the child's head immediately following birth. Among African Americans, a child born with a veil is considered to be blessed with the ability to prophesy and is thought to be selected, chosen, or ordained by God to be a religious. So important is the veil as an index to a child's future personality and the manner in which he will be regarded—even if he does not appear to immediately manifest his calling—that parents and grandparents will frequently hold and cherish the veil as a keepsake, typically in small wooden boxes.

Robinson reported that Pierce took his first name seriously.[25] Surely Pierce's mother had in mind Elijah, the ninth-century B.C. Hebrew prophet of I Kings of the Old Testament, when she named her son. The naming was, perhaps, far more apt than Nellie Pierce may have realized. A leader in both the secular and the sacred worlds, Elijah was a political activist of sorts, on God's side. And he, like Elijah Pierce, resisted his calling until a visitation from the Lord convinced him, compelled him, to become a religious champion. Born the second youngest, and the youngest boy, into a large family of nine children and a small and relatively close-knit community, it is unlikely that the young Elijah ever escaped interpretations of his religious destiny. The woods became a sanctuary for the bright, independent-minded, venturesome Pierce, and here he could indulge his dreams, strengthen his determination to leave his father's farm to seek the bright lights of points north, and generally construct a psychological secular existence unfettered by his family's powerful Christian centering.

This is not meant to suggest that Pierce was antagonistic toward his family's religious foundation. There is little in his material to indicate that he was. Pierce was, in fact, profoundly influenced by the family's daily prayer sessions and Bible readings, by his father Richard's unbending independence and his refusal to yield psychologically or physically to the system of enforced servitude into which he was born and from which he freed himself, and his mother's apparently gentle humanity and abiding faith and strong resolve.[26] And each of these elements is found in abundance in Elijah Pierce the mature adult. Still, as a young adult Pierce struggled mightily to balance his sense of mission, greatly intensified by the quality of his family's religious life, his community's expectations, and his own needs as a young man. Interestingly, as the following anecdote testifies, this essential, appropriate, and necessary tension in Pierce's young life was frequently resolved in sacred contexts.

> After I was a young man and had left home, I was up to a New Year's Eve dance. Something I had never did. The bells was ringing and we was on the floor dancing, people were hollering and singing, we were gliding over the floor. In fact I love to dance. But that night while I was dancing, the hall was singing and I heard my mother praying, just like she was in the dance hall. And when I heard her call my name, ask the Lord to take care of Elijah wherever he may be, I turned my girlfriend a-loose and ran and sit down and cried like a baby. This is something I never did, dance a New Year's in and the old year out. And over all that noise I heard her praying just like she was right there in the room and saw her with my eyes. I said she is broadcasting and televising to [me] and I will never dance anymore if the Lord will forgive me.[27]

Chronologically, this experience probably came after the more widely reported experience that may have lead to Pierce's formal conversion as an adult, and his decision to be ordained and licensed as a preacher, an event that took place at the Mt. Zion Baptist Church in Baldwyn on September 26, 1920. Pierce has summarized this latter experience, the subject of his *Obey God and Live (Vision of Heaven)*, 1956 (cat. no. 6), numerous times in interviews. The version of this critical experience offered below, taken from the 1971 Hall interview with Pierce and probably the fullest text of the narrative ever published, has been described by Jane Connell as, "if not the earliest post-contact recording of Pierce's words, then one of the most candid and private interviews [of Pierce] ever recorded."[28]

> The one where I was laid out for dead? . . . oohwee . . . That picture kind of gets under my skin . . . But it's kind of like this . . .
>
> One day when I was down home in Mississippi where I lived, my mother and I and my sister stayed together after Father died. She [mother] moved to town and lived in my home. So one day I was doin' my evening chores and I was told to read a certain passage of scripture in St. Matthew. I think it's around the sixteenth chapter. And instead I went into the house and sit down in my chair beside a short table. Mother was on one side and I was on the other.
>
> She and I used to read in the evenings the Bible—different passages of scripture. And that day Sears and Roebuck sent a catalogue. A brand new catalogue came in the mail. And I saw it on the table and I reached over the Bible with my left hand and picked up the catalogue to thumb through it lookin' at the sights and different things that were in the catalogue. And as I did so, the power from above—seems as though a hand touched my head. And when that happened, I began to fall out of the chair. And mother looked at me fallin' out of the chair on the floor. She jumped up and came to my rescue and asked me what was the matter. And as I was goin' through that fallin' out of the chair, I heard the voice of God told you to read the Bible, and you disobeyed him, and I'm just showing you my power.
>
> So my mother and sister drug me into the bedroom and laid me on the bed. And I went out just like the sun going behind a cloud. And they put camphor to my nostrils. Last thing I remember, mother asked me, "Honey, what's the matter?" And I couldn't say anything, although I didn't have any more pain than I have now. But I went on out, and they pronounced me as being a dead man.
>
> And my mother and sister began to scream and cry and the neighbors heard them, came in to see what was the matter. And they said I was dead. I didn't have any pulse beat and neither my heart was beating or breathing or anything. And they said that I had passed away. And the house

was filled with neighbors as I was laying there on the bed. And they made preparations to get the doctor and the undertaker . . . yes . . . [Pierce's voice breaks and he clears his throat].

So finally—I don't know how long I was in that condition—but finally I came back just like I went away, like the sun comin' from behind a cloud. And I heard the voice of God just showing you his power. He [Pierce] was disobedient, and I got a chance to speak. I said, "Hush Mother. I'll tell you what's the matter . . ." [pause, Pierce begins to sob]. She said, "Lord, honey, tell me." I said, "God told me to read the Bible and I reached over the Bible to look at a magazine and he just laid his hands on my head." I want to stop. [Here Pierce begins to cry uncontrollably. He asks Hall to turn off the tape recorder until he can regain his composure.]

And people was in the house looking frightened and some was backing toward the door as though they were afraid. And I stood up and walked around and they all were looking. I didn't have any pain, but I found out that it's bad to disobey God; that he will speak to you today just like he did in the days of old, that he spoke to the prophets and told them what to do. And he was showing me that it's bad to disobey.

I thank you.[29]

There are several points to be made from this intensely personal narrative. The first is to observe the structure of the iconographic representation of the narrative in Pierce's carving *Obey God and Live*. The second is to determine whether this structure approximates in any definitive manner the prototypical structure of the performed African American sermon as defined in academic literature. Finally, it is appropriate to examine the means by which Pierce, as an African American folk artist, may have come by his knowledge of carving and preaching structure and transferred those technologies to the aesthetic rendering of images.

Elsewhere I have identified what I consider to be the "minimal requirements for the realization of an African American sermon."[30] It is amazing that this conceptualization holds true across African American denominational boundaries. The minimal requirements are:

A. The preacher informs his congregation that his sermon is not his own, that he did not arbitrarily decide the text of his sermon. The African American preacher must indicate to his congregation that the text of his sermon was provided by divine intervention, by God.[31]

B. The next obligatory step in the development of the African American sermon is the identification of the sermon's theme. Usually theme identification is followed by a supporting Bible quotation.[32]

C. The final phase of the obligatory introduction in the development of the sermon is the threshold of the sermon formulaic systems. Following the Bible quotations, the preacher is obliged and expected to interpret, first literally then broadly, the quoted biblical passage.[33]

D. The body of the African American sermon is constructed of independent theme-related formulas. Each unit of the formula develops or retards a secular and sacred tension and moves between abstract and concrete example. Each generated formula is an aspect of the argument of the announced theme and advances the discovery and examination of the sermon theme.[34]

E. There is rarely a closure to the African American sermon. The sermon is open-ended and compares favorably with the open-ended nature of African American performance forms generally.[35]

In *Obey God and Live,* it is clear the distinct elements in Pierce's carving approximate the narrative formulas in the African American sermon. In some of his "sermons in wood," Pierce deliberately sets each of his elements apart from others through some form of bracketing, frequently using narrow frames or borders within the large carved or pieced border that frames the entire composition. It is instructive that Pierce has said of his carving, "Everything I carve, I want it to tell some kind of a story." Pierce continues, "It don't seem like nothing to me if it don't tell a story. I think that anything that don't have a story behind it, I don't know, I just don't understand it. I wouldn't call it junk. Beautiful work. Good work. But it don't tell nothing. It don't move me. It's not strong. I don't see nothing it tells."[36]

For Pierce, it would appear that there were equivalences between the episodic nature of sermons or tales, as he may have heard them performed, and the structure of many of his carvings. While this may be regarded as an artist's organizing technique, a kind of mnemonic device, it is equally clear that a great deal of African American narrative and material form seem to be composed of sequentially related elements.

In the case of *Obey God and Live,* a work in which each element is distinct, one has a handsome working out of a distinct cultural—African American—aesthetic structure, which compares rather favorably to the organization of the African American performed sermon summarized above. Moreover, Pierce's multi-episodic carvings are recognized and accepted as narratives, or as having a high narrative quality, by many African Americans. Such a consistent recognition obviously requires a sound cultural base shared by the artist and his community.

There are seven distinct episodes or structural units in *Obey God and Live,* a couple of which hold dual properties. The first, of course, is the text "Obey God and Live," which has both sacred and secular applications. It is the abstract religious principle against which the concretized secular Pierce experience is mounted. The next two elements are positioned by Pierce around the table on which the Sears Roebuck catalogue and the Bible are located — the Sears Roebuck catalogue located on the right side nearest Pierce's mother; the Bible positioned on the left in front of Pierce. This is the beginning of the narrative proper. Element two represents Pierce

and his mother sitting at the table preparing for prayer and Bible reading; in a profoundly intimate, religious setting, element three captures Pierce's interest in the world, which unwisely causes him to flaunt well-established social custom and reach across the sacred Bible to pick up the secular merchandise catalogue. The fourth element is the representation of the heavenly power reaching down to touch Pierce on his head, rebuking him for his lapse. Pierce falls comatose from his chair in element five and in element six is surrounded by people who think him dead. Element seven depicts the general community watching the proceedings.

Without belaboring the correspondences, it would appear that element one satisfies phases A and B of the performed African American sermon structure. The element is weighted heavily in Pierce's secular life but positioned against an abstract sacred principle well known in Baldwyn. This is both the secular theme of the carving and acceptable as the religious text. Sermon phase C is accomplished by elements two and three, Pierce's setting up of the essential confrontation between his worldly needs and the religious nature of the family gathering. Sermon phase D is realized through elements four through six, and perhaps seven. In element seven, Pierce returns the import of the carving and the message to the secular world, and, as in all African American sermons, he personally assumes responsibility for the impact of the message, even as he makes it clear that it is intended for a more general application in the daily lives of the people of his community.

While there may be some slight variance from religious carving to religious carving, in most ways this admittedly academic analysis is useful if one is to more fully appreciate the sermonic character and the distinct cultural provenance of Pierce's work. Pierce was an *African American* folk artist who mined and trusted the rich stores of African American traditional aesthetic systems to guide his hand and heart as he set knife to wood. Much has been made of the fact that Pierce considered himself self-taught. This is not to challenge the representation of idiosyncrasy in causing Pierce's interest in wood carving, but having been raised on a farm which probably exposed the young Pierce to at least some rudimentary knowledge of carpentry and wood working, and having a favorite uncle who was himself a carver, may have had a great deal to do with Pierce's choice of avocation. Certainly, he would have gathered his knowledge of African American preaching structure from church attendance and from a familiarity with the variety of community narrative expressive forms which abound in any African American traditional family environment.

A query was raised near the beginning of this essay concerning which of several competing standards of excellence should be used to evaluate the genius of a traditional African American folk artist. One set of standards habitually denies the existence of community categories of excellence and thereby denies any linkages between an artist and his historical, social, and cultural foundations. The absurdity of such standards is most easily recognized in language that speaks of the folk arts as "quaint," or "idiosyncratic," or "dying out," or "the province of the old, the unlettered, the poor, the dispossessed, the marginal."

This retrospective exhibition focuses on the life work of an African American man, a most excellent and respectful manipulator of steel against wood; a preacher who was born in the rural South and whose soul found sweet rest in the urban North; this man who was saintly because he knew intimately the ways of the world; this most gentle spirit who treated his wood with respect and who welcomed all to his embrace; this man who could fix a person with one eye while the other roamed seeking nuance, this man, this Reverend Elijah Pierce. This exhibition puts the lie to those who think the folk arts dead and simple and quaint, and folk artists marginal and anachronistic. Pierce, as were most folk artists, was dynamically aware of his world. Through his art, the rich complexity of daily, secular living finds momentary repose as we walk through the galleries of his personal quests, his wondrous visions of African American ideas and heroes, his community perspectives on national events and political figures, his relationship with his God, and his elemental belief that *his* people are good people. This tall, elegant, superbly presented man was no mere simple soul. His life and his art are metaphors for the dynamism of life and the legitimization of the power of African American aesthetic structures.

> And I usually pray over a piece of wood before I ever put a knife into it. I'm depending on him for my inspiration and he give it to me. He said, "Ask and you shall receive."[37]
> So I think as long as you have lived and after you have died your work will live on. That's one thing I have to believe. I've made some history and after I've passed off this old sinful world I live on.[38]

Gerald L. Davis is Associate Professor and Chairperson of the Department of Africana Studies, Rutgers University.

1. The title of this essay is taken from the title of a double-headed multimedia collage portrait of Elijah Pierce by Columbus artist Aminah Robinson, and it is used with her permission.
2. Many scholars, among them Gladys-Marie Fry, Steven L. Jones, Mary Arnold Twinning, John M. Vlach, Roy Seiber, and Lawrence Levine, have noted the historical connections and relationships between patterns in African fabrics and textiles and African American quilt tops. But few commentaries have approached the precision and confidence of art historian Robert Ferris Thompson in his *Flash of the Spirit: African and Afro-American Arts and Philosophy* (New York: Vintage Books, 1984), pp. 207–222, and collector-scholar Eli Leon in his catalogue for his exhibit of the same title, *Who'd A Thought It: Improvisation in African-American Quiltmaking* (San Francisco Folk Art and Craft Museum, 1987), pp. 22–28 esp.
3. Gerald L. Davis, "Afro-American Coil Basketry in Charleston County, South Carolina: Affective Characteristics of an Artistic Craft in a Social Context," in *American Folklife*, ed. Don Yoder (Austin: University of Texas Press, 1976), p. 177.
4. Gwendolyn Brooks, *The World of Gwendolyn Brooks* (New York: Harper & Row, 1945, 1949, 1959); reprinted in Stephen Henderson, *Understanding the New Black*

Poetry: Black Speech and Black Music as Poetic References (New York: William Morrow & Co., 1973), pp. 169–170.

5. Ibid.

6. Pierce's discovery is thought to have resulted from the artist's meeting in 1970 with Boris Gruenwald.

7. Pierce was an honorary member of Master Lodge 62 of the Ancient Free and Accepted Masons, Columbus, Ohio. Originally thought to have been a thirty-third degree Mason, Pierce was in fact an eighteenth degree Mason. Apparently, Pierce became a Mason earlier in his life and was reinstated to active membership in his later years. In any event, Masonry was a powerful force in Pierce's life, and Masonic symbols figure prominently in many of his works.

8. Ellis, May 12, 1984.

9. During a three-hour interview in her Columbus home on June 21, 1991, Aminah Robinson shared with E. Jane Connell and myself some of her thoughts on Pierce's life and art. It was an extraordinary interview, and I am indebted to Ms. Robinson for her candor, trust, and grace.

10. The appellation "sermons in wood" may have originated, as Michael Hall suggests, as journalistic hype. The phrase appears on the Sunday, November 11, 1979, cover of the *Cleveland Plain Dealer Magazine* and in an article inside the Sunday supplement, "Elijah Pierce, An American Original," by Jay Hoster, pp. 22–29. However, the conceptualization of "preaching" by carving religious images and narratives in wood Pierce attributed to his second wife.

11. Marsh, p. 55.

12. Ibid.

13. Ibid.

14. *Artists Among Us.*

15. Marsh, p. 56.

16. Ibid.

17. Wolf interview.

18. Hall interview, fall 1971.

19. William H. Wiggins, Jr., "The Wooden Chains that Bind: A Look at One Shared Creation of Two Diaspora Woodcarvers," *Black People and Their Culture: Selected Writings from the African Diaspora,* ed. Linn Shapiro (Washington, D.C.: Smithsonian Institution Press, 1976), pp. 29–34.

20. From interviews with Isiah Holoman, Lonnie Cumberlander, and Dewell Davis, Jr., all members of Pierce's Gay Tabernacle Baptist Church. Both Davis and Cumberlander are, as well, thirty-third degree Masons. I am deeply appreciative of their willingness to share with me their memories of Pierce. Davis was among those who received a Pierce carving in church.

21. In a personal correspondence, friend, general savant, and African American literary theorist Erskine A. Peters supplied the following clarifying note on the meaning of the "woodpile." "If you were living in a rural area down south and your father said 'If he doesn't straighten up I'm going to *put him on that woodpile* out there,' what is meant is that the subject would be assigned the task, the arduous and trying task, of chopping firewood."

22. Hall interview.

23. Ibid.

24. From a videotaped interview of Pierce by Jeffrey Wolf at the opening of Corcoran Gallery of Art's *Black Folk Art in America, 1930–1980* exhibition, 1982.

25. Aminah Robinson, June 26, 1991, interview.

26. Ibid.

27. *Artists Among Us.*

28. Personal correspondence, July 19, 1991.

29. Hall interview.

30. Gerald L. Davis, *I Got the Word in Me and I Can Sing It, You Know: A Study of the Performed African-American Sermon* (Philadelphia: University of Pennsylvania Press, 1985), p. 46.

31. Ibid., pp. 67–70.

32. Ibid., pp. 70–74.

33. Ibid., pp. 74–76.

34. Ibid., pp. 76–80.

35. Ibid., pp. 80–82.

36. *Artists Among Us.*

37. Hall interview.

38. *Artists Among Us.*

Hands-on Work

Style as Meaning in the Carvings of Elijah Pierce

Michael D. Hall

It was late fall in 1970 and I had just walked into Elijah Pierce's barbershop and was standing face to face with the carver for the first time. I introduced myself, and he replied, "I'm pleased to meet you—I sure am." Then he reached out and shook my hand. Beyond my recollections of Elijah's reserve, dignity, and civility, I remember the man's hands. His right hand enfolded mine completely. My full-size adult hand disappeared in his welcoming grip. This tall, elegant, soft-spoken black man named Elijah had the largest hands I had ever held. On the occasion of this retrospective exhibition, I am brought again to thoughts of this Columbus barber/carver and the compelling images his large hands coaxed from the pine and cedar he whittled into American folk art history.

The search for meaning in Pierce's work has historically gone in two quite different directions: one focused on Pierce and his art in an aesthetic discourse and the other addressed to his carvings as ethnographic information. In the aesthetic arena Pierce is celebrated as a self-taught folk artist notable for his naive polychromed narrative carvings—carvings that fortify popular art-world myths about the simplicity and honesty of primitive art. In ethnographically focused studies Pierce is celebrated as a cultural hero—an African American barber from Ohio who created objects remarkably informed by, and expressive of, the collective experience of black people in the United States. An in-depth look at the whole of Pierce's work suggests that the aesthetic and the ethnographic are not exclusive concerns.

Pierce once told me that his knife almost never slipped out of control when he worked. He believed that some divine power guided his knife and that his hand was only a tool in the service of some greater hand. It falls to others to trace the impact this belief had on his art. For my part, I find myself increasingly interested in the secular (rather than the divine) forces that guided Pierce's knife and brush. As someone interested in the study and interpretation of art as a condition of culture, I try to listen to Pierce's art directly in order to understand its sources, its meanings, and its usefulness to its audience. To interpret Pierce's work, I turn to an inspection of the Pierce style in search of the social, political, and temporal impulses that led the artist's hands through the creative process.

Webster defines style as the characteristic manner of expression, execution, construction, or design of any art. Inquiring into the Pierce style, we ask: What characteristics make a Pierce a Pierce? Only after we answer that question can we speculate on what makes a Pierce work significant.

The Pierce style is a consequence of the ways in which Pierce, the artist, consciously and unconsciously directed and infused his creative impulses into the physical processes necessary to the production of his work. Pierce drew, carved, painted, and composed. He depicted particular subjects in his work and ignored others, and he habitually realized his work at a certain scale. If style gives form to concepts, then Pierce's artistic concepts and intentions should be legible in the marks that characterize his art making. How Pierce drew, carved, and composed tells us about the artist and his world. Those things in the Pierce style that reflect matters of choice tell us about the artist's disposition and taste. Aspects registered as a matter of habit tell us about Pierce's upbringing and about the ethnic and social traditions that shaped his world and the world around him. Issues of race, gender, and class all informed Pierce's thoughts, responses, and perceptions. His art, then, as a body of made objects encoded with the stylistic marks of his hand speaks to us of human activity and belief bounded and prescribed by very particular cultural permissions. A decoding of the gestures created by the extraordinary hands of this carving barber enriches our map of the world of human experience.

Drawing is an important aspect of the Elijah Pierce style. When we think of someone who can draw, we typically recall someone we once knew who with a few deft strokes of a pencil could render an outline image that successfully captured a likeness of a person or an object. Such drawings rely heavily on the visual information conveyed by contours and the edges of forms. Pierce, in imitation of this rather mundane model, began all of his work with a rudimentary outline drawing. Next he elaborated with secondary lines, creating folds in a robe, features in a face, or ripples on water. Filling in details and texturing with line, Pierce completed his drawing to the point where he had effectively described his images. Drawing in anticipation of carving, he developed a drawing style that was informational rather than expressive.

Pierce's approach to drawing reflects his exposure to the ordinary informational drawings that he saw throughout his life. Outline drawings filled the Sunday school books and illustrated bibles that shaped his early religious training. Line illustrations and schematic diagrams were standard fare in the mail order catalogues and "how-to" books he read as a young man. Finally, there was the spate of cartoons and caricatures that papered the 1930s and 1940s barbershop world where he earned his livelihood as an adult. As a consequence, Pierce the artist understood drawings as lines and edges filled in with simple details. His gift was his ability to utilize such drawings as blueprints for his carving.

In the strictest sense, Pierce's panel pictures are relief-enhanced polychromed line drawings in which shallow engraved lines are used for details and where bold, deeply cut passages define and emphasize major images. Unschooled in drawing, Pierce drew in an unsophisticated yet pragmatic manner, sketching simple profiles or frontal outlines of his subjects. Figures rendered in more complicated poses involving turning, twisting, or bending were created through a selective process of copying. Generally, these figures are readily recognized because they retain the look of forms traced or otherwise lifted from book and magazine sources. In *Indians Hunting*, 1943 (cat. no. 62), Pierce copied or traced feathered warriors scouting, canoeing, fishing, and hunting. By contrast, in *Samson*, 1942 (cat. no. 108), he generated his own frontally posed Samson figure flanked by Delilah in profile. Adding textured tresses to Samson's head and placing a jawbone in his hand, Pierce created a strongman hero of his own that is just as effectively drawn as are his appropriated Indians.

As a draftsman, Pierce repeatedly combined self-generated schematic representations and selectively borrowed illustrations. The peculiar alloy formed from this mix becomes identifiable as part of the Pierce style. Flat Pierce figures often meet fully modeled and anatomically detailed copy figures in the same narrative, and these simultaneously overlay landscape vistas and architectural interiors drawn both from the artist's imagination and from appropriated sources. Ultimately, it fell to Pierce's knife to bring all this disparate drawing into artistic synthesis. His carving unifies the work visually. Unconcerned with drawing for itself, Pierce grounded his art in a vocabulary of line that both limits and informs everything he sought to communicate to his viewers.

The Pierce hand that penciled outlines and textures also wielded a paintbrush. Like many sculptors, he was not a colorist. He had almost no painterly concern for paint, but he did have use for color in his art. He used it basically in two ways. First, as with drawing, he used it as information.

He used it to identify figures and objects in his narratives and to unify or separate forms across his relief surfaces. Second, he used color as decoration. Paint and, of course, glitter frequently embellish his work, adding much to its visual appeal.

Color as information is an interesting proposition. To use color informationally, an artist must presume that his or her art contains some informational message that is to be visually transmitted to an audience. Further, the artist must identify color as part of a code to be used in that transmission. Some artists create their own codes and expect their audiences to break the code in order to read their paintings. Others choose to telegraph their meanings using codes already commonly legible in their world. Pierce was an artist of the second sort.

White robes identify the virgins in Pierce's *Wise and Foolish Virgins and the Man with the Clean and Soiled Heart*, n.d. (cat. no. 170). The pure heart in the same work is colored bright red, while the soiled heart is spattered with black blotches—a code for its stains. Elsewhere we note that blues in Pierce's work generally refer to the sky, while greens are for fields, trees, and nature. Suns are gold, moons are silver. Satan comes in both black and red. Christ figures are cloaked in the white of purity and chastity, while kings wear royal purple or burgundy. Convention dictates many of Pierce's color codes. He chose to reinforce popular style conceits to assure his audience that he understood the visual conventions of his culture and he fully expected such conventions to communicate their traditional meanings in his art.

Pierce's decorative use of color is more arbitrary. Patterns of contrasting stripes and dots and spots accent many of his painted works. He striped animals at will (alligators, even), and he habitually tossed striped shawls over the shoulders of many of his biblical apostles. Both Marys in *Crucifixion*, mid-1930s (cat. no. 99), are set off by brightly spotted tunics. Further, most of the cows and horses in the carver's animal menageries are of the piebald sort. In other works, the artist often filled in the incised lines that texture his forms with fanciful inlays of color to clarify and accentuate his drawing. Finally, we see Pierce using decorative color simply to enrich his art and to make it appear more resplendent. Metallic golds and silvers are found in many of the message signs, and the mix of greens, golds, whites, and maroons used in *Pilgrim's Progress*, 1938 (cat. no. 140), creates an opulence that captivates viewers with the seductive power of color as pure embellishment.

Pierce's use of straight-from-the-can color keeps his art direct and balanced. Limiting his palette, he extended his authority with paint. In *First Meeting of Jesus and John*, 1940 (cat. no. 110), he saw no place for paint and simply varnished the panel, leaving the wood itself to speak through the amber glaze that sealed it. For *Noah's Ark*, 1944 (cat. no. 103), he painted the entire background landscape bright green but left the ark and the parade of animals unpainted. Isolated in a field of green, the varnished animals, two by two, rhythmically cover the surface of the panel like cuneiform marks on an ancient tablet. In *Obey God and Live (Vision of Heaven)*, 1956 (cat. no. 6), Pierce polychromed an entire panel. Across the frieze, he identified characters in the narrative with colors that allow viewers to follow a stop-action story through several frames of an episodic sequence. Above the action, he painted an aurora of gold and red rays behind the commanding heavenly hand of God and then enhanced this image of glory with a field of sparkling glitter. To the far left of the action, he carved an admonishing sign appropriately emblazoned with red paint that reads "Obey God and Live."

Once he had painted a work, Pierce typically sealed it with a heavy coat of varnish or shellac. Frequently he would then sprinkle commercial glitter over areas of the wet finish, accenting the work with a metallic sparkle. Something interesting is to be learned from this aspect of Pierce's work. Why, we ask, did he favor such a garish finish for his labors? Some commentators have described these gloss and metallic surfaces as the funky side of today's so-called folk-art aesthetic (glitter signals that this is truly anti-good-taste, hence anti-academic, art). To others, Pierce's gloss and glitter are assessed as signs that some informing ethnicity directed the carver's hands as he worked—that certain black traditions and cultural histories found their way into Pierce's paint and finish.

Putting aside folk art adages and issues of ethnicity, I would argue that something else may have led Pierce to varnish and glitter his work. Popular culture, the mass culture of modern America, reveals itself as the major shaping force in the Pierce style. The 1930s and 1940s were the great periods of the American home-shop and hobby-craft movements. In this period, craft and antiques magazines went into national circulation and found themselves being sold side by side on vendor shelves with a host of how-to, home-shop journals such as *Popular Mechanics*. Also in this period, Montgomery Ward introduced its versatile home-shop line of tools, and its Shopsmith woodworking machine became synonymous with the do-it-yourself life. The Shopsmith was part table saw and part lathe with a drill press and sander all rolled into one. America could not get enough of this little wonder, and by 1950, at least seventy thousand homes sported a hobby shop in the garage built around a Shopsmith or one of its several cousins.

Hobby- and craft-fixated Americans popularized decoupage, figurine painting, copper craft, paint by numbers, and mosaic art, each in its time. Glitter came into its own in the hobby movement and found dozens of applications in everything from string art to Easter egg decorating. Similarly, spar varnish, spray lacquer, and quick-dry shellac became preferred finishes for everything from copper-craft pictures to hand-rubbed shadow boxes and laminated coffee tables. For lower and middle class America from the 1930s into the 1950s, varnished knotty pine was homey and a redwood fence rubbed with linseed oil was elegantly rustic. Varnish, in popular applications, transformed ordinary pine and cedar into approximations of more exotic and elegant woods—woods worthy enough to be used in the making of expensive furniture and fine violins. Glitter became the hobby world's decorative analogue for gold leaf, and varnish became the poor man's rubbed lacquer.

Pierce, in the midst of this ferment, was predictably drawn to glitter and varnish. If his Christ figures were to dazzle viewers with their luminous halos, gold glitter was there to do the job. If judgment fires were to attend a depiction of the Second Coming, then red glitter was there to set the stage. Varnish, for its part, gave tone to his work. The deep gloss over the natural wood surface of *First Meeting of Jesus and John* dignifies an image Pierce obviously sought to imbue with portent solemnity.

The style of Pierce's carving (unlike that of his drawing and painting) evolved and changed dramatically over the years. Considered in terms of its technical refinement, Pierce's work can be divided into roughly three periods of stylistic development. His earliest surviving carving, *The Little Elephant* (cat. no. 21), is believed to date from the mid-1920s. Works created through the 1930s are from the artist's early period. Pierce's middle period runs through the 1940s and into the 1950s, and his late period runs through the 1970s and arguably into the early 1980s.

Works from the early period exhibit a characteristic flatness that is clearly the mark of an artist learning how to translate flat drawings into three dimensions. Outlines and detail lines rather than sculptural modeling give form to Pierce's early images. Works such as *Suffer the Little Children*, n.d. (cat. no. 112) exhibit the flatness typical of Pierce's first efforts. Here the surface plane of his panel—the top surface of the plank he was carving—is everywhere present and retains its recognizability as a plane of origin. The figures, trees, and clouds, like chain paper dolls, are silhouetted across a tentative and shallowly cut background. Textures in this and in many other early works are only crudely cut or scratched into the wood, and some images, such as bushes and grass, which the artist would carve in detail in later works, are only sketchily indicated with quick dabs and splashes of paint.

This tentativeness would not last long. Building his skills as well as his ambitions, Pierce, in certain early works, began to carve deeper and more confidently into the wood. Heads, arms, and shoulders (though still rather flat) are stacked in front of and behind each other. At this point, Pierce discovered undercutting as a technique for making his figures float above a background. In some cases, he carved through the plank to create three-dimensional cutouts held in a frieze configuration by the edges of the panel he left as a frame around them.

The same ambition that caused Pierce to move from relief carving to open-cut work also pushed him to find new formats for the presentation of his carving. In the 1930s, he began to combine cutouts and small reliefs into large assemblages. By 1935, this technique allowed him to work in the largest scale he would ever investigate. Some of these assemblages, such as *Monday Morning Gossip,* 1934 (cat. no. 153), were mounted on paper and cardboard and framed for presentation as large wall pieces. Others were mounted into large vertical frames that were then hinged together as freestanding architectural screens. The screen entitled *Bible Stories,* n.d. (cat. no. 169), consists of at least eighteen separately carved and painted vignettes along with a number of spacing blocks that fill the gaps between irregular-size picture panels. All of these components are fitted like interlocking puzzle pieces into the frames of the screen. Whether Pierce used the screens as portable teaching aids is not known, but their design strongly suggests that they may have been built as display units or stage props.

It is known that the early assemblage *Book of Wood,* circa 1932 (cat. no. 100), was a visual aid used by Pierce in his ministry. The assemblage panels that make up the pages of the book are meant to be read in a sequence. An early photo shows Pierce holding the *Book of Wood* like the Bible. Most collectors visiting the barbershop in the 1970s remember Pierce opening the book on the stand where it rested in his gallery and hearing him narrate as he turned each page to reveal yet another story.

Book of Wood was the last work Elijah showed me on my first visit. His obvious sense of theater made him save what he thought was the best for last. Lowering his voice and pointing toward the book, he said, "I bet you've never seen anything like that before!" Then he deliberately turned to stand beside it and positioned the work so that it opened facing me. He paused and then gestured with his hand across the image on the book's first page. "I bet you don't know what this tells," he said. "Well, this is the story about the time. . . ." Elijah was preaching to me, and I began to understand his art in its necessary and right relationship to its maker and his world. Time rolled back and I was experiencing early period Pierce.

It was also in his earliest period that Pierce built the majority of his three-dimensional constructed sculptural tableaus. The most important of these was *Crucifixion.* The piece remained on view in the center of the barbershop gallery until the early 1970s, when the artist dismantled and rebuilt it as a wall relief. In its original tableau configuration, the piece stood as a complex figural narrative built into a three-dimensional stage space. The figures carved for this work were stacked on a series of wood strips built in the manner of a five-tiered bleacher. Soldiers and onlookers occupied the first two tiers of this stage. The crucified Christ and the two thieves were mounted on the center tier. On yet higher levels, Pierce set up more soldiers and a backdrop landscape consisting of some trees flanked by a grieving silver moon and an ominous black sun. Two mourning Marys and a number of frightened disciples also found their way onto various tiers of the display bleacher, and a jubilant devil popped up on the level below the Christ figure to raise his arms and trident in a gesture of malicious glee.

Arranging his figures in rising and receding planes of vertical space, Pierce created sculpture that, despite its three-dimensionality, was emphatically not sculpture in the round. His *Crucifixion* was intended to be viewed frontally. The story was enacted in a space separate from the viewer. The static, flat planar character of the piece is yet another example of the the way in which Pierce avoided complex manipulations of sculptural form in favor of simple presentations that served his didactic (as opposed to plastic) understanding of art. Similar in form to crèches and other popular religious tableaus, *Crucifixion,* nonetheless, had its own uniqueness. It was rich in detail and ambitious in conception, but it needed to be confronted in person to be fully appreciated. Along with the *Bible Stories* screen and *Book of Wood, Crucifixion* must be numbered among the master works from Pierce's early period.

Pierce's middle period is distinguished by his improved craft and by the increased sophistication of design that he seemed interested in bringing to what his hands could make. Having defined his issues and having mastered the skills he needed for his work, Pierce seems to have become more interested than he was previously in adding nuances and decorating his art. His interest shifted from a focus on the informational relationship between foreground images and their backgrounds, to an investigation of forms that could be developed in midground spaces. His work, in short, became more pictorial and less graphic.

In this period, Pierce began to rhythmically modulate his carving through his panels and to explore space and texture in new ways. His knife technique remained bold and direct, but he carved with new finesse. His relief compositions became formally more active and complex, playing flat and round forms against each other. Strongly undercut and modeled forms are juxtaposed against areas of simple engraving and texture. Figures stack against each other more subtly than before, and foreground shapes recede into background spaces in ways that create more believable illusions—illusions that allow the artist considerably more freedom with his storytelling. The hard, bold forms of the early panels with strong knife marks disappear and in their place we see delicate and carefully incised drawing complementing modeled and carefully sanded images.

These middle works have a classical look about them. From *Pearl Harbor and the African Queen,* 1941 (cat. no. 155), to *Obey God and Live (Vision of Heaven)* (cat. no. 6) of the mid-1950s, Pierce showed himself

to be in control of his media and fully mature in his vision. His work became increasingly secular. Sports heroes, popular entertainers, politicians, and other public figures were his subjects. He became particularly fond of celebrating the achievements of black Americans: Joe Louis, Jessie Owens, and George Washington Carver all found their way into commemorative panels from his middle period. In addition, Pierce depicted stories from the community around him, as well as historic events. In these works he puns, he plays, he entertains. Most important, he celebrates his own artistic maturity. His carving is disciplined, his paint is elegant, and his work as a whole achieves a certain condition of resonance in the world. In the 1940s, Pierce's hands seem to have become conduits for impulses drawn from art and life in equal measure.

The third period is marked, again, by subtle but important changes discernible in the artist's carving style and follows a long hiatus in which he produced almost no work at all. For reasons yet unclear, Pierce, having filled his barbershop gallery with panel carvings and other constructions, seems to have stopped carving after the mid-1950s. Perhaps the artist felt that his statement was complete; perhaps he turned his attention to more community-related activities (his lodge and church); or perhaps something in his personal life distracted him from his art.

This dormancy, however, ended with Pierce's discovery by collectors of folk art. By 1972, the barbershop was deluged with visitors and Pierce was overloaded with commissions. He began actively producing an entire new body of work, which anthropologists would refer to as "post-contact" production. Pierce's creative energies were galvanized by new appreciation and demand for his work, but they were also redirected to meet the expectations of a new audience quite different from the one he had sought earlier at state fair exhibitions and church showings.

Earlier, Pierce brought to life stories and images that were familiar to his peers in the black community around him. The 1970s folk art world was a white world quite distanced from the artist and his Columbus community. It was cosmopolitan, generally college educated, and conditioned to understand his art through the lens of modernist art history. The moderns collecting folk art placed Pierce and his carvings in a primitivist myth of their own making. For these collectors, folk art exemplified a cultural longing for a lost, innocent world and a rediscovery of the honest and earthy in art. For them, Pierce's pantheon of prophets and apostles were less characters from a real history than charming signs of naive belief. Likewise, the illustrational and narrative strategies Pierce used for orchestrating the arrangement of figures in his panels were understood by collectors only as intuitive and spontaneous approaches to pictorial composition rather than as conscious pedagogical recitations.

Nonetheless, meeting his new world of 1970s admirers, Pierce began to carve actively again. New heroes (for example, John F. Kennedy, Martin Luther King, Jr., Nancy Wilson) joined the prophets and sports figures from earlier works. New book and magazine illustrations were available from which to appropriate new images and ideas. Old skills were summoned up, and hands now growing old were asked to respond. By 1974, Pierce was busily carving small animals and ambitious large panels between haircuts in the barbershop. Sitting in the shop watching him razor trim around a customer's ears one afternoon in the mid-1970s, I complimented him on his skill. "Yes," he replied, "my hands have always had the knack. Carving and barbering are a lot alike to me. I enjoy both." Five minutes later, with his customer checked out in a mirror, brushed off, and out the door, Elijah was back carving the panel he had put aside earlier. The carver, seated in his barber chair, was cutting on the plank cradled in his lap as we talked.

Two formal qualities readily distinguish the artist's late works. Like those from his formative period, they are flat; modeling is abbreviated and midground areas in the reliefs are not well defined. These carvings are generally brighter in color than their predecessors. The enamel paints Pierce used after 1970 have not mellowed and the varnish has not yellowed. Without patina, the late works seem even more graphic and raw than the works from Pierce's earliest years. Overall, because late period works are less precise and have fewer nuances than works from the previous period, they often have an expressive physicality that can be very interesting and desirable. Conversely, because the surfaces of the late panels are often rough, they can also seem carelessly made and even unfinished.

The artist's age certainly accounts for some of this. Older hands can be slower, weaker, and less deft than younger hands. Concentration, too, can wane with age. Pierce sometimes complained to me in the 1970s that it was harder for him to carve than it had been in his youth. Nonetheless, a good number of original and compelling new panels as well as sculptures issued from the barbershop in the late period. Few visitors left the shop without some small piece in hand. Pierce, for his part, seemed to enjoy making the small objects that kept his expanding circle of visitors coming back again and again.

By 1978, many of the original early works in the barbershop gallery had been sold to collectors and museums. Pierce seemed of two minds about these sales. Sometimes he seemed despondent watching his work trickle out the barbershop door, but at other times he seemed happy to know that he had found a certain immortality. He frequently noted that the artworks now scattered in collections all across the country would speak for him long after he had passed on. Despite feelings of conflict, he began restocking the gallery and drew firm lines as to what he would and would not sell from his remaining trove of historic pieces (*Obey God and Live* was always off limits). In this process he found himself increasingly responsive to collector requests for second versions of earlier works. Replacement pieces began to show up on the gallery walls, and large early constructed works were occasionally cannibalized to allow their components to be incorporated in new smaller panels backed and framed for wall presentation and collector consumption. The gallery came alive, but the artist was pushed to keep up with the demand for his work.

Through all his periods, Pierce relied on pictorial composition, as he did on color, to clarify his messages. Although his compositions are not purely intuitive, they are also not ruled by formalized concepts of design or theoretical principles. Typically, Pierce composed his works using every means available to make his point. His figures could be bold or subtle depending on how adamantly he carved and painted them. Images could be central or peripheral according to their placement in the visual field. Information could be sequential or casual, flowing or interrupted, all in relation to whatever strategy the artist chose as the organizing principle for a given composition.

Examining the corpus of Pierce's work, we find one compositional tendency that seems to be stylistically consistent throughout. Forms within his pictorial constructions are almost always hieratically schemed. To achieve clarity, Pierce stacked and overlaid image information in simple lines and columns. His compositions thus have more in common with Egyptian wall painting than they do with European Renaissance art. Pierce, like the Egyptians, depicted his important figures as large and placed them in the lower (front) areas of his panels. And also like the Egyptians, he structured many of the narrative passages in his work into linear friezes intended to be read from left to right across the composition. Significantly, however, Pierce's work can also be read up and down and sometimes diagonally. Narration and free association live together in surprising ways in the art of Elijah Pierce. His compositional schemes clearly indicate that Pierce himself understood seeing as a function of recognition. As a consequence, he viewed his task as an artist to be one of representation rather than self-expression.

In the most complex of his works, such as *Story of Job,* circa 1936 (cat. no. 105), the narrative moves freely through the panel, addressing viewers who are preconditioned to be able to pick their way through image information and to recognize the story being told. Pierce selected the points where he wanted his audience to enter the story, beginning the recitation with the Lord and the Devil making their wager and then confidently leading the viewer through the highlights of Job's trials. As he worked, his hand selectively and artistically condensed and edited the text he was illustrating.

To complement his images, Pierce frequently interjected language into his work. Words distill meaning and clarify the artist's intent, and reflect Pierce's roots in an oral tradition. Word texts range from the cryptic to the blatant. *Pearl Harbor and the African Queen* is punctuated with a carved sign that barks "duty." Emblazoned in a frieze across the top of *Father Time Racing,* 1959 (cat. no. 159), are the names of Old Testament prophets. In *Story of Job,* snippets of text are laced through the composition forming a running commentary on the action being shown pictorially. In the upper left, the Lord seeks "a perfect and upright man." In the lower center, Job laments, "Though he slay me yet will I trust him," and in the lower right, Pierce, the storyteller, has the last word: "Cuss God and die!"

Speech and the speech patterns of storytelling translate into composition in Pierce's art. Pierce's was a world of spoken communication—a world of preachers sermonizing, elders reminiscing, neighbors gossiping, and barbershop clients chatting. His was also a world of radio—radio commentary, radio sports, and radio gospel. Pierce and his community were conditioned to form pictures from words broadcast both from church pulpits and from radio studios. They also read pictures through simple captions like those found in illustrated Bibles, on postcards, and across the pages of *Life* magazine.

In much the same way that a speaker telling a story, issuing a command, or recalling an anecdote modulates and paces speech as sound, Pierce modulated and paced the forms in his panels as visual images. Similarly, as the voice can intone, implore, entreat, and cajole, Pierce expected that his hands could shape forms—including the forms of writing—to admonish, explain, narrate, and teach. His was emphatically not a plastic approach to the problem of composition. But his work, perhaps ironically, is filled with plastic invention. Approaching his work additively (a seeming contradiction to the fact that carving is a subtractive process), he freely built each of his compositions. His hands, however, marked his works with a recognizability that is as identifying as a voice print. Composed on the architecture of speech, Pierce's works are direct, intimate, and conversational in character. Like storytellers throughout history, Pierce invented images and collaged tales, and as an artist he sought to reshape with his knife and brush a graspable, believable, and durable world.

The subject of the Pierce style does not just end with broad descriptions of the drawing, carving, and composition that characterize the carvings of Elijah Pierce. Nor does it end with the grouping of his work into neat stylistic periods or even with the identification of the beliefs and events that inspired his knife. Reliable attributions, based on stylistic analysis, are increasingly important as newly discovered works said to be Pierce carvings find their way into private and museum collections. Because these works are often unsigned and their provenance is unknown, they must be submitted to stylistic scrutiny to be reliably declared as having issued from Pierce's hands.

The most complicated challenge to Pierce attributions involves the assessment of certain very late works that are known to have come from Pierce's shop. Sometime in the last year or two of the 1970s, the look and feel of many Pierce carvings subtly changed in ways that depart from the pattern of norms in the Pierce style. Style is a funny thing. Because it involves expressions of the subconscious, it is less a diagnostic absolute than it is a range of possibilities. On the other hand, because style is so tied to habits and because habits are so hard to change, style has a lingering predictability about it that makes it a curiously reliable measure of artistic authorship.

Close inspection of many of the works said to have been made by Pierce between 1978 and 1982 reveals a number of stylistic marks that are uncharacteristic of the artist. The stylistic aberra-tions identifiable in these works cannot be fully explained by Pierce's aging or by the demands of collectors. A best-guess argument suggests that the atypical marks registered here could have been those made by a young artist named Leroy Almon, who came to apprentice with Pierce in the late 1970s.

Are the crudeness and seeming ineptness visible in very late Pierce works the mark of the untrained hand of an apprentice? Not necessarily. Pierce, over eighty years old, was not carving with the strength and dexterity he had once possessed. Similarly, is the felt-tip marker substituting for enamel paint in many late works the addition of an apprentice? Again, it is hard to say. Pierce by the mid-1970s had already experimented with markers, and by the time he met Almon he was consistently using felt-tip pens to sign and date the backs of his panels and to initial the bases of his small sculptures. Still, the carving and coloring in the late works do not always reflect Pierce's hand.

Pierce had a habit of carving with a flaking knife stroke. His blade was held in such a way as to allow him to peel a small chip off his work. He repeated this caressing, whittling gesture until a form was revealed. Almon, in contrast, attacked his wood directly. He used a chopping and gouging method of removing wood from his block. Almon's method (as seen in the works he carved and showed in the barbershop; see fig. 2) was much faster than Pierce's but left less time for contemplation and risked over-commitment in a way that the whittler's method does not. Also, Pierce typically flowed his paint on his work with a loaded brush. His color saturated the wood and unified his forms. Almon, perhaps less patient with paint that needed to dry, used markers. He could produce overlapping areas of transparent color that were dry to the touch almost immediately by quickly scrubbing the marker tip over his carving. Almon's marking gesture leaves an agitated, energetic trail rather than a flat field of unifying color on his work. However, both men did emulate each other's techniques, and Pierce, seeing the practicality of his assistant's technique, often assigned him to rough out and even

Fig. 2. Leroy Almon, b. 1938, *Simon Bearing Jesus'
Cross*, 1980, carved and painted wood relief,
14 x 32 in. (35.6 x 81.3 cm), Columbus
Museum of Art: Museum Purchase

finish certain works. True collaborations resulted
from these interactions.

The apprentice, in some ways, revitalized the
master. We see this most directly in the choice of
images that become the focus of Pierce's late works.
Almon, like Pierce, was attuned to his generation's
popular culture. The world he knew was filled with
the images of 1970s black politics and the signs from
the black awareness movement that included illustrations from newly published histories of the African
American experience. Most important, Almon
shared Pierce's view of art as teaching, and he encouraged Pierce to focus on new lessons for a
changing world. Almon understood art as power,
politics, and economics; he was eager to find his
way into Pierce's world of collectors and in return to
bring Pierce into his own world of urban politics
and entrepreneurship.

Almon's hand is clearly discernible in the one
major collaborative work that both carvers signed
and acknowledged as a joint effort, a piece entitled
Cruelty of Slavery, n.d. (cat. no. 171). The panel
depicts various scenes from African American history. Slave cabins and a cotton field spread below a
large sun with extending rays. Carved in the center

of the sun are the words "Eye of God"—a text
which is found in many early works by Pierce. The
cabins are foreshortened and simplified in a way
that strongly suggests they were copied from a typical Pierce-selected book illustration. The field with
its pickers is a schematic representation punctuated
with white-painted cotton balls. So far, we are looking at vintage Pierce.

Elsewhere, however, new images and a new
hand flesh out the panel. The detailed line carving
of a slave auction incised into the lower right quadrant of the panel is simply too tight, too flat, and too
detailed to be Pierce's. Similarly, the freed slave
reaching heavenward with broken chains still dan-
gling from his wrist in the upper left is also too flat
and linear to have been executed by Pierce. In addition, this image is sentimentally mannered in a
decidedly un-Pierce-like way. These passages stylistically must be attributed to Almon. Finally we
examine the slave-whipping scene in the center
right, of this panel. Here we find both the teacher
and the pupil. The drawing and carving in this
schematic representation are pure Pierce. The
source for the whipping image, however, is Almon.
This vignette is from the 1977 television miniseries

Roots. Pierce and Almon, reviewing the black experience through the eyes of Almon's generation, depict Alex Haley's Kunta Kinte tied and spread-eagled between two posts, his body forming a cruciform. This media image transposed into the panel is marked by both men. Pierce's didacticism and Almon's activism are perfectly married here.

Almon left the Pierce shop in 1981 and went on to establish himself in Georgia as a folk carver in his own right. His work owes much to his apprenticeship in Pierce's barbershop on Long Street, but his disposition to his own brand of flatness, linearity, expressive carving, and coloring, as well as his concern for contemporary image sources, became the marks of his own style. The absolute identification of his hand in Pierce's work remains a study yet to be seriously undertaken. Such a study would surely also have to consider the possibility that other hands, including that of Pierce's wife, for example, could be found in the artist's later works. Beyond this, the carvings themselves argue that Elijah Pierce, for his part, maintained an active and serious presence in his work to the end.

Whatever else Pierce's art may have been, it was always dynamic. The push and pull of time, place, and events can be felt throughout the work. Pierce's personality collides with the collective psyche of culture to create a peculiar tension in his work, and the original images generated in the private vision of an artist continually grapple with conventions of representation informed by clichés and stereotypes. Pierce's art is both original and dialectical, and it confronts the world as both a document and a critique.

Pierce's art was, from the outset, answerable to a world grounded (as we have seen) in the culture around the artist. His immediate culture was the black community of his church, his lodge, his barbershop, and his neighborhood. Beyond this world, however, Pierce was also a full citizen in the community of popular middle-American culture. He belonged to the world of do-it-yourselfers: the color-blind, mid-century, spar-varnish world collectively manufacturing the millions of yellowing knick-knack shelves and copper-craft pictures that flood contemporary flea markets (along with a few more idiosyncratic and ambitious things that we call folk art). Finally, Pierce's work became resonant in the extended, predominantly white, community of late-century American art collecting. Here, it was perceived both as a quaint talismanic relic and as a sign of a living folk aesthetic.

Pierce mediated between all of these worlds. His was an engaged rather than disengaged persona. Despite what appeared to be his humble and accommodating manner, Pierce was a proud and even stubborn man. I saw evidence of his healthy self-esteem one night in 1971, when I went to visit him and his wife at their residence on Margaret Street. I had arranged to tape an interview with him, and he was visibly excited about the project. His first words into the microphone were: "I'm very glad to have you in *my* home!" Elijah took charge. His statement had an encompassing and self-assured ring to it. He was welcoming me to his world—the world of his life, his beliefs, and, of course, his art.

Recent studies on the subject of material culture persuasively argue that all art is culture bound. Accepting this, we need to look for a new and enfolding art appreciation that will acknowledge the cultural conditions that shape art and at the same time permit it. Ideally, folk art would, from a cultural perspective, be an expression of community and tradition. At the same time, in a contemporary art context it would have to be answerable to aesthetic issues and tested against the modern concept of the artist as an individual creative self. Elijah Pierce the artist and Elijah Pierce the citizen were one and the same. His carving bears witness to this fact. It provides us with palpable new text for the study and appreciation of art as a cultural production indelibly and dynamically marked by the singular hands of a maker. The carvings of Elijah Pierce issued from hands that were both receivers and transmitters—hands that in putting aside the barber's shears and taking up a carving knife became the hands of an artist.

Michael D. Hall is an artist and a critic.

"Your Life Is a Book"

The Artistic Legacy of Elijah Pierce

John F. Moe

Elijah Pierce is one of the most significant African American folk artists of our time. In 1992, on the occasion of the one-hundredth anniversary of his birth, it is important to recognize his role in African American art, culture, and history. During his lifetime, Pierce played a central role in his community; he was an articulate and thoughtful interpreter of his surroundings, and his art reflected and told the story of his times. Yet Pierce's own history and personal experience, formed in the context of African American and American culture, were the primary influences on his art and his development as an artist.[1]

Pierce's career as a woodcarver can be divided into stages that relate both to his artistic competence and to his development of a religious philosophy. Early in his career as a barber, wood carving was already an important venue for his religious and social aims and ambitions. As early as the 1930s, Pierce's goal was to articulate religious messages in his art. For inspiration he often used religious images he had found in magazines, Sunday school books, and other publications. By the 1940s and 1950s, he had yielded to his own personal "call to preach the word of God" and intensified his wood carving to better aid his preaching. Though Pierce had carved religious images before this time, and the earlier works were also born of religious beliefs, the later works sprang from the deeper wellsprings of his calling to preach.

During the 1960s and early 1970s, Pierce was carving his best work, both technically and philosophically. From about the mid-sixties until the early seventies, he arrived at a point in his career where his independent philosophical perspective was well formed and his experience and skill in his craft were fully developed. Like many artists, Pierce reached this point late in life, when he was in his seventies and early eighties. In his late eighties and nineties his carving gradually became less proficient, but the strength of his vision remained intact and his images continued to reflect the power of his convictions.

Pierce understood his mission in life: God had given him a talent to carve the messages of the Bible and it was his responsibility to carry out this mission. Many times, as we sat and talked, he would say to me in rhythmic tones and with complete conviction, "God speaks to me. I know his voice. 'Elijah, your life is a book, and every day you write a page, and when you are done you won't be able to deny it because you wrote it yourself.'"[2]

The art and life of Elijah Pierce provide an excellent illustration of the importance of the biographical and artistic framework for the analysis of folk art. The existence of a large body of biographical information and materials pertaining to Pierce helps us to gain a meaningful understanding of his work and to learn much about the role that community plays in the making of folk art.[3] In the case of Pierce, we are also given much to learn about the wealth of art and expression in the African American community.

When he died in 1984 at the age of ninety-two, Pierce had carved the subjects he had observed throughout most of the twentieth century. He had depicted his impressions of the major events of African American history as well as—and distinct from—American history. He carved images of slavery, work gangs in the South, U.S. presidents, black community leaders, and important events such as the integration of the U.S. Armed Forces. He also carved the personal stories of his youth in the South and his adulthood in Ohio. He carved important universal messages for the community that concerned sacred themes such as that in *Put Your Trust in God and Not in Man* (cat. no. 136), and secular themes such as the importance of neighborliness in community behavior.

Elijah Pierce's discovery by the art world did little to affect his self-image. Though he was undoubtedly pleased that people appreciated his art, he seemed to take most pride in the fact that his own African American community in Columbus had appreciated and displayed his works in their homes and businesses for years. By the time he was in his seventies, Pierce had experienced enough of American culture to understand completely the implication of his discovery. He accepted the recognition but allowed himself to enjoy only a moderated sense of success through his later years.

Certainly fame did little to alter his attitudes toward either his art or his understanding of American culture. He did, from time to time, carve pieces that were similar to or almost the same as pieces he had carved before, and he often intended these for sale. In this he was merely acknowledging the importance of providing for his family, and he recognized that his fame allowed him to do this better than before. During interviews, he frequently remarked about his father's struggle to provide for his family, adding that this was the duty of the family patriarch.

Pierce thought a good deal about the idea of duty, of seeing one's obligation in life and fulfilling it. His reflections on this concept are portrayed in *Pearl Harbor and the African Queen*, 1941 (cat. no. 155), in which he examines the concept of duty in the particular life of his community and in African American life in general. In this work, the word

"duty" is prominently placed. In the upper left of the picture, Pierce portrayed a young black man and woman appealing to Uncle Sam to accept their services during World War II. Pierce's sense of humor is seen in the image of a dog, a characteristically faithful animal, carrying a bone; yet another bone below the dog probably refers to Aesop's fable in which the dog is lured by a larger bone. Next to the dog and the bone, Pierce placed the Rose of Sharon, a symbol of Christ. Pierce used the dog and the fable as a means of reminding the viewer that duty is complex and often interferes with personal ambitions. The representations of Uncle Sam and the Rose of Sharon are clearly the most important images in the picture.

Pearl Harbor and the African Queen is a sophisticated work that touches on many aspects of the relationship of black people to American society. Most significantly, we can see in this work the complexity of race relations during a time of war. Historically, African Americans have volunteered for the armed services in times of national crisis, perhaps evidencing an ultimate aim to come to positive terms with an American society that once kept them in bondage. Pearl Harbor and World War II would be natural subjects for an African American artist who in his fifties was too old to fight. Pierce completed this work in 1941, when the outcome of the war was still very much in doubt.

What most influenced Pierce's religion, philosophy, and activities, and thus became the subjects of his carving, is deeply embedded in his experience as a citizen and as an African American. Pierce's story, like those of so many other African Americans, began in the South, in Mississippi, where he was born on March 5, 1892. He grew up in the northeast corner of the state, not far from Tupelo. He lived with his family on a plantation outside of Baldwyn, in a part of Mississippi that was known for its logging industry. Early on, Pierce was surrounded by woods and acquainted with the business of timber cutting, and he became well accustomed to both. The northeast quadrant of Mississippi, where Pierce spent his boyhood and teenage years, was more rugged hills and woods than the so-called black prairie usually associated with the state's plantation and cotton-growing delta. The Mississippi of young Elijah was home to both whites and blacks who farmed the land, growing cotton, peas, corn, and peanuts. The hilly land, reminiscent of the land described in the fiction of William Faulkner and Eudora Welty, was divided into small farms and some plantations. In that part of the lowland South, close to where Mississippi, Alabama, and Tennessee meet, small towns were often predominantly either white or black.

Pierce's hometown, Baldwyn, was one of the most economically depressed areas in the South. With people relying on logging and small farming, there developed a poor record on social and racial democracy. Statistically, Mississippi in general, and northeast Mississippi in particular, had a high number of incidents of violence against blacks. Segregation and discrimination continued well into the post–World War II period of American history.

The circumstances of Elijah Pierce's youth appear to be mixed. Of course, growing up in the Deep South when he did, he was exposed to the worst of racial prejudice and violence. In interviews, however, and in his art, Pierce described his family life and relations with people who lived around his family as positive. Pierce's parents provided a sound and healthy family background. He loved and wanted to emulate his father, but he held a special place for his mother. Pierce said he had five sisters and three brothers; he was the second youngest among the nine children. He remembered that some of the children, especially the girls, would be sent or "hired out" to provide domestic help. He always remembered in warm and loving terms his immediate family as well as extended family and other families who lived on the same plantation. During my interviews with Pierce, I noted his childhood memories were in stark contrast to what I had learned of the harsh realities of everyday life in the segregated South at the turn of the century.

Pierce often carved images from his boyhood depicting scenes of his family, especially his mother. Again and again he returned to these images as sources of inspiration. Not only did he carve family pieces in several versions, but he also tended to keep them and not sell them. When he did sell one, he generally regretted the sale. He told me that once he sold an art piece in which the subject was his mother, and he tried to buy it back. He was genuinely surprised and disturbed that the purchaser would not sell it back to him. It was, after all, his own depiction of his own mother.

The painted wood relief entitled *The Place of My Birth*, 1977 (cat. no. 1), is perhaps the most significant of the family pieces and is certainly one of the most striking. Pierce carved the work to depict his home in Baldwyn; it shows a typical plantation house of the area, a type of vernacular architecture known as a dog-trot or turkey-trot house. Popular among both whites and blacks, the house, pictured in the middle of Pierce's carving, is typically two rooms on either side of a passageway. Pierce accurately pictured the chimneys at opposite ends of the house, on the outside wall, an architectural feature designed to warm the entire interior of the house in the most efficient way. In the hot summer climate, it was necessary that a house should not accumulate heat. Pierce recalled that these houses were particularly suited for hot weather, for even a faint summer breeze could flow through the entire house. Pierce recalled that during the summer he slept with his head on the windowsill many times in order to stay cool through the night.

When talking about *The Place of My Birth*, Pierce noted that you could see the cotton field in the lower left and the "cotton house" in the lower right of the picture. Two families on a plantation would share a cotton house; each cotton house was typically eight feet wide and twelve feet deep with two doors in the front. The cotton house would store the season's production of cotton, which then would be taken to the plantation owner's mill, and the families would receive credit at the company store for their proceeds. Pierce remembered the exact layout of the dog-trot house, and he also remembered the cotton house in this carving that was made nearly sixty years after he left his Mississippi plantation home.

The Place of My Birth is a bucolic plantation landscape that describes how Pierce felt about the circumstances of his youth, or at least how he remembered these. The scene pictures four children playing in a wagon next to the cotton field, with no hint of the work in the field that presumably lay ahead. Two other children are to the side of the dog-trot house and are playing with either dogs or small horses. Another child is in the outhouse (Elijah always peopled his outhouses). Pierce's father is shown above the house, behind the plow, and his mother (or older sister) is shown on the right. There are nine people in the carving, of which probably seven or eight are children. The mother, who appears so prominently and with such a natural focus in *Mother's Prayer,* 1972 (cat. no. 8), and *My Home,* 1978 (cat. no. 2), is most likely the figure to the right of the house, although in this piece, Pierce simply did not give her the specialness of position that he gave her in other works. Shade trees on the upper left and right over the house and the outhouse make a statement about the need for cool refuge in the Mississippi summer. Additional animals in front of the house and other outbuildings to the side of the house contribute to the rustic nature of the setting.

Above the house and the man with the plow are the sun, a star, and the moon. Both the sun and the quarter moon have faces, evoking an impression that a child imagined the scene or that Pierce intended the scene to be imagined as by a child. Pierce also put faces on the sun and moon in other pictures, such as *The White House,* 1977 (cat. no. 84), and *Crucifixion,* 1930s (cat. no. 99), personifying these celestial spheres so that they seem to reflect and comment on earthly events. The overall presentation of Pierce's *The Place of My Birth* gives the impression of a very happy and contented childhood and family life. Pierce said that when he grew up the family had "acquired a milk cow," an important possession, and they had other animals includ-

ing "horses, mules, chickens and ducks. . . . We had quite a few chickens; mother raised them. She had a little basket and everyday she'd gather up eggs. We had all kinds of eggs 'cause we had all kinds of chickens. We didn't have anything special," he remembered, adding, "Well, we did have some Dominics and Rhode Island Reds."

His memory of farm, family, and childhood reflects the importance of these themes to Pierce during his later years. At about the same time that Pierce created *The Place of My Birth* he also completed *My Home,* a painted and carved wood relief that is likewise a warm and peaceful view of his Mississippi homeland. In *My Home,* however, a log cabin with end chimneys is the focus of the work, not the dog-trot house of *The Place of My Birth,* which is likely the more accurate representation of his actual childhood home. Nonetheless, Pierce has again pictured the cotton field at the lower left of the composition, with a man in the lower right behind a plow. The cotton house is in the upper right of the picture and an outhouse is to the left of the log cabin.

Fewer children are pictured in this work, but again we have an overall impression of the bucolic nature of the plantation farm. The cotton is in bloom, a shade tree overlooks the field, and, perhaps most significantly, Pierce has placed his father in a rocking chair next to the field. Throughout his adulthood, Elijah attempted to make life easier for his parents. Clearly, he missed them both. He made his mother a miniature house (see cat. no. 86), carved furniture for the small house, and made other carvings of his mother in a rocking chair. Pierce said "I would do anything for my mother, 'cause she is the one who gave me life itself. I love my mother." After he carved the dollhouse for his mother, he said, "you know, I made a house for my mother with all the furniture . . . and I put a nurse in the house for my mother. I would give her anything. Of course," he added, "it was only a playhouse. But, I would have given her anything she wanted."

Pierce had a more problematic relationship

with his father. His father was evidently much older than his mother. Pierce said "I loved that old man. He could be very hard, but I admired him a good deal. He was a man to be respected." But it is also clear from Pierce that his father was somewhat distant; Pierce spoke about his Uncle Lewis, who was younger than his father, as someone who might have been emotionally closer to Pierce than his father. Pierce's attitudes toward his parents reflected traditional values during the late nineteenth and early twentieth centuries. It was always clear that the love he had for his mother was different from the love and respect he had for his father.

Pierce's memories of his youth also reflect the history and culture of Mississippi, including slavery. His father was an old man when Elijah was born, old enough to have been a slave during the latter part of the antebellum period. Pierce remembered that his father told him he had been "sold three times 'cause he would fight. . . . He would fight and they [sold him] for fear that it would learn some others to fight, protect themselves." Elijah had strong memories of his father and his father's influence on him. He said proudly, "and they never fooled with Daddy 'cause he'd fight. I would too when I was younger. I just wanted to be like my old man."

Pierce's father was twenty or thirty years old when Emancipation came. "Oh," Elijah recalled, "he'd been married and had four or five children" by the time of the Emancipation, "'cause my mother wasn't the first. . . . We were in the second family. . . . But I didn't like a lot of them [those in the first family]." Elijah was as much as thirty-five to forty-five years younger than the children from the first marriage. Certainly his father was a man of considerable survival skills. It was due to his father that Elijah's family had a good place to live. He recalled that the plantation was owned by Lee Prather: "He had a thousand acres of land. Down to the bottom. Trees growed, oh, big things. He logged it." Pierce's father played a significant role on the plantation. Elijah remembered that Mr. Prather "lived in town. He didn't know how much land he

had himself. Had three or four boys. I used to play with 'em. 'Course some was a lot older than I."

One of his most pleasant memories from childhood was the summer fish fry on Prather's plantation. "Every summer they'd have a big fish fry. And your family, my family . . . they all cook," he recounted. "Farmers from twenty miles would come to get in the gang." The summer fish fry on Prather's place was remembered by Pierce as an extremely good time; it was an unusual time as well. "That's one time it wasn't segregated," he said. "Blacks and whites be together."

Although Pierce's work is well known and widely represented in folk art collections, current interpretations of his art tend to ignore important aspects of his life as an African American. It is true that Pierce possessed exceptional expressive abilities that made him unique. Nevertheless, the content of his work and the nature of his occupation existed in concert with the values and structure of his community. Indeed, in the three primary areas of his life—as an artist, a barber, and a lay minister—Pierce lived at the very heart of African American community life. In his daily life, he was surrounded by signs and symbols that spoke not only of the hereafter but also about life as an African American in what seemed an inhospitable country. For Pierce, and for other African Americans, the nature of American society was a fact of life that always had to be reckoned with. He was constantly dealing with apprehensions about the hereafter and religious salvation and with the anxieties of living in a society in which people like himself were not always welcome. Pierce's oeuvre is replete with works that negotiate these two worlds, the world of the now and the world of the hereafter.

Although his messages encompass the sacred and the secular, in the end, only one message was paramount for Elijah Pierce, and that was the experience of salvation. For Pierce, all of the daily life and the trials that people were forced to endure amounted to preparation for everlasting life. In this battle, Pierce hoped he had endured. He believed he had done his best toward that end. He attempted to demonstrate through his art and actions the intensity and wisdom required to survive all earthly trials. In many ways, Pierce was a stern man. He believed in his community and he believed in his God.

When Pierce arrived in Danville, Illinois, in the early 1920s, he joined hundreds of thousands of African Americans who had begun to move to the North in search of new opportunities. This movement was the greatest demographic and cultural change for the American population since the period of slavery. Pierce eventually settled in Columbus and established himself in the black community, in the northern section of the city. His barbershop was located on Long Street, a major thoroughfare in the 1920s to the 1960s and one of the black community's business, social, and religious hubs. Pierce thrived in this environment. Before urban renewal eliminated much of the walk-in barber trade, Pierce's barbershop was one of the places to stop by and catch up on the news of the neighborhood. During his most productive period as a woodcarver, Pierce had other barbers as partners. He explained that when he became particularly involved in a wood carving, he would ask one of the other barbers to take over his customers.

In Columbus, Pierce continued his lifelong commitment to Christianity and became a member of the Gay Tabernacle Baptist Church on Gay Street. Toward the end of his life, he was also a member of the Seventh Day Adventist Church, primarily because his wife was a member. Though he was first of all a Baptist, he shared his deep Christian beliefs with both churches.

In 1947, Pierce joined the Master Lodge 62 of the Ancient Free and Accepted Masons. One of the principal organizations that united aspiring black men in the community, the black Masonic Lodge was originally organized by Prince Hall, one of Boston's most prominent blacks during the time of the Revolution. The black Masons provided African American males the same protection and insurance that other immigrant groups found in their respective fraternal orders. Pierce was a member for

twenty years; he left the lodge in 1967 but rejoined in 1979 as an honorary member. In fundamental ways, the two areas of black community life, the lodge and the church, were critically important. Pierce recognized this fact in his carved images of Masonic symbols, which often included a symbolic Rose of Sharon.

Throughout his development, Pierce carved with the conviction of one who understood his mission in life. A particularly personal work, *Obey God and Live (Vision of Heaven)*, 1956 (cat. no. 6), tells the story of Pierce's conversion to faith in God and Jesus Christ. The carving depicts the time when the artist was a young man, perhaps in his early twenties. His mother had instructed him to read the Bible, but the young Pierce was tempted instead to look at a new Sears Roebuck catalogue that had recently arrived in the mail. In the images on the right, Pierce is being punished by God for running away from the teaching of the Lord. Pierce remembered that God touched him on the side of the head and something happened that made him appear to be dead. The family gathered around; Pierce knew he was not dead, but he did not know how to come back to life. As he explained his recovery, when he confessed his faith in Christ, he was restored to good health.

Pierce was the second youngest child of his father's second marriage. Richard Pierce, a slave who was freed in Raleigh, North Carolina, and then traveled to Mississippi, first married a woman named Mattie and had four children (named Tom, Richard, Ella, and Carrie). After Mattie's death, the elder Pierce married Nellie Wallace and had four more children (Willie, Jesse, Elijah, and Minnie). The youngest child, Elijah's sister Minnie, for whom he had great affection, is pictured in *Obey God and Live (Vision of Heaven)*.

The theme of running away from the teachings of Christ can be found in many of Pierce's works. *Home and Prayer (Obey God and Live)*, 1977 (cat. no. 7), is one such work. By the end of his life, Pierce felt he had completed his God-given task and had created a collection of art work that conveyed the importance of religious faith and salvation. He had created his own art gallery in which he could illustrate to visitors the messages he had received that related to life's religious, social, and political dilemmas. Indeed, he was satisfied with his work and felt that he had made, to the best of his ability, an answer to God's challenge: "Your life is a book and every day you write a page." In Pierce's book there is certainly a profound personal witness to his faith through preaching and art combined.

Pierce was especially pleased by the aesthetics of his well-known storyboard carvings. He was also very generous with these carvings. "If someone liked my carving," he said in 1982, "then I would just give it to them." Pierce found pleasure not only in the act of making art but also in making gifts of his works. He said that he might make a sign for someone in the church who just got a new job, or had a baby, or who needed to be reminded of something. Some examples are: *Don't Lie* (cat. no. 138), *Your Life Is a Book*, 1978 (cat. no. 133), *God Grants Wisdom* (collection of Robert and Marge Piper), and *Have Faith in God / He Will Save You* (collection of the author). In this way, Pierce was always giving, always preaching to the community. As a lay minister at his Baptist church, he often sent people home with personal messages reminding them of homilies that could guide them in their daily lives. I was with Pierce in the winter of 1981–1982, when he was carving a piece entitled *God Is Love* (cat. no. 139). When I asked him why he was making the sign, he told me simply, "Well, it's true, isn't it? I just carve these signs for people to remind them of things."

Carving wood always held a special fascination for Elijah, even from his childhood. When asked if he could remember when he started to carve, he said, "In a way, yeah. I've been carving for as long as I remember." At seven, he began carving farm animals. "Anything I could picture that I could carve, I used to carve it. Horses, cows, dogs, chickens." Over the years Pierce answered the question many times for people who were curious about his personal history. In 1983, he told me his standard response was: "But I just naturally loved

the knife when I was a kid. Pocketknife was the greatest thing I thought Santa Claus put in my stocking. . . . I would have been disappointed if I didn't get a knife for Christmas." Then he would say, "My dad was Santy Claus."

Like many traditional artists, Pierce was influenced primarily by one person. "My uncle carved, he did a lot of carving. Lewis, my mother's brother, Lewis Wallace." Pierce said his Uncle Lewis made chairs and baskets, and did some "regular carving." Pierce said that it was Lewis who taught him how to work in wood, what kind of wood to use in carving, and how to enjoy carving.

Wood seemed a natural medium for Elijah Pierce; it was available. And the enjoyment derived from wood carving was a natural extension of the environment. "I dream things the way they ought to be. I can see them in my mind and I know what they are going to look like." Not unlike many traditional artists, Elijah Pierce perceived that he had special powers to see things that, perhaps, others did not see.

When Pierce was in his teens, he determined that he did not want to be a farmer. He said many times that he did not like farming, but it appears that he left farming because he wanted to get on in the world. In any case, as the youngest son in the family he did not have the rights to the farm. He began laying track for the railroad. He said once that the crew he worked on laid timbers for the track and that the timbers were delivered by train and dumped on the ground. "We always had a lot of broken timbers that way. So I figured out a way of unloading the timbers without breaking them all. So I told the foreman and he thought it was a pretty good idea. We tried it and, well, it worked. He then told his boss, but he didn't tell him that it was my idea; he pretended that it was his idea. Well, it was then that I realized that I would never get anywhere working for the man. The man I worked for never said a word to me about it. Isn't that just amazing?"

Pierce recognized early on that he wanted independence and a trade that would allow him to function on his own. He said, "I needed a trade where I could be independent. I didn't need to work for nobody. And, I liked barbering. I knew a barber in town and I was just fascinated by cutting hair. That man would allow me to learn barbering from him and so I did." Actually, he had started to learn barbering earlier. When he was young, he trimmed his father's beard. "I'd trim 'im up sometimes," he recalled. "I started barbering, I was about in my early teens." He said simply, "I like it." He also said that being a barber would allow him to have a job anywhere. He wanted to go to a city, and barbering would be the most practical profession for an aspiring young black man in the early part of the century. Barbering was also an important occupation in the African American community because white people would not barber for blacks. "I like to cut hair. Cut anybody's hair that come in the shop," Pierce said, with characteristic affection for humanity. Typically, an African American not only tended to the hair of customers but performed small surgical tasks as well, such as removing ingrown hairs and boils, procedures not generally performed during a doctor's visit even if a doctor were available.

When Pierce was probably in his early twenties, he married Zetta Palm. "She was the love of my life," he said. "We were very happy together. I was barbering and we had a little home." They had one year together in Mississippi and according to Pierce it was perfect. At the end of a year, Zetta died. "I never knew what it was. She seemed healthy and all, but one day she took sick and then in a couple of weeks she died. . . . Well after that, I just didn't have anything to stay around for and I left. That's how I got to Ohio."

After he learned to barber and after the death of his first wife, Zetta, Pierce decided to follow the migration of thousands north to the cities. By train, he traveled first to Illinois, living in Champaign, then Danville, and then moving on to Ohio. "I never had any problem getting a job 'cause every town needed a barber. So I worked wherever I stopped." It was in Illinois that he met his second wife, Cornelia. She was from Columbus, Ohio, and

he followed her there; they were married September 8, 1923.

The second marriage ended in 1948 with Cornelia Houeston Pierce's death at the age of sixty-one. At this time Pierce began to come into his own as a mature artist, and his life took yet another direction. He became known as an accomplished artist and, literally, a folk hero. His fame spread nationally and, to some degree, internationally. His life began almost anew when he was sixty. On June 2, 1952, he married Estelle Greene, who was then forty-six. Pierce needed her attention and devotion in his later years, and she enjoyed his sense of life and his imagination. In many ways, they complemented each other. She was devoted to religion and preaching, and he could provide the stage or the pulpit in terms of his art and his own faith. Both of their initials were E.P., and sometimes she painted the "E.P." signature on his works.

Pierce carved in wood from the turn of the century until only a few days before his death. During the time I knew him, he worked on several carvings at the same time. He said that he always worked that way, though when he was more active as a barber he probably did less. He would work on large storyboard relief carvings at the same time that he made smaller figures in-the-round, as he called them. Overall, he spent much more time making relief carvings than he did smaller standing sculptural figures. During the periods when Pierce was carving small figures to sell at local fairs or in his shop, he always had a good supply of finished pieces. These small figures took little time compared to the complex relief carvings.

During his marriage to Cornelia, Pierce spent considerable time at county fairs and other exhibitions where he displayed his crafts. He seemed to have a dual purpose at the time: to preach and to sell some small figures. Later, he began to mount the figures on flat board, in a manner recalling the relief carvings. Apparently Pierce did not see much difference between relief carving and gluing flat, carved pieces on board, except that the latter took less time. He was pleased particularly when the result (see, for example, *Crucifixion*, cat. no. 99) was successful in his preaching.

Many of Pierce's friends and colleagues take credit for encouraging him to mount his flat figures onto board. At least one from central Ohio affirmed that he helped Pierce mount the figures which became the final presentation of *Book of Wood* and assisted him in preparing the frames. The early cardboard mounting disintegrated in time and the figures had to be remounted on wood panel.

Elijah Pierce died on May 7, 1984. He had been sick only two days. But, during March and April he complained that he felt tired and worn out. He said toward the end, "I've had ninety-two years of backaches and ninety-two years of headaches, I'm tired of all this work." But even in the end, he recognized the importance of his calling. "I'll stay as long as I'm needed. We never know what he [God] will want of us."

During his last month, he waited for Easter. He did not celebrate Easter the way most Americans do. He said it was a time for mourning and recognition. The last full piece he created was a magnificent crucifix, made of one piece of wood. It was, he said, a gift for someone in his church. He finished the crucifix only a few days before Easter. He died shortly after.

John F. Moe is Fulbright Professor of American Studies, University of Bergen, Norway, and Adjunct Associate Professor of Ethnology and Art Education, The Ohio State University. Dr. Moe's research on Elijah Pierce was completed with a Senior Individual Research Fellowship from the National Endowment for the Humanities.

1. For further discussions of Pierce's personal history, see Moe, 1990, and Moe, 1991.

2. All quotations used in this essay are from the author's fieldwork interviews with Pierce over a number of years.

3. Folklorists have long been interested in the relationship between the artist and his or her community and the performance of the art. Some excellent treatments of the subject are available: see, for example, Henry Glassie, "Folk Art," in Richard M. Dorson, *Folklore and Folklife: An Introduction* (Chicago: University of Chicago Press, 1972), pp. 253–280; and Henry Glassie, *The Spirit of Folk Art* (New York: Harry N. Abrams in association with the Museum of New Mexico, Santa Fe, 1989).

   On the relationship of an artist and his or her personal history to the history and culture of the community, see John Michael Vlach, *Charleston Blacksmith: The Work of Phillip Simmons* (Athens, Georgia: University Press of Georgia, 1981).

   For a discussion of the role of community and autobiography in the folk artist's world, see Moe, 1987. Much of my own analysis of the role of community in an artist's work is indebted to Henry Glassie's work in his monumental study, *Passing the Time in Ballymenone* (Philadelphia: University of Pennsylvania Press, 1982); for an excellent discussion of the community's belief systems, see particularly Part One: "A Territory of Wits," pp. 11–87.

ELIJAH PIERCE AND THE AFRICAN AMERICAN TRADITION OF WOOD CARVING

REGENIA A. PERRY

During the eighteenth and nineteenth centuries and well into the twentieth, a school of African American woodcarvers flourished along the coastal areas of Georgia as well as in Alabama, Louisiana, and Mississippi. The tradition of carving figures, canes, walking sticks, and bird, animal, and serpent imagery may be traced directly to West Africa via the importation of slaves to the United States during a two-hundred-year period.

As African Americans migrated from the Deep South following World War I, most moved northward to cities such as St. Louis, Chicago, Detroit, Columbus, and Milwaukee, rather than to locations along the northeast coast or the west coast. That migratory pattern is reflected in the lives of many African American woodcarvers, in particular Elijah Pierce of Columbus, Ohio; William Dawson of Chicago; and Josephus Farmer of Milwaukee. An investigation of the lives and careers of these three artists reveals a number of striking similarities. All were born on farms in the South; two of the three were ministers and barbers (Pierce and Farmer);[1] and all were elderly before they received their first artistic recognition. Pierce was the most celebrated member of the trio, the one who practiced his craft for the longest period of time and the only one to receive international recognition during his lifetime. The works of Pierce and Farmer, both of whom were evangelical lay ministers—of the Baptist and Pentecostal denominations respectively—evidence the closest iconographic, stylistic, and technical similarities. Although Pierce, Farmer, and Dawson were the most celebrated mid-twentieth-century African American woodcarvers—and all migrated northwestward—an equally talented group of carvers, including Ulysses Davis, George White, George Williams, and Luster Williams, remained in the South and practiced their craft.

THE FIRST GENERATION

ELIJAH PIERCE (1892–1984)

Born in a log cabin on a farm near Baldwyn, Mississippi, on March 5, 1892, Elijah Pierce was reared in a devoutly religious Baptist household.[2] His father, a former slave, was a deacon for forty years, and his mother required her children to read the Bible regularly. Those early religious influences were later reflected in a number of Pierce's carvings. Pierce's interest in wood carving began at the age of about eight when he began to cut names and designs into the bark of trees on his father's farm and then carved small animals and hickory walking sticks. Pierce later recalled that one of his maternal uncles carved wooden figures and that he had been greatly influenced by him. During his early boyhood, Pierce did not like farm life and, unlike his siblings, yearned to see the bright city lights. Pierce attended school through the eighth grade, and learned the trade of barbering when he was about eleven by observing local barbers in Baldwyn.

Between 1914 and 1917, a number of important events occurred in Pierce's personal life. Around

1914, he was converted at Mt. Zion Baptist Church in Baldwyn. During the following year, he married his first wife, Zetta Palm; their son Willie was born and Zetta died shortly afterwards. Two years later, Pierce's father, Richard, also passed away. Undoubtedly saddened by the loss of his wife and father and unhappy with his rural Mississippi environment, Pierce left Baldwyn when he was about twenty-five years old and began a hobolike existence hitching rides on boxcars and working on bridge gangs in Tennessee, Missouri, and Ohio. Pierce later described those years of wandering as a time when he "dressed well, danced well, and played the piano well." However, Pierce was apparently unable to disassociate himself from his southern roots entirely, and he visited his mother in Baldwyn intermittently. Pierce's mother informed him during his early childhood that he was born with a "veil over his face,"[3] meaning he possessed psychic powers. Although he initially resisted a calling to preach, Pierce received his preacher's license on September 26, 1920, following his ordination at his home church in Baldwyn. Still unsettled, Pierce left Baldwyn and moved north once again, living briefly in Champaign, Illinois, and later moving to Danville, Illinois.

While living in Danville, Pierce met Cornelia Houeston from Columbus, Ohio, who apparently worked in Danville for several years, then returned to Columbus in 1923. Although he had intended not to remarry, Pierce missed Cornelia greatly. He followed her to Columbus; the couple were married on the day of his arrival. Pierce's second marriage lasted until Cornelia's death in 1948. In 1952, Pierce married his third wife, Estelle Greene, who survives him.

Shortly after Pierce's arrival in Columbus, he obtained a job as a barber, which remained his primary livelihood until his retirement in 1978. Pierce worked for another barber, then in 1951 opened his own shop on Long Street in the heart of Columbus's African American community. Having finally found happiness with his new wife and job, Pierce apparently lost interest in the nomadic lifestyle and rediscovered his early passion for wood carving. One year during the late 1920s, Pierce was unable to afford a birthday gift for his wife Cornelia. Instead, he carved a small elephant for her, which pleased her so greatly that he promised her an entire zoo.

Cornelia's menagerie, or the promise of the same, was probably the impetus for some of the figures and panels Pierce began carving during the late 1920s. His earliest works were based on ideas from cartoons and popular images. By the early 1930s, biblical subjects had become the dominant themes in his carvings. A number of his later works were also inspired by Old and New Testament topics. "Every piece of work I got carved," stated Pierce, "is a message, a sermon. Preacher don't hardly get up in the pulpit and preach but he don't preach some picture I got carved."[4]

Pierce's earliest Columbus works were small three-dimensional figures, which he began mounting on cardboard and wooden backgrounds during the 1930s. From that stage he progressed to carving panels in bas-relief. During the 1930s and 1940s, Pierce and Cornelia packed their car with his carvings and traveled during their summer vacations to revivals, churches, and fairs in a number of states. The Pierces staged informal programs and explained the iconographical and moral implications of each carving. Although they never charged admission to their programs, a donation plate for "silver offerings" and the occasional sale of a carving paid their expenses.

The most ambitious work of Pierce's long wood-carving career is *Book of Wood* (cat. no. 100), which he completed during a six-month period circa 1932. Originally carved as individual scenes, the pieces are mounted in a book format. *Book of Wood* consists of seven relief carvings representing the seven great churches of Asia Minor and thirty-three scenes representing the thirty-three years Christ lived on earth. The scenes are arranged—not always in chronological order—across the entire surface of the wood panels. The backgrounds are painted green and serve as an effective foil for the brightly colored bas-relief carvings.

Pierce's wood carvings, with their direct approach, humor, simple imagery, bright colors, and moral lessons, are important additions to American folk art. Although Pierce was a woodcarver for more than sixty years, his first major public recognition did not occur until 1971, when he had his first one-artist exhibition—at Ohio State University in Columbus. The most distinguished honor of Pierce's long career occurred in 1973, when he was awarded first prize at the International Meeting of Naive Art in Zagreb, Yugoslavia.

On May 7, 1984, Elijah Pierce passed away in his adopted city, Columbus. During more than sixty years as a woodcarver, Pierce sold and gave away hundreds of examples of his art. However, by establishing the Elijah Pierce Art Gallery in his Long Street barbershop, he retained a large body of the carvings he considered the most significant. Pierce was the first among his generation of African American woodcarvers to perceive the significance of his work and to present it to the public in a gallery setting.

JOSEPHUS FARMER (1894–1989)

The career of Josephus Farmer parallels that of Elijah Pierce more closely than that of any other first-generation twentieth-century African American woodcarver. Like Pierce, Farmer migrated from his southern birthplace, was a licensed minister, began carving during his childhood, specialized in religious subjects, and considered his works to be "sermons in wood." Both carvers were also circuit preachers and musicians: Pierce played the piano and Farmer was an accomplished guitarist.

Farmer was born on August 1, 1894, in rural Gibson Courts, near Trenton, Tennessee. When he was around twenty, he moved to St. Louis, where he found employment in an Armour meat-packing house.[5] The year 1922 was probably the most momentous of Farmer's life. That January 15, Farmer heard the voice of God calling him to join the church. Several weeks later he was baptized, and, filled with the Holy Spirit, he "spoke in tongues" for the first time.[6] Farmer was called to the minis-

try and on May 14, 1922, preached his first sermon. He obtained a permit to preach on the streets of St. Louis. During that same year, Farmer met and married Evelyn Griffin, from Prairieville, Missouri. The couple's only child, Joseph, was born in 1924.

During the next several years the Farmers moved frequently, living in Missouri, Illinois, Indiana, California, Oregon, and Washington. Farmer followed his evangelical calling, while working as a laborer to support himself and his family. On weekends he held tent revivals or preached in storefront churches; he founded his own church, El Bethel, in South Kinlock, Missouri, in 1931. Farmer also was pastor of churches in Murphysboro and Harrisburg, Illinois.[7] In 1947, Farmer moved his family to Milwaukee, where he remained until his retirement in 1960.

Farmer's artistic proclivities were, like Elijah Pierce's, evident from his early childhood, and he recalled carving a wooden duck at the age of ten. As a young boy, he also fashioned animals from baling wire, made string puppets, and carved animals from peach stones with a pocketknife.[8] Shortly after his retirement in 1960, Farmer began carving relief panels, primarily depicting biblical and patriotic themes, largely inspired by images he faithfully copied from newspapers, magazines, and books. One of the earliest groups of Farmer's relief carvings, dated to the 1960s and early 1970s, is in the collection of the Milwaukee Art Museum. Farmer's panels from this period frequently depict President John F. Kennedy and his wife Jacqueline and the White House; they clearly reveal that Kennedy was Farmer's hero. These panels are carved in low relief, with innumerable details, and painted with bright enamel colors. Farmer's works fall into four categories: relief carvings, tableaus, banners, and three-dimensional figures.

Most of Farmer's works are relief panels carved from a variety of softwoods—redwood was his preference—obtained from lumber yards and hardware stores. He made preliminary sketches directly on the wooden panels and employed pocketknives, chisels, and drills during the carving process.

Fig. 3. Josephus Farmer, 1894–1989, *Welcome to St. Louis*, 1985, carved and painted wood, 18 x 72 x 21 in. (45.7 x 182.8 x 53.3 cm), Private Collection

Farmer was alone among the leading twentieth-century African American woodcarvers in his extensive use of the power drill in his works.

As Farmer grew more confident and skilled in his handling of wood, he began drilling small holes close together in his panels to create negative spaces in the designs. Farmer sometimes carved and painted both sides of his panels, unlike Pierce, whose essentially flat figures were mounted on cardboard and wooden backgrounds. In the third phase of his career, Farmer constructed large, three-dimensional tableaus of biblical and historical scenes. While not as numerous or as well known as his relief panels, the tableaus were the pieces he cherished most.[9] Farmer's preference for large three-dimensional constructions was apparently unique among twentieth-century African American woodcarvers. Pierce completed several impressive tableaus, including *Sacrifice of Isaac*, 1952 (cat. no. 92), and *Paul and Silas in Jail*, n.d. (cat. no. 98), but he preferred carving relief panels. A major difference between Pierce and Farmer is that Farmer rarely carved three-dimensional animals that were not intended for his tableaus.

The earliest examples of Farmer's religious and historical tableaus were completed during the late 1970s, when he began to attach three-dimensional figures to plywood bases. Farmer's use of additional materials in these constructions was very imaginative. He used green flocking to simulate grass on the bases, and in scenes recalling his childhood, such as *Promise of Liberty* (private collection) and *Dixie Land* (private collection), he used wood putty to fashion bolls on cotton plants; Farmer made trees of wooden dowels and attached leaves of cellophane painted green.

One of the finest of Farmer's three-dimensional constructions is *Welcome to St. Louis*, which he completed in 1981. Four years later he enlarged the composition. Farmer repeated this theme in several additional constructions during his late period; however, these lack the power and clarity of the original enlarged version (fig. 3). In Farmer's scene, Adolphus Busch, the city's wealthiest citizen, at one time the owner of St. Louis's largest brewery, is depicted driving a Budweiser wagon drawn by a team of four Clydesdale horses. The wagon is shown entering a replica of St. Louis's famous arch, above which perches a bright red cardinal (symbolic of that city's baseball team, owned by Anheuser-Busch). A soldier on horseback in the original version represented General Ulysses S. Grant, who owned a farm near St. Louis that was purchased by Busch and converted to an animal reserve.[10] Farmer later increased the team of horses from four to six, eliminated the figure of General Grant, and added two houses and a descriptive plaque commemorating an early settlement in St. Louis. Additional tableaus by Farmer portray farming and cotton picking; religious subjects such as *Noah's Ark, The Nativity,* and *Flight into Egypt; Casey Jones,* Kentucky's legendary train engineer; and *The Village Blacksmith,* which was inspired by Henry Wadsworth Longfellow's poem.

A category of Farmer's art that distinguishes him from Pierce is a series of painted banners, which he initially used as teaching aids in his Pentecostal services. Most of the banners were painted on window shades and combine text and illustrations in often extremely elaborate biblical iconography. Another category of Farmer's works consists of a number of three-dimensional carved single figures including crucifixions, the Statue of Liberty, trains, pistols, and a delightful pair of bears inspired by the design on St. Louis police badges.

Like Pierce, Farmer received considerable public recognition for his carvings during the final years of his life. He exhibited regularly in Milwaukee community art festivals and exhibitions and was awarded a first prize in sculpture in 1981. The following year, the University of Wisconsin in Milwaukee mounted a large retrospective of Farmer's work with an accompanying symposium and a well-illustrated catalogue.[11] In 1985, he received the Governor's Heritage Award, and in 1986, six of Farmer's early relief panels were presented to and installed in the permanent collection of the Milwaukee Art Museum.[12]

Widowed and in declining health in 1987, Farmer moved from Milwaukee to Joliet, Illinois, to be near his son. He moved into an apartment in a senior citizens' building and continued his wood carving with great fervor. Failing eyesight and crippling arthritis did not diminish Farmer's determination to construct complex tableaus, still employing power drills extensively. By the summer of 1989, Farmer was experiencing equilibrium difficulties and could no longer care for himself. He was admitted to Sunny Hill Nursing Home in Joliet, where his days were spent reading the Bible, receiving visitors, and attending church services with his son several times a week. On November 15, 1989, Farmer suffered a heart attack in his room at the nursing home and was taken to a local hospital, where he passed away several hours later.

WILLIAM DAWSON (1901–1990)

William Dawson was born in Madison, Alabama, on the outskirts of Huntsville, in 1901. Unlike Pierce and Farmer, Dawson settled in one place —Chicago—and remained there until his death in 1990. He worked at a number of jobs before starting his thirty-five-year tenure at E. E. Aron Produce Company, where he began as a laborer and rose to the position of produce supervisor.

Following Dawson's retirement from E. E. Aron in 1965, he attended several adult education classes in painting and ceramics. However, his interests quickly turned to wood carving, and he began carving without the benefit of classes in this area.[13] Unlike Pierce and Farmer, Dawson did not carve during his boyhood. Undoubtedly, however, it was on his father's farm near Huntsville that he developed an affinity for the animals and birds that appear frequently in his works.

Dawson's best-known figures are totems depicting human faces that initially were carved from furniture legs (fig. 4). His decision to carve totem figures was apparently not influenced by American Indian or other similar carvings. In addition to the totems, which range in height from three to five feet, Dawson carved birds, animals, humans, and popular themes such as *Chicken George* (inspired by Alex Haley's *Roots*) and *Idi Amin Walking His Pet Pig* (fig. 5). Included in Dawson's oeuvre are numerous boxy architectural constructions.

Fig. 5. William Dawson, 1901–1990, *Idi Amin Walking His Pet Pig*, 1977, carved and painted wood, 13½ x 6½ x 2½ in. (34.3 x 16.5 x 6.4 cm), Collection of Chuck and Jan Rosenak

Fig. 4. William Dawson, 1901–1990, *Totem*, 1982, carved and painted wood, H. 19 in. (48.3 cm), Private Collection

Dawson was unlike Pierce and Farmer in that the majority of his carvings depict secular subjects. Dawson stood out among his generation of African American wood carvers for a small but significant group of bone "sculptures" which he constructed from discarded chicken, beef, pork, and fish bones and attached to wooden bases with nails and glue. Dawson embellished his bone sculptures with enamel paint and often incorporated found objects and wooden forms into the design. He assigned titles to his bone sculptures, such as *Ship of Fools* and *One Flew over the Cuckoo's Nest*.

Toward the end of his career, Dawson completed a number of paintings showing yet another facet of his artistic versatility. Working in acrylics on paper and board, and often varnishing the completed paintings, Dawson created jewel-like compositions that usually reflected the same subject matter as that in his carved works, including the well-known totems.

The scale of some of Dawson's late figures increased dramatically. Several totems and single figures approach five feet in height and, like their predecessors, usually have movable arms, which were carved separately and attached with nails.

Dawson spent his final years carving daily in one of the bedrooms of his apartment in downtown Chicago, which served as his studio-gallery. He purchased his wood from local lumber yards, and, like his peers, Pierce and Davis, he painted his figures with enamel paint and added sequins, rhinestones, and glitter. To his later carvings of female figures Dawson frequently attached hair obtained from wigs. He used a minimum of tools, carving primarily with a pocketknife, chisel, and file, and he did not employ power drills. Dawson rarely discarded scraps of wood, using these to create a variety of small serpents, animals, and birds.

The majority of Dawson's figures retain the blocklike character of the wood from which they were carved, and large painted eyes are trademarks of his designs. Dawson created innumerable variations of the totem theme. Human heads, ranging in size from a few inches to five feet, were carved singly or in combination with houselike bases and painted in an array of vibrant hues. Although Dawson carved a veritable menagerie of real and imaginary animals, serpents, and birds, his totem figures are the objects for which he is best known. They are also the most original category of his prodigious output.

In January 1990, Dawson was honored with a large retrospective exhibition, and an accompanying catalogue, at the Chicago Public Library. Six months later, in July, he suffered a stroke in his apartment. He was admitted to a Chicago hospital, where he passed away several days later from complications of pneumonia, which he had unknowingly contracted weeks earlier.

ULYSSES DAVIS (1914—1990)

Ulysses Davis, born on January 13, 1914, in the tiny south-central community of Fitzgerald, Georgia, never ventured far from his roots. His interest in wood carving as a sideline to his barbering profession parallels the career of Pierce, and, to some degree, of Farmer.

Davis gave his first haircut at the age of ten and laughingly remembered receiving one penny for his efforts. He dropped out of school in the tenth grade to help support his younger sisters and brothers. In 1933, he married his childhood sweetheart, Elizabeth, and in 1942, he moved his family to Savannah, Georgia, where he remained until his death.[14]

Davis did not practice barbering full-time until the early 1950s, when he was laid off from his job as office helper for the railroad. During that period of unemployment, he built a small barbershop behind his house and decorated the screen door, trim, and window frames with colorful designs, carved and stamped into the wood with dies he fashioned from automobile bushings. Similar dies provided embellishments for many of Davis's carved designs.

The majority of Davis's carvings are three-dimensional; however, he also carved relief panels. His subjects include a variety of animals, familiar and imaginary; religious subjects; scenes recalling

Fig. 6. Ulysses Davis, 1914–1990, *Busts of Presi-*
dents, 1970s, carved and painted wood,
Each 8 x 4 x 2½ in. (20.3 x 10.2 x 6.4 cm),
Estate of Ulysses Davis

his rural childhood; and patriotic and civil rights
figures, such as George Washington, Abraham Lincoln, John F. Kennedy, and Martin Luther King, Jr.
The most celebrated among Davis's hundreds of
carvings is a series of small busts of forty U.S. presidents, from George Washington to George Bush,
and the presidential seal.

Not unlike Elijah Pierce's barbershop, Davis's
functioned as a studio and gallery for his numerous
carvings, which neatly lined shelves and counter
spaces, often two and three deep. Davis's earliest
figures and reliefs were painted with enamel while
the majority of his later carvings were simply
varnished and occasionally accented with color.
Rhinestones, sequins, and glitter were liberally
used by Davis, who referred to such materials as
"twinklets" and frequently acquired them from
his wife's broken costume jewelry and cast-off
evening gowns.

During the late 1930s in Fitzgerald, Georgia,
Davis carved and painted several reliefs of scenes
from his rural boyhood. These panels were of
great sentimental value to Davis, and he retained

them until his death. To that group belong two
farm scenes, *Boy Milking Cow* and *Airplanes,* and
two religious panels, *Crucifixion* (see fig. 11, p. 62)
and *Samson and the Lion.* Although Davis carved
religious subjects throughout his career, they were
not his specialty; his best examples were completed
during the 1930s and 1940s. Childhood scenes do
not appear in his more mature and later works.

Davis followed the tradition of Farmer and
Pierce in his representation of well-known people.
However, Davis was quite unlike Farmer and Pierce
in that his most celebrated figures are not religious
but political subjects. During the early 1970s, Davis
began carving his series of small portrait busts of
U.S. presidents with an accompanying presidential
seal. All of the figures but one are carved of
mahogany (that of Buchanan is of pecan), and all
are approximately eight inches high and four inches
wide. Viewed as a group, this impressive array of
small figures appears monumental, almost transcending the realm of folk art. Some of the figures
wear miniature eyeglasses fashioned by the carver.
These portraits are the most widely acclaimed

among Davis's carvings and probably his most out-standing works (fig. 6).

Most of Davis's prolific output consists of humans, animals, reptiles, and hybrid creatures, both naturalistic and chimerical. Davis stated that he often envisioned subjects in his dreams the night before he began carving them. Grimacing monsters, many-headed creatures, and other visionary figures with rhinestone eyes and elaborate surface patterns appear among Davis's subjects.

Davis delighted in bestowing unusual titles on some of his pieces, such as *No-No Bird; Man from Jupiter; When, Where;* and *Nimrod.* Some single figures are Janus-faced, while others have as many as four faces. Davis's earliest sculpture, a hand-size figure entitled *The First Man,* which he carved when he was ten, still survives. One of the most personal pieces among his carvings is *Elizabeth—The Goddess of Peace and Love.* Dedicated to Davis's wife, Elizabeth, a quiet and gracious lady who predeceased Davis, the goddess is depicted holding a heart in one hand and displaying the sign of peace with the other.

A group of hand-carved tables is also among Davis's works. The tops of the primarily medallion-shaped tables were carved in elaborate relief patterns, often employing a large central floral motif bordered by geometric patterns or multifloral designs. Davis was probably alone among his generation of African American wood carvers in the production of decoratively carved tabletops featuring foliated and geometric designs.

Davis's talents were first noticed and encouraged in 1953 by Virginia Kiah, a local public schoolteacher and collector who later founded her own museum of African American art in Savannah. Kiah exhibited some of Davis's carvings in her classroom and was instrumental in arranging his first one-artist exhibition, in the local YMCA building. In spite of numerous requests, Davis sold only a few of his carvings during his lifetime. He preferred to keep his more than three hundred objects together as a legacy for his children and grandchildren. The majority of his carvings are currently housed at King-Tisdale House, an African American museum in Savannah.

On November 10, 1990, Ulysses Davis died suddenly of a heart attack while engaging in his favorite activity, the carving of yet another whimsical figure.[15]

GEORGE W. WHITE, JR. (1903–1970)

Of all the woodcarvers mentioned thus far, George White was the only one who developed a sense of his artistic significance early on. He was born in Cedar Creek, Texas, and died in Dallas; his extensive travel itinerary during the intervening years reads like a Marco Polo diary. White boasted that he was of Mexican, American Indian, and African ancestry, which accounted for his "ginger cake" complexion. His father owned a farm, where young George spent his boyhood working closely around the animals, farm machinery, and implements he would later depict in his carvings. White attended Evo Elementary School in Cedar Creek; apparently he did not attend high school. He remained on the family farm until 1920, then moved to Austin to work in the oil fields. White began his nomadic lifestyle during the late 1920s. He enlisted in the army in 1932. According to White, he traveled to West Africa during his military career, and there he learned the art of wood carving.[16]

In 1957, shortly after marrying his second wife, Lucille, White dreamed he would become a famous artist, and on the following day he carved and painted his first relief, *Rodeo Scene.* During the next twelve years, he produced scores of drawings, painted reliefs, three-dimensional tableaus, collages, carved canes, tooled leather items, painted gourds and bottles, miniature wooden chairs in bottles, carved pipes and musical instruments, and replicas of farming implements and machinery. White adamantly refused to sell or exhibit any of his works during his lifetime as he hoped to buy a bus, convert it into a traveling museum of his works, and sell his bathtub-brewed cure-all liniment as admission.

Fig. 7. George White, 1903–1970, *Emancipation House*, 1964, mixed media: wood, cloth, and oil, 19¹⁄₂ x 23¹⁄₄ x 18¹⁄₂ in., National Museum of American Art, Smithsonian Institution, Washington, D.C.: Museum Purchase, 1976.60

Fig. 8. George White, 1903–1970, *Wrestling*, 1968, carved and painted wood relief, 21¹⁄₂ x 24 in. (54.6 x 61.0 cm), Collection of Jean and Bill Booziotis

The most intriguing category of White's works are his three-dimensional tableaus, including *Old Ladies Washing and Ironing, Mules Pulling Hay Wagon,* and *Butchering the Pig;* scenes inspired by his travels, such as *Rooster Fight, Oil Drilling,* and *Rodeo Rider;* and images of popular culture such as *Joe Louis in Shoe Shine Parlor, Jack Johnson Boxing,* and *We Are Having Hell with This Old Ford.* Many of White's tableaus are mechanical, and some were fitted with coin-operated motors in anticipation of his traveling museum. White's well-known *Emancipation House,* 1964 (fig. 7), depicts two black men and one white man applying shingles to the roof of a small cabin. A magazine illustration of Abraham Lincoln is attached to the side of the house, and in the yard is a stereotypical image of a black woman holding a gigantic slice of watermelon. While some of the images in this and other tableaus have been perceived as negative caricatures of African American life, this was apparently not the intent of the artist, who enjoyed depicting scenes from his own perspective. Many of White's three-dimensional constructions and painted reliefs display magazine illustrations, which are sometimes incorporated into the designs. The interesting mixed-media technique coupled with the innovation of movable parts is a unique aspect of his work.

White's carved and painted relief panels also constitute a large body of his work. Among several splendid examples is *Wrestling* (fig. 8). This unusual relief is fitted with a hinged panel at the center. When the panel is turned to the left, a scene of the wrestling match is seen; when the panel is moved to the right, the viewer sees the winner declared and his opponent lying helpless on the floor.

White did not create his first work of art until he was fifty-eight, and his artistic career spanned a period of only twelve years. He did not live to realize his dreams of operating a traveling museum of his works. On January 1, 1970, George White, Jr., died of blood poisoning at the Veterans Administration Hospital in Dallas. His death followed surgery to amputate an infected toe, which White apparently caused by trimming a corn with one of his carving knives. White was buried in the cemetery behind Shiloh Church in Cedar Creek, Texas, which he attended during his boyhood.[17]

White was one of the most talented and innovative African American woodcarvers of his generation, yet his works have not received as much public exposure as those of Pierce, Dawson, and Farmer. A posthumous one-artist show of seventy-seven works was held at the Creative Arts Center in Waco, Texas, in 1975. Clearly White's large body of works bears silent and sometimes eloquent testimony to an artist whose life and art were far from commonplace.

THE SECOND GENERATION

LEROY ALMON (B. 1938)

The most celebrated member of the second generation of twentieth-century African American woodcarvers, Leroy Almon is the only practitioner who was born in the South (in Tallapoosa, Georgia, a small town northwest of Atlanta), then migrated to the North, and then returned to his southern birthplace, where he currently lives and works. Trained by Elijah Pierce in Columbus, Ohio, Almon is also the only well-known African American woodcarver of this century who served an apprenticeship under an older master.

Following studies at Kentucky State College for two years and a six-month assignment in the United States Army in 1961, Almon returned to Cincinnati and married his high school sweetheart, Etta Mae Lewis, in 1962. Almon found employment in Cincinnati as a shoe salesman for Schiff's Shoe Company and after two years was transferred to a Columbus branch of the company. Shortly after moving to Columbus, he became a salesman and marketing specialist for Coca-Cola Bottling Company.

While residing in Columbus, Almon visited a number of African American churches in quest of a home church and was particularly impressed with the services at Gay Tabernacle Baptist Church. One Sunday in 1978 while visiting Gay Tabernacle, Almon heard Elijah Pierce deliver a sermonette and saw him present a small woodcarving to a member of the congregation. Inspired by Pierce's message and impressed with his largess, Almon decided to visit the elderly gentleman at his barbershop on Long Street several days later. He was received warmly by the preacher-carver, and the Pierce-Almon relationship began.

Initially, Almon was not interested in wood carving or art but anticipated a successful corporate career. Almon and Pierce developed a close friendship of a father-son type, based on mutual admiration and benefit. Almon frequently drove Pierce to affairs and appointments and assisted him in conducting tours of the Elijah Pierce Art Gallery. In 1979, Almon lost his job at the Coca-Cola Bottling Company and began visiting Pierce's barbershop daily. Pierce paid him a small salary, and Almon became the curator of the gallery. Almon credits Ursel White Lewis, a prominent African American educator in Columbus, for the beginning of his artistic career. Lewis was also an early and avid collector of Pierce's wood carvings. During one of her trips to Pierce's gallery in 1980, she suggested to Almon that he should attempt to carve and benefit from his direct exposure to Pierce's talents.

Almon considered Lewis's suggestion for several weeks before selecting a piece of wood from Pierce's scrap box and sketching a three-part design depicting Noah's Ark, the Garden of Eden, and the Tower of Babel. Pierce provided the pocketknife and chisel for Almon's earliest carving, which was remarkably accomplished for a neophyte. Pierce encouraged his young apprentice, and Almon soon began carving a number of panels while collaborating with Pierce on some of his designs. Almon's apprenticeship with Pierce was of relatively brief duration. However, he benefited immensely from Pierce's instruction and from observing the techniques of the older carver. Although Almon was very enthusiastic about his budding avocation as a woodcarver, his personal life was unsettled. Shortly after losing his position with Coca-Cola in 1979, he and his first wife were divorced. Lacking steady employment and yearning for his southern roots, Almon decided to return to Georgia in 1981.

He initially moved to Atlanta, where he remained for a year, working as an assistant manager of a fast-food restaurant. In 1982, Almon decided to return to his tiny hometown of Tallapoosa.

Almon produced no wood carvings during his Atlanta sojourn or during the first year following his return to Tallapoosa. It was a very difficult period financially until 1984, when Almon was hired as a radio dispatcher for the Tallapoosa Police Department, a position he still holds. By 1985, Almon, had resumed woodcarving and, unlike his master, Elijah Pierce, developed a system of executing small preliminary sketches on paper for all of his proposed carvings. These sketches are transferred to wooden panels and carved in the low-relief method, which has become Almon's trademark. Since early on, Almon, who developed a preference for softwoods such as redwood, basswood, and birch, has executed his designs primarily with a pocketknife and chisel. Not unlike his mentor and peers, Almon paints his panels with bright enamel colors.

From the beginning of his career, Almon has been keenly interested in depicting contemporary, historical, and religious themes. Unlike Pierce, Almon has completed few animals or three-dimensional woodcarvings. The wooden panels of Leroy Almon are frequently commentaries on African American and American life in general: he has described in his works such subjects as temptations confronting young people; President and Mrs. Reagan steamrolling poor African Americans; slavery scenes; death as the wages of sin; and hell, with tortured faces surrounded by a blazing red inferno. There are also portraits of Mona Lisa, Elvis Presley, and Martin Luther King, Jr., as well as a centaur inspired by an illustration in a children's storybook.

In the past several years, Almon has begun painting to expand his preliminary sketches. He paints on paper and panels with acrylics and depicts religious themes, self-portraits, still lifes, abstractions, and geometric designs. During a three-month period in 1990, when his hands were sore and weak from many months of incessant carving, Almon produced an interesting series of framed small paintings on panel, embellished with glitter, depicting many of his familiar themes.

Almon is perhaps the only major African American woodcarver who is also a folk artist–environmentalist. The meticulously landscaped yard surrounding his boyhood home on Sugar Hill (which Almon restored several years ago) is dotted with signs referring to his wood-carving pursuits and ministerial calling. Almon is a nondenominational evangelist. In the front yard of the Almon residence is a large outline of the name Jesus, illuminated by Christmas lights. A number of small paintings by Almon are suspended on a line on one side of the driveway leading to the backyard. Directly behind Almon's residence are a large gazebo, prayer tower, and baptismal pool.

The octagonal meditation gazebo is screened and furnished with comfortable chairs. Seven of the eight sides of the gazebo's exterior display vibrantly painted panels which were completed by Almon in 1987. These panels—his finest paintings to date—are: *Cleanliness is Next to Godliness, The Crucifixion of Christ, Angel in Orbit, Satan Fishing, A Dream, Boyhood Farm Scene,* and *The Holy Trinity.*

Almon erected the prayer tower for his own private meditation and for the use of family members and anyone else who desires to use it. This small, but impressive, white stucco two-story building has a square plan on the first floor, surmounted by a circular second level. Immediately beyond the entrance to the tower is a small altar, covered with dark blue velvet and displaying an open Bible. A ladder in one corner of the room provides access to a circular balcony with a splendid open-timber ceiling whose radiating beams are painted in bright hues of green, blue, red, and yellow. The only examples of Almon's art in this unusual edifice are four angels placed near the ceiling in each corner of the main prayer room.

The final member of the architectural trio behind Almon's home is a small baptismal pool lined with concrete, which is used for baptisms of new converts and for those who wish to renew their spirituality. On a hill above the pool, Almon has erected three wooden crosses and a sign which reads, "Be baptized unto repentance." This composition functions as a poignant reminder of the baptism and crucifixion of Christ.

Leroy Almon is now apparently at the height of his artistic powers. Although his most sought-after works are carved panels depicting religious subjects, he also produces panels dealing with aspects of African American life and history. His most recent series, entitled African American Life, includes fifteen panels depicting pimps and prostitutes, street people smoking and drinking, winos sharing a bottle, nightclub scenes, women at wash pots, people going to church, cotton picking, baptisms, and funerals. In the upper left corner of each panel is an all-seeing eye of God, and each panel bears Almon's trademark signature—"LA"—carved in block letters within a vertical bar painted gold. Almon has taken part in a number of exhibitions in the United States, and his work was recently included in an international exhibition entitled From Atlanta to Paris. In 1985, he received the Georgia Governor's Award for the Arts. Almon has remarried, and he and his wife Mary Alice are the parents of a son, Elisha Leroy.

ELIJAH PIERCE AND LEROY ALMON—
MASTER AND APPRENTICE

When Leroy Almon made his initial informal visit to Elijah Pierce's barbershop-studio in 1979, few could have suspected that the visit would lead to an important and successful collaboration between the elderly preacher-woodcarver and the considerably younger career man. During the course of repeated visits to Pierce's shop, Almon carefully observed the older master's methods of carving and asked numerous questions about his techniques.

As in the case of his mentor, Almon has become a minister; he was ordained at Mt. Newly Baptist Church in Tallapoosa on July 6, 1986. Almon has converted two of the three rooms in the basement of his house into a studio and gallery, where he displays his carvings and paintings and con-

ducts tours as he did for Pierce in Columbus. Almon is an articulate and enthusiastic interpreter of his works and constantly refers to the spiritual element that pervades his life and oeuvre.

Single figures of angels and panels depicting Satan fishing are among the most avidly collected of Almon's carvings, and both of these themes are Pierce-inspired. While Almon was working with Pierce in Columbus, Pierce gave him an angel he carved in 1935.[18] Based on Pierce's figure, Almon created a similar design which is a model for his numerous angels. Pierce's Satan Fishing theme depicts the devil with a fishing pole from which many enticing allurements are suspended: women, money, cards, liquor, and other symbols of entrapment. Almon has expanded this theme, calling it Mr. and Mrs. Satan Fishing and adding more contemporary lures such as drugs. Mr. and Mrs. Satan appear in a recently completed panel called Hell (fig. 9), which describes Christ's last days on earth, between his resurrection and ascension to heaven. In Almon's panel, Jesus has descended into hell and chained Mr. and Mrs. Satan, who kneel helplessly beside their weapons. Clad in white and surrounded by a golden aura, Jesus holds a large key to the padlock that imprisons the satanic couple. A galaxy of tortured faces representing the races of mankind, arranged in tiers throughout the panel, is surrounded by leaping flames that enframe the entire composition.

Almon carves and paints scenes from his early childhood in a manner recalling that of Pierce; he has also carved canes and walking sticks. Almon almost invariably employs colors that are brighter than those of Pierce; however, the use of glitter in the works of both carvers is similar. Almon does not carve freestanding three-dimensional figures or tableaus; he does not apply cutout designs to backgrounds; and he does not make frames for his panels as did Pierce. The level of relief in Almon's panels is consistently low, whereas Pierce sometimes combined high and low relief and negative areas in the same work.

Fig. 9. Leroy Almon, b. 1938, *Hell*, 1990, carved and painted redwood, 36 x 24 in. (91.4 x 60.9 cm), National Museum of American Art, Smithsonian Institution, Washington, D.C., Gift of an Anonymous Donor, 1991.127

Although Leroy Almon has expanded his repertory of themes, mediums, and techniques beyond those of Pierce, he has remained a humble man. Almon gives credit to two masters: to Pierce, under whose tutelage he developed his remarkable woodcarving talents, and to God, whose presence pervades all aspects of his art, life, and recently embraced calling as a preacher.

HERBERT SINGLETON (B. 1945)

The background for the artistic career of Herbert Singleton was the rough environment of the urban African American neighborhood in New Orleans where he was born. The oldest of eight children of Herbert and Elizabeth Singleton, Herbert Jr. attended school through the seventh grade. After dropping out of school, Singleton spent most of his time hanging out on the streets of New Orleans and associating with gangs, pimps, prostitutes, and drug dealers. Between 1967 and 1986 Singleton spent some thirteen years incarcerated in the Angola State Prison in Louisiana for various narcotics offenses.

Singleton's encounters with law enforcement officials have been frequent and traumatic. In 1980, one of his sisters was shot to death in her bathtub in an early morning raid by three police officers searching for suspects in the murder of another police officer. After the raid, Singleton and several others were taken to police headquarters, where they were allegedly beaten and tortured in attempts to obtain confessions. Singleton recalls that he and other suspects were detained for over twelve hours, and a plastic bag was placed over his head in an attempt to elicit a confession. The incident enraged many citizens of New Orleans, which eventually awarded sizable monetary settlements to Singleton and several others.[19] Singleton depicted his harrowing experiences at police headquarters in one of his carvings, in which he is seen strapped to a chair with a white plastic bag over his head. In view of Singleton's background, it is not surprising to observe numerous scenes of violence and police brutality among his carvings.

Like his elders among early twentieth-century African American woodcarvers, Singleton exhibited artistic impulses during his boyhood. He recalls walking along the banks of the Mississippi River as a young child and amusing himself by fashioning snakes from mud. "I would reach in and pull out a snake, just like that. I'd let it dry in the sun, but it would fall apart." Unhappy with the impermanence of his clay figures, Singleton decided to work in wood and began by picking up pieces of driftwood from the river when it was low.[20]

Around 1975, Singleton began carving walking sticks from ax handles. His clients were buggy drivers in the French Quarter, pimps, and drug dealers with whom he hoped to exchange his work for cocaine and heroin. Singleton's walking sticks and staffs were also used in voodoo ceremonies and Mardi Gras parades. The sticks were eagerly sought after by the street people who were his associates. Singleton recalls that a well-known pimp called Big Hat Willy "never went night-clubbing without one of my sticks in his fist." Singleton stopped carving his trademark walking sticks after a buggy driver on Jackson Square killed a would-be robber by splitting his head open with one of Singleton's sticks. Following that incident, Singleton's walking sticks were dubbed "killer sticks," and he received so many requests from persons with less than honorable intentions that he vowed never to carve them again.[21]

Singleton's more recent three-dimensional sculptures and relief panels are carved from pieces of driftwood he finds on the levees of the Mississippi River: logs, tree trunks and stumps, old doors, and panels from discarded furniture. That all of Singleton's sculptures are carved from pieces of found wood—he never purchases precut panels—contributes to the powerful, emotive quality of his work. Singleton paints virtually all of his sculptures in bright enamel colors, as do most of his peers and predecessors.

Singleton's carvings may be grouped into three categories: religious scenes, scenes of contemporary African American life, and social and political subjects. Singleton's religious sculptures are frequently stagey interpretations, as in *He Be the One* (see fig. 13, p. 63), or they may depict the duplicity of religious leaders as in *Preacher Pimp and Sister Church* (Barrister's Gallery, New Orleans), in which a minister and a pregnant woman are engaged in a provocative dance. Most of Singleton's sculptures depict scenes from his own experiences: police bru-

tality and harassment, lynchings, tavern brawls, dishonest card playing, prostitution, and scenes of prison life. Other sculptures by Singleton are acidic commentaries on national and international issues, as in *Blood in Exchange for Oil* of 1991 (Barrister's Gallery, New Orleans), a carved relief panel alluding to the Persian Gulf crisis.

Two of the most intensely personal panels among Singleton's works are *Point Man* (fig. 10) and *Ant Hill* (private collection), inspired by his experiences as a heroin addict and a prison inmate, respectively. *Point Man* (the term is street slang for a man who injects heroin with a needle and a syringe) is a self-portrait in which Singleton, in blue bib overalls with a red handkerchief tied on his right arm, is seen kneeling against a vivid yellow background. His right hand holds a large white syringe, and in the left is a small white package containing powdered heroin. Singleton's kneeling posture and upward turned head and eyes allude not to prayer or subservience but to slavery and servitude to drugs. According to Singleton, at Angola State Prison the validity of complaints from ill inmates was sometimes tested by requiring the complainant to lie on a gigantic ant hill. If the inmate were feigning illness he would be unable to remain immobile from the attacking ants, whereas the sincerely ill person would remain essentially motionless. The figure in Singleton's carving waves his limbs wildly in an attempt to avert the numerous gigantic ants that are sprinkled over the panel's surface like little calligraphic characters.

A prolific artist, Singleton estimates that he has carved more than two hundred works. Some of his sculptures are large scale—up to seven feet in height. He does not make preliminary drawings, preferring to sketch his designs directly onto the wood. He carves primarily with pocketknives and chisels and does not incorporate negative areas in his panels.

Given their frequently uncomfortable subject matter, Singleton's sculptures have not been as widely collected as those of some of his peers. However, as Singleton's sculptures gain wider

Fig. 10. Herbert Singleton, b. 1945, *Point Man*, 1990, carved and painted cedar board, 35 x 18 in. (88.9 x 45.7 cm), Collection of Erwin Rappaport

exposure, more collectors and scholars of self-taught artists will begin to appreciate his powerful and innovative themes and will recognize the contribution of this gifted artist.

Given that none of the most prominent twentieth-century African American woodcarvers was aware

of the others' work, with the exception of Leroy Almon, who was apprenticed to an older master, an unusually large number of common themes exist in the works of two generations of carvers. These stylistic and iconographic parallels provide additional credence for the theory that African American folk art is, indeed, a distinct stylistic entity within the vast spectrum of American folk art.

Each of the woodcarvers included in this study carved canes, staffs, or walking sticks at some point in his career. Pierce was probably the leader in this category. Farmer recalled carving canes in Tennessee; White made glitter-embellished examples; Dawson carved canes; Singleton created "killer sticks"; and Almon carved a small number of canes during the 1980s. The African American tradition of cane carving has been well documented from its West African roots to its dispersal on the Georgia coast and inland, then northward where it survived well into the twentieth century. One of the earliest known carvers in the United States was Henry Gudgell (ca. 1826–1895), the most celebrated African American woodcarver of his generation, whose wooden objects are known only through two surviving walking sticks of the 1860s. Gudgell moved from Kentucky, his birthplace, to Livingston County, Missouri, in what constitutes the earliest documented northwestward migratory pattern.

A common theme depicted by most of the artists discussed here, excluding Dawson and White, is the Crucifixion of Christ. African American folk art is frequently religious in subject matter, and many of its practitioners are ordained or self-styled prophets, missionaries, and ministers. The most celebrated crucifixion carving is the example completed by Pierce in the mid-1930s (see cat. no. 99). Pierce carved additional crucifixions, one in 1975 (cat. no. 96) and another in circa 1980 (cat. no. 97), which are stylistically similar to two that were completed by Josephus Farmer in 1985. One of the finest figures from Ulysses Davis's oeuvre is his large *Crucifixion* (fig. 11) of 1946. The figure is carved from a single piece of cedar, and Christ's crown of thorns is of mahogany studded with toothpicks.

Fig. 11. Ulysses Davis, 1914–1990, *Crucifixion*, 1946, carved and painted cedar, mahogany with toothpicks, 40¹/₂ x 13¹/₂ x 6 in. (102.9 x 34.3 x 15.2 cm), Estate of Ulysses Davis

Crucifixion themes in the paintings and wood carvings of Leroy Almon follow the tradition of his master and were undoubtedly inspired by examples he observed while serving as curator of the Elijah Pierce Art Gallery. Almon has carved a number of panels, including *Christ between Two Crosses* (fig. 12), an unusual concept in which the two arms of a cross and the upright member terminating in a head represent the Father, Son, and Holy Ghost. This Byzantine iconlike image is apparently an Almon innovation; at least he is not aware of this concept being used previously.

A crucifixion entitled *He Be the One* (fig. 13), carved by Herbert Singleton in 1991 on a wooden door, reveals the tremendous strength of that artist's talents. This large-scale and forceful work is boldly inscribed with a verse from Matthew (7:7): "Ask and it shall be given you; seek and ye shall find; knock and it shall open unto you." Singleton used the door's projecting cross-shaped central panels for the cross and at the bottom carved the kneeling Mary Magdalene. The three Marys, a man nailing Christ's right arm to the cross, a centurion, and two soldiers gambling for the seamless garment are included in the door's central zones. Four white skeletons with large red eyes, carved on the bottom of the door, describe the scene as a place of death. On the door's outer panels are thirty pieces of silver, carved in relief, painted silver, and bordered with red, in reference to the "blood money" Judas received. The projecting central panel of the door serves as the foreground of the composition. By eliminating the projecting panel of the door's upper section, Singleton created a planar surface for the inscription. Thus this remarkable artist converted a discarded door into one of the most poignant representations of the crucifixion of Christ made by any twentieth-century American artist.

Other common subjects seen in the works of African American woodcarvers are U.S. presidents and Martin Luther King, Jr.; the Statue of Liberty and other patriotic images are also found frequently among African American folk artifacts. Josephus Farmer incorporated the Statue of Liberty into some

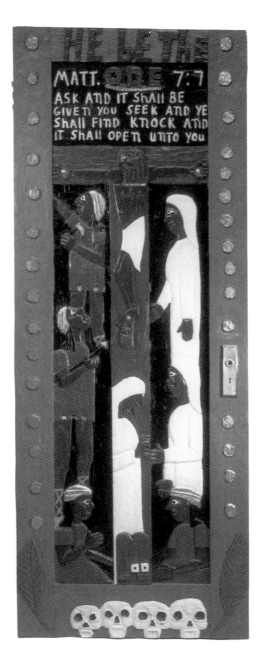

Fig. 12. Leroy Almon, b. 1938, *Christ between Two Crosses*, 1989, carved and painted redwood, 24 x 12 in. (61.0 x 30.5 cm), Collection of the Artist

Fig. 13. Herbert Singleton, b. 1945, *He Be the One*, 1991, carved and painted cypress door, 80 x 30 in. (203.2 x 76.2 cm), Collection of Chuck and Jan Rosenak

of his tableaus and also created some examples that were wired and fitted with Christmas lights to symbolize the flaming torch.

Although contemporary African American painters outnumber woodcarvers, the tradition of woodcarving still survives. The artists included in this brief survey represent only a few of the talented woodcarvers of African descent who have made important contributions to the field of American folk art. These artists have lived, or still reside, primarily in the South and Midwest. Among the first generation of woodcarvers from the South, Luster Willis (1913–1990) and George Williams (b. 1911) of Mississippi are noteworthy. Prominent second-generation woodcarvers include Jeffrey Williams (b. 1954) of North Carolina, Isaac Smith (b. 1950) of Texas, and others. Given the long tradition of woodcarving—from West Africa to the United States—it seems reasonable to assume that the art will live on.

Regenia A. Perry is Professor of African and African American Art History, Virginia Commonwealth University.

1. Although Farmer was not a licensed barber, he informed the author that he frequently cut hair in his home in St. Louis.
2. Biographical information concerning Pierce was taken from files at the Columbus Museum of Art.
3. This expression is commonly used in African and African American societies and refers to a section of placenta membrane covering the baby's face at the time of birth.
4. Columbus Gallery of Fine Arts, unpaginated.
5. Josephus Farmer, in interview with the author, May 8, 1984.
6. Cubbs, p. 8. "Speaking in tongues," or glossolalia, is said to be a spiritual state in which the speech is non-decipherable and supposedly indicates the presence of the Holy Ghost.
7. Interview, May 8, 1984.
8. Ibid.
9. Ibid.
10. Ibid.
11. Dean Jensen, "Museum's Farmer Collection Celebrates a Local Treasure," *Milwaukee Art Journal*, Sunday, July 13, 1986.
12. Ibid.
13. William Dawson, in interview with the author, January 8, 1982.
14. Virginia Kiah, "Ulysses Davis, Savannah Folk Sculptor," *Southern Folklore Quarterly* 42 (1978): 271–285.
15. Michelle Davis, granddaughter of the artist, in conversation with the author, September 10, 1991.
16. All biographical information concerning White is taken from a biography compiled by Murray Smith, Dallas, Texas, and an exhibition catalogue by Murray Smith, *The World of George W. White, Jr.* (Waco Creative Arts Center, 1975).
17. Bill Porterfield, "The Genius," *Texas Observer*, November 1, 1974.
18. From a resume provided by Leroy Almon and conversations with the artist, July and August 1991.
19. Bill Grady, "The Algiers Killings–10 Years Later," New Orleans: *Times Picayune*, November 8, 1990.
20. Andy Antippas, *10 Southern Black Folk Artists* (exh. cat., Houston: Icon Gallery, 1990), unpaginated.
21. Ibid.

A HOLY PLACE

A Tribute to Elijah Pierce

AMINAH ROBINSON

I knew there was something holy about the corner at Long Street and Washington Avenue as I stood, many days after art classes were over, waiting at the bus stop to go home. Back in the mid-fifties, while I waited for the bus, I would sit on the curb and sketch the chain of storefront churches and the women who came out of the storefronts doing the Holy Rock Dance and talkin' in tongues. Out on the street the preacher followed with his sermon, his words echoing through this holy stretch back and forth to passers-by. I would always cross the street to feel a better view. It was more than just drawing the storefront scene; it was embracing from deep within a small chapter about the culture of a people. As the preacher sang out his songs upon the streets, I quietly sat on the opposite side of the street facing the chain of storefront churches and the Holy Rock Dancers talkin' in tongues with no idea that I was drawing in front of a Holy Place.

In 1968, the International Art Festival, organized by Fran Luckoff, was held at the YWCA on Fourth Street in Columbus. This was my first encounter with Elijah Pierce, who was displaying his carvings on the second floor. My son was a year old and Mr. Pierce handed him a small animal carving depicting a bull and a dog. Mr. Pierce looked at me and said: "This is the way you teach a little child, you have to scoot it, make it do." I did not meet Mr. Pierce again until 1971, when Ursel White Lewis, my friend, mentor, and mother-in-art, introduced us formally.

Those early years in the 1970s with Mr. Pierce were quiet times for us, especially during the mornings before his customers came in for a haircut. Sometimes Mr. Pierce would ask me to sketch animals or sketch in his *Slavery Time,* 1973 (cat. no. 5), which he was carving for a second time. Anything Mr. Pierce wanted me to draw, I would draw for him. He spoke often of his dear friend Boris Gruenwald, a sculptor and student at the Ohio State University. Mr. Pierce related to me many times that this was the man who discovered him and told him that he was going to make sure the world knew about his art! I never had the privilege of meeting Boris Gruenwald, but I knew he was a special friend to Mr. Pierce and that he brought his work and life before the world.

The barbershop was a gallery in itself, but it was not the room that housed most of his works. That room was next door. The presence and spirit of this barbershop changed as the seasons changed. In the summertime, outside Mr. Pierce's barbershop were beautiful ripe tomatoes and flowers growing in the two plots that Mr. Pierce had cultivated, one on each side of the steps. As you walked up the steps and to the left, the aroma of fresh flowers and vegetables followed you into the shop, transcending the intense heat of summer days. I don't remember ever feeling the heat. There was an Air-Soul that circulated in and out of the barbershop, never leaving and never staying. The stillness of Mr. Pierce and the flow of this Air-Soul aroma wandered in and out throughout the summer months.

Fig. 14. Aminah Robinson, b. 1940, Neighborhood of Pierce's Barbershop, pen and ink drawing. Copyright 1991, Aminah Robinson.

Sometimes when I went to the barbershop to see Mr. Pierce, my friend Ursel White Lewis would have just left or sometimes she had just arrived, bringing with her a bag of shell peanuts for Mr. Pierce, which he dearly loved. They were always deep in dialogue: shop talk! Community people from all over the city and especially the artists would come visit Mr. Pierce at his shop.

During the early seventies artists came to paint or to sculpt or just to interview Mr. Pierce. Elijah Pierce was loved by the entire community, which reached beyond Columbus, Ohio, as time went on and became an international community. Mr. Pierce's community was not a black community or a white community. His community transcended the boundaries of race or color. Elijah Pierce's community was born out of *Love*. His was a community of love that brought people together in search of truth.

Many times, artists would bring Mr. Pierce art that they had created for him. We all wanted to give something back to this genius who had given and shared so much of his life's work, time, and love with each of us.

Elijah Pierce was a righteous and Christian man who walked with dignity and love, who loved God more than anything else in the world. He lived by his own sermons, which were turned into works of art. One of his favorite carved sermons was *Your Life Is a Book, and Every Day Is a Page* (private collection). Mr. Pierce would look at me and say: "You cannot deny the pages of your own book, because you've already written into the pages of life. And that life will be open in the eyes of God. When the book is finished, you cannot deny it." So, Mr. Pierce goes on to say, "Walk slow! Nobody can catch up with Father Time. Just walk. And walk it

Fig. 15. Aminah Robinson, b. 1940, In the
Barbershop: Aminah Drawing, Pierce
Carving, pen and ink drawing.
Copyright 1991, Aminah Robinson.

slow." Not only was Mr. Pierce my friend and mentor, but he was also my spiritual counselor. Our friendship was a very special friendship as were those of all of his friends. In those early years of the 1970s, the barbershop became a meeting place. A prayer house. A praise house. A holy place.

Was the barbershop yet another storefront church that preached its sermons in wood? Across the street the storefront churchgoers still sang the Lord's praises in Holy Rock Dance and talkin' in tongues. Sometimes it seemed that Mr. Pierce's carvings would jump out at you and talk in tongues too. Yes, these little storefront churches were there even in the 1970s until the Columbus College of Art and Design expanded its facilities.

Long Street and Washington Avenue was a holy place! At Broad Street and Washington Avenue is the Columbus Museum of Art, which was founded in 1878. Behind the museum is the art school of 113 years. Across the street at 90 North Washington Avenue was the Kojo Photo Art Studio, which closed its doors in 1981 to make room for a new parking lot. Kojo Kamau, owner and manager of the studio, began to give African American artists an

opportunity to exhibit their art and to give poetry readings. But most of all, the studio assisted artists to go to Africa to study. During the four years of the art studio, Kojo Kamau kept a permanent exhibit space of Mr. Pierce's carvings in his art studio. As you walked north on Washington Avenue a block away from the Kojo Photo Art Studio, you were at Long Street, where the storefront churches were still alive. Across the street at 534 East Long Street was the Elijah Pierce barbershop. Sometimes I wonder if the street corner at Long Street and Washington Avenue should have been renamed "A Holy Place/Elijah Pierce Boulevard."

Here at Long Street and Washington Avenue, as the sun set on the eve of an autumn day, Mr. Pierce would catch the bus to return home. It was the soul and spirit of this whole environment, this Holy Place, that followed Mr. Pierce back to his home, to 2290 Margaret Avenue and to the Shepard Community, an established old residential neighborhood in northeast Columbus, at the end of a day spent working at the barbershop.

Everywhere we were surrounded and rejuvenated by the deep oranges and sunlight yellows and especially those brilliant reds. The morning walks became shades of autumn. The Pierces and I lived a block away from each other in the small Shepard Community. On many mornings, Mr. Pierce, my son, and I would take our walks. The red leaves that fell to the ground would turn almost to a purple-blue that reflected not only the light of the morning but the brilliance of Mr. Pierce's genius. One brisk fall morning, right before Mr. Pierce took the bus to leave for work, we took our morning walk through the community. As we walked we could hear only the songs and cries of nature and the bristling sounds of the wind as the leaves fell to nature's floor. It was in this spirit that Mr. Pierce led me through spiritual journeys that would eventually become many. Mr. Pierce picked up a leaf that had turned as orange as a sunset. Mr. Pierce said, "The laws of nature, the laws of God, are the laws man should live by and be in tune with. Not sometimes, not every now and then, but all the time."

We had walked quite a lot that morning even though Mr. Pierce had an appointment with a fellow artist from Detroit named Elwyne Bush. Mr. Pierce had consented to sit for Bush to create a sculpted bust of him. Mr. Pierce sat for a whole week in his barbershop as Bush created this wonderful sculpture.

After its completion, Elwyne Bush had the Pierce bust cast in bronze, and in February 1975, he donated it as a gift from the artist to the Columbus Gallery of Fine Arts, which is now the Columbus Museum of Art. I remember people crowding the Elijah Pierce barbershop as Mr. Pierce sat for Elwyne Bush, just watching. Fellow artists, friends, and customers came back every day that week to watch this artist transform clay into a beautiful work of art. This was one of the most joyful times I spent in Mr. Pierce's barbershop.

As the days moved on into the cold winter months, we would sit close to the heat of the old wood-burning stove, where Mrs. Pierce had left Mr. Pierce's lunch to warm on top. Around the barbershop were many old photographs and newspaper clippings that had been framed but had yellowed with age. Carvings crowded the walls, tables, and windows, and sat among growing plants, speaking in silence to each other. I remember the door opening and snow rushing in with an old and loyal friend, who came every week at the same time as he had the past twenty years. His friend takes off his coat and sits in the special red barber chair. Mr. Pierce smiles, puts down the carving he had been working on, and walks over to his friend who is about to get a haircut. Mr. Pierce picks up his clippers with his huge, slender hands and puts a white sheet over the front of his friend to protect his suit and tie from the hair droppings. The spiritual journey begins again—with another friend, another dialogue, deep in shop talk!

The transformation of the Elijah Pierce barbershop to the Elijah Pierce Art Gallery in the spring of 1980 brought renewal to the life of Elijah Pierce. With the help of Leroy Almon, apprentice to Elijah Pierce, the gallery opened its doors to community artists, inviting them to exhibit a piece of their work in this newly transformed space. Today, Leroy Almon makes his home in Tallapoosa, Georgia, and continues to carry on the Elijah Pierce folk art tradition of carving wood with only a pocketknife and a hand chisel.

Elijah Pierce affected the lives of so many people—especially artists in the community like myself—who had the privilege of knowing him during his lifetime. There is something about Columbus, and indeed all of Ohio, where the Elijah Pierce influence has been greatly felt. As I view the works of fellow artists throughout Ohio, I see the burning torch of Elijah Pierce, who has left his mark. And this is good, for the indescribable spirit and life of Elijah Pierce continue to permeate the world, and somehow we manage to know that truth speakers are timeless. Timeless beginnings. Timeless endings. The presence, knocking at the door. Take my hand.

Aminah Robinson is a Columbus artist who was a colleague and friend of Elijah Pierce.

CATALOGUE OF THE EXHIBITION

E. Jane Connell

Nannette V. Maciejunes

Slavery Time (detail, cat. no. 5)

AUTOBIOGRAPHICAL WORKS

Many of Elijah Pierce's carvings are strikingly autobiographical in content. During his sixty years in Ohio—especially during the last two decades of his life—it became important for Pierce to document his past, to explain and validate his roles as woodcarver, barber, and lay minister in the African American community of Columbus. Scenes of his early life in the South, of the history of American slavery, and of his religious calling—as well as symbols of his affiliation with Freemasonry—are strong personal statements and rich expressions of African American culture.

While his carvings were intended to inform, they were also meant to inspire. Pierce was a master storyteller. He often illustrated dramatic accounts of personal history and related these to themes of faith, obedience, and salvation. His narratives are bold in composition and vibrant in color and include written words as cues for his messages. He sometimes placed his scenes within the familiar context of contemporary theater and cinema, and embellished the stories with the moods and rhythms of gospel music. As reflections of the multimedia culture that surrounded and informed him, Pierce's autobiographical works are sophisticated and compelling. Their messages are accessible to all.

1. THE PLACE OF MY BIRTH

1977
(cat. no. 1)

2. The Little White Church

1936

(cat. no. 3)

3. SLAVERY TIME

ca. 1965–1970

(cat. no. 4)

4. Slavery Time

1973

(cat. no. 5)

5. OBEY GOD AND LIVE

(VISION OF HEAVEN)

1956
(cat. no. 6)

6. Mother's Prayer

1972

(cat. no. 8)

7. Picking Wild Berries

1979
(cat. no. 9)

8. Masonic Plaques

(cat. nos. 13, 12, 14, 11)

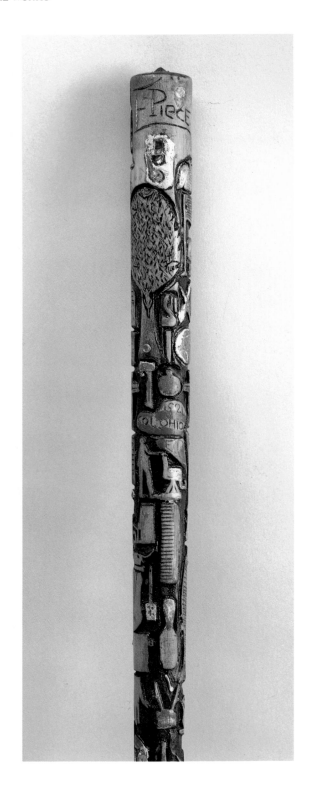

9. PREACHING STICK

ca. 1950

(cat. no. 15)

10. MY SAYINGS

n.d.

(cat. no. 20)

Horse and Rider (Paul Revere) (detail, cat. no. 41)

FREESTANDING CARVINGS: ANIMALS AND FIGURES

The first subjects of Elijah Pierce's boyhood carvings were the animals on his family's Mississippi farm and in the surrounding woods that he so loved. His choice of animal subjects for his carvings was as natural as his fascination with the act of carving itself. When he began to carve seriously as an adult, he naturally turned again to animals for subject matter. Pierce's first significant carving, *The Little Elephant*, was so admired by his wife that he promised to carve an entire zoo for her.

> And I began carving every animal that I ever saw in the circuses and in the parades and in street carnivals—cows and horses and dogs and squirrels and any kind of animals that I could think of. Sometimes I'd see some animal in a paper or in a magazine and I'd carve it. Being in the shop, men would come in and tell [me], "You can't carve a lion," or "You can't carve a tiger," and different things. I'd carve it! Sometimes I'd carve something just to pass time or to satisfy my mind—little animals and other things. But it's a story—that's a turtle or that's a lion. Even in the first chapter of Genesis everything God made was good and very good. And I did have in my mind, if I didn't sell these little animals and different birds and things and snakes that I carve, someday if it was pleasing to God I would make an ark.[1]

Pierce's comments about his animal carvings reveal how fully integrated his vision was. His animals exist simultaneously as part of the sacred and secular worlds. They are the animals of Genesis and of street carnivals and magazine illustrations. They are tributes to God, and they also allowed Pierce to interact with his community, enjoying the good-natured challenges his customers posed. Moreover, they are part of the African American tradition of storytelling in which animals play a key role. Though many of these oral traditions are made manifest in his narrative reliefs, they are also implicit in his freestanding pieces.

Like the animals, the carved figures are derived from a rich variety of sources—popular culture, American folk legends, African American history, and popular proverbs and parables. They draw on common cultural traditions with which his audience would have been very familiar. Pierce was a concerned, insightful member of his community, and his work reflects the values and interests of his audience. Pierce was deeply interested in the world around him. He always had the radio on in his shop and frequently greeted visitors with the question "Did you hear the news?"[2]

Pierce's numerous freestanding figures date from early in his career, emanating from the youthful impulse that made him believe, "Anything I could picture, I could carve."[3] Less demanding to carve than his major reliefs, the small figures had a broad public appeal and were frequently offered for sale at local fairs and later in his shop. Many were given to friends and members of the community.

1. Jones and Kook.
2. Communication from Margaret Armbrust Seibert.
3. Jones and Kook.

11. FROG, DINOSAUR, ELEPHANT, DOG,

MONKEY, TIGER

(cat. nos. 36, 28, 22, 24, 30, 27)

12. Alligator

1974
(cat. no. 34)

13. OWL IN TREE

1973

(cat. no. 37)

14. Horse and Rider (Paul Revere)

ca. 1970s

(cat. no. 41)

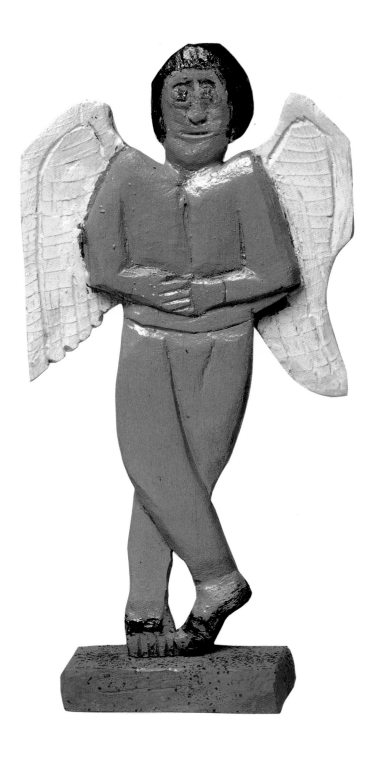

15. ANGEL

1980

(cat. no. 45)

16. Archie Griffin

1976
(cat. no. 47)

17. SULKY DRIVER, FIGURE (MAN WITH
PURPLE BOTTLE), MAN (SAMMY DAVIS, JR.),
FIGURE (MAN WITH CIGARETTE),
SEATED LADY, MOTHER AND CHILD,
JITTERBUG

(cat. nos. 43, 53, 46, 54, 61, 60, 52)

18. MAN IN THE MIDDLE

n.d.
(cat. no. 57)

19. MIGRATION NORTH

1976, 1977
(cat. no. 59)

The White House (detail, cat. no. 84)

SECULAR RELIEF CARVINGS

Though Pierce discussed his carvings of secular subjects less frequently than either his religious or autobiographical reliefs, and they have traditionally received little attention in the literature on the artist, they are integral to his body of work and vital to understanding the precepts by which he worked and lived. Pierce believed that everything in life was connected. He believed that one should live a balanced life, following the laws of both God and Nature. Pierce was not, as he was once portrayed, a religious savant with little interest in the things of this world. He was a shrewd man who was very much a part of his community.

Pierce's secular works are filled with his enjoyment of the world in which he lived. In his relief carvings and freestanding figures, subjects of specific interest to the African American community mingle with those drawn from mainstream culture. Indeed, Pierce often chose subjects whose appeal transcended racial differences. When looked at as a whole, his secular works reveal several aspects of Pierce's personality—his interest in national politics, his love of baseball, boxing, and horse racing, his enjoyment of comics and the movies, his deep patriotism, and his admiration for a number of American heroes who fought for justice and civil liberties. In his popular culture reliefs Pierce seldom emphasized or even distinguished the race of the figures. When asked, Pierce would often say that his figures were neither black nor white but represented Everyman.

Popular culture often provided not only subjects for Pierce's work but visual source material as well. Several of his carvings are appropriated images from published photographs or popular prints. In each of these works Pierce produced not a derivative cliché but an original image with its own expressive integrity.

20. Indians Hunting

1943

(cat. no. 62)

21. Louis vs. Braddock

n.d.

(cat. no. 67)

22. POPEYE

1933

(cat. no. 70)

23. MR. AND MRS. HANK AARON

1974
(cat. no. 75)

24. PRESIDENTS AND CONVICTS

1941

(cat. no. 77)

25. ABRAHAM LINCOLN

ca. 1975

(cat. no. 78)

26. MARTIN LUTHER KING JR. AND THE

KENNEDY BROTHERS

1977

(cat. no. 79)

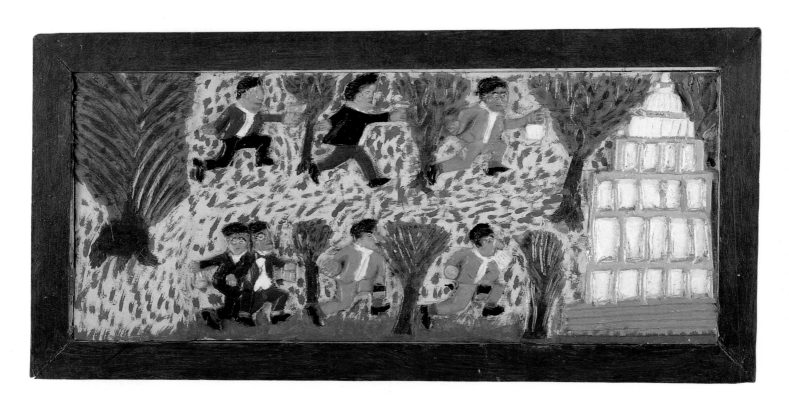

27. NIXON BEING DRIVEN FROM THE

WHITE HOUSE

1975
(cat. no. 82)

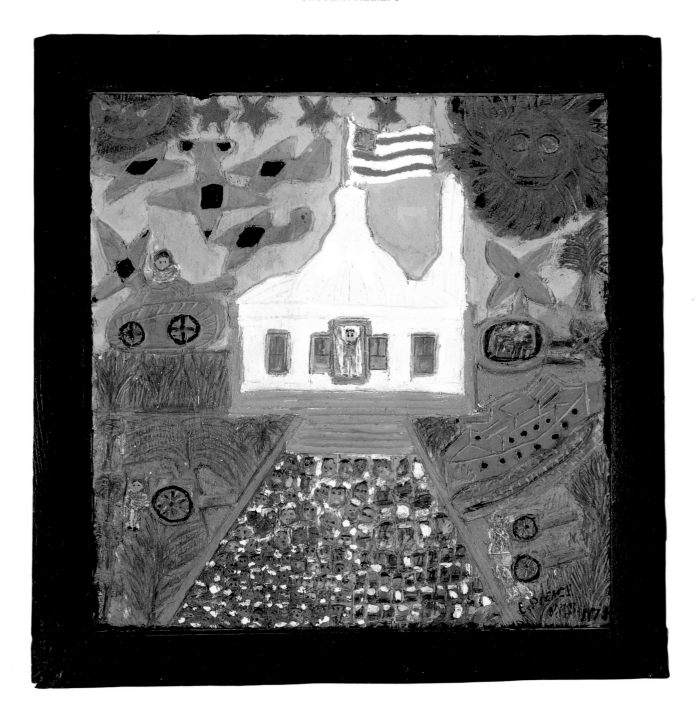

28. THE WHITE HOUSE

1977

(cat. no. 84)

Card Players (detail, cat. no. 89)

TABLEAUS

Elijah Pierce's interest in tableaus dates from at least the mid-1930s when he created his masterful *Crucifixion*. Although Pierce chose to reformat *Crucifixion* in the early 1970s when he mounted the individual figures on panel, he continued to create tableaus throughout the decade.

The scale and subject matter of his tableaus reflect the same remarkable range found in the individual relief carvings that encompass both the sublime and the humorous. In his tableaus Pierce could create a whole world, stage a religious drama, present an imaginary story-scene to teach a moral lesson, or depict a fragment of the real world. The tableaus gave Pierce the opportunity to create entire environments for the types of animal and human figures he depicted in his freestanding works. Frequently, independent figure groups relate strongly to figures found in the tableaus, or favorite subjects and motifs in his relief carvings are translated into tableaus.

29. DOLL HOUSE

before 1948

(cat. no. 86)

30. MUSIC BOX

n.d.
(cat. no. 87)

31. CARD PLAYERS

1940s — after 1964

(cat. no. 89)

32. CHRIST ENTERING JERUSALEM

1942

(cat. no. 94)

33. SACRIFICE OF ISAAC

1952
(cat. no. 92)

34. Abraham Sacrifices His Son

1979
(cat. no. 93)

Christ Walking on the Water (detail, cat. no. 117)

RELIGIOUS RELIEF CARVINGS

Religious work, I enjoy that the most. You know, some great
writer once said, "One picture is worth a thousand words."
And I thought of that book, the Bible: one picture is worth a
thousand of those words! So my mind just went thatta way.[1]

Religious relief carvings constitute Pierce's largest body of work. They were his spiritual livelihood, touchstones for his own beliefs, and the focus of many a barbershop lecture. A veritable anthology of biblical tales and heroes—from the Book of Genesis, in which Adam and Eve are described among the delights of the Garden of Eden, to the Book of Revelation and John's visions of the Second Coming of Christ—filled the walls of the shop, and many of these works were acquired by collectors and museums. Favorite heroes were Noah, Jonah, and Job, whose personal tribulations, followed by divine reward, have carried special meaning for African Americans since slavery times. The life of Christ—he is viewed as friend, counselor, and redeemer—was of particular interest, especially in the miracle stories and the Passion.

The religious carvings have been called Pierce's sermons in wood, the works that gained for him the title preacher in wood. These are the works that are most commonly associated with Pierce and around which his myth has been built. His words, "I ran from the ministry. I had a calling to preach, so God put me on the woodpile. I have to carve every sermon I didn't preach," are now legendary.[2] While Pierce's religious vocation was fervent and his inspiration profound, his religious works are not visionary in the mystical sense. Instead, imagery is often drawn from vernacular sources like Bible illustrations or, more important, from personal experience.

1. Columbus Gallery of Fine Arts, unpaginated.
2. Aschenbrand, p. 25.

35. CRUCIFIXION

mid-1930s

(cat. no. 99)

36. Panel 1, recto

37. Panel 1, verso

38. Panel 2, recto

39. Panel 2, verso

36–42a. BOOK OF WOOD

ca. 1932

(cat. no. 100)

40. Panel 3, recto

41. Panel 3, verso

42. Panel 4, recto

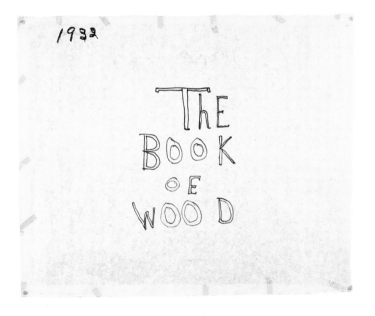

42a. Panel 4, verso

43. ADAM AND EVE

1971
(cat. no. 101)

44. NOAH'S ARK

1944

(cat. no. 103)

45. JONAH AND THE FISH

1949

(cat. no. 104)

46. Story of Job

ca. 1936

(cat. no. 105)

47. SAMSON

1942

(cat. no. 108)

48. FIRST MEETING OF JESUS AND JOHN

1940

(cat. no. 110)

49. SUFFER THE LITTLE CHILDREN

n.d.

(cat. no. 112)

50. CHRIST WALKING ON THE WATER

ca. 1970

(cat. no. 117)

51. JESUS BEFORE PILATE

n.d.

(cat. no. 121)

52. CHRIST OF THE APOCALYPSE

1940s
(cat. no. 123)

53. I Am the Door

ca. 1940

(cat. no. 128)

54. POWER OF PRAYER

1960

(cat. no. 130)

Your Life Is a Book (detail, cat. no. 133)

MESSAGE SIGNS

The powerful language of sermons and folktales permeates many aspects of African American life, and verbal skills, particularly in oral but also in written form, are thus highly esteemed. Quite naturally, then, Elijah Pierce had a reverence for words. He often incorporated words into his pictorial carvings, and he also regularly used sayings (*Put Your Trust in God and Not in Man*), incentives (*Courage*), admonitions (*Don't Lie*), and phrases from hymns and popular songs (*What the World Needs Now Is Love*).[1] Pierce used the signs to encourage others to lead a good life. The message signs were hung in the barbershop, and Pierce often gave them as gifts. Made of pine or lightweight commercial wood paneling, these small works fit comfortably in the hand and could be easily accommodated on a wall.

The written signs give permanence to Pierce's words of guidance. The messages are either carved in relief or incised into the wood; sometimes they are inscribed on the surface. Words are colored with paint and marking pen, ornamented with colorful outlines and daubs, and often embellished with glitter. Pierce's signs have a strong, sometimes dazzling, visual intensity and are invested with an emotional charge reflecting deep personal feeling. Every message is intended to be universal.

1. The Burt Bacharach–Hal David tune *What the World Needs Now,* first recorded by Jackie De Shannon, became a hit in the summer of 1965. It was on the Top Ten pop charts for fourteen weeks in a row, from July 3 through the week of October 2, and was the number one hit during the weeks of August 21 and 28. See Elston Brooks, *I've Heard Those Songs Before: The Weekly Top Ten Hits of the Last Six Decades,* vol. 2 (Fort Worth, Texas: The Summit Group, 1991), pp. 214–215. The song was also recorded by Mahalia Jackson, Dionne Warwick, and others.

55. MESSAGE SIGNS

(cat. nos. 132, 133, 134, 135, 136, 137, 138, 139)

Devil Fishing (detail, cat. no. 145)

Moral Lessons

Pierce's relief carvings of moral subjects are secular counterparts to his didactic religious works. Their purpose is to teach the wisdom of collective experience and to advise on the serious concerns of community life. For all their seeming simplicity and informality, the moralizing works are some of the most sophisticated and versatile of Pierce's oeuvre. They are also the most abstract, embodying universal philosophies concerning personal conduct, good citizenship, and the brevity of life in a unique pictorial language.

The repertoire of sources from which Pierce drew his imagery reflects the wide range of African and European oral and written traditions that were absorbed into the folk life of the South. The Bible and John Bunyan's *Pilgrim's Progress,* ''The Signifying Monkey'' and ''Snow White,'' parables and proverbs, newspapers and comics provided a rich context for Pierce's personal brand of commentary. The punning, alliteration, and metaphor of the titles add to the meaning of the works and endow them with poetic charm.

Like his religious subjects, these works appeal to an enlightened audience that is familiar with the stories and sayings Pierce has illustrated. Both telling and viewing are reciprocal, participatory. As a storyteller, Pierce used many theatrical devices: words are transcribed into their literal visual equivalents, dramatic action is portrayed as gesture and mime, inflection and emotion are translated into vivid color and exaggeration of form. The results are compelling, often humorous, and sometimes even nonsensical. The works reflect the African preference for indirect narrative, in which much is learned about how life ought to be lived through the exemplary actions and antics of characters, both human and animal.

56. PILGRIM'S PROGRESS

1938

(cat. no. 140)

57. PEARL HARBOR AND THE

AFRICAN QUEEN

1941
(cat. no. 155)

58. Parable of the Gnat and

the Camel

1974
(cat. no. 141)

59. CROCODILE AND UNWARY COW

ca. 1945

(cat. no. 142)

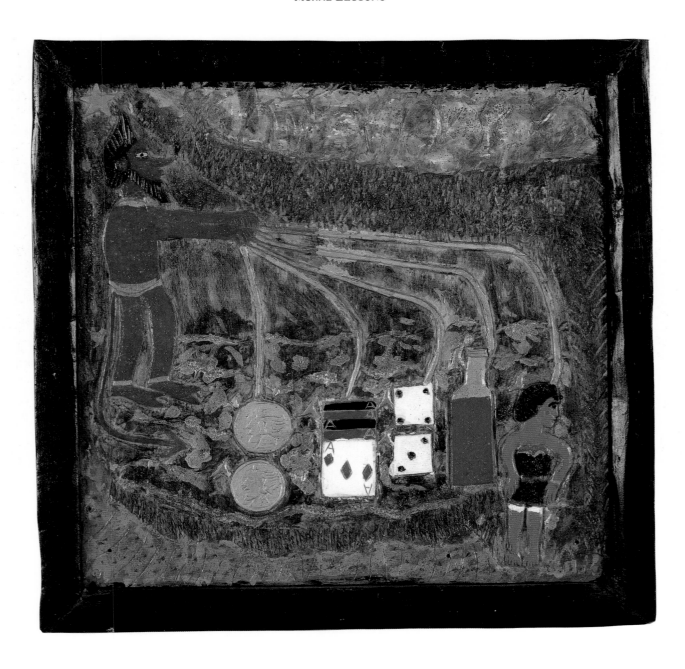

60. DEVIL FISHING

n.d.

(cat. no. 145)

61. THE PICKUP

1973

(cat. no. 146)

62. THREE WAYS TO SEND A MESSAGE:

TELEPHONE, TELEGRAM,

TELL-A-WOMAN

n.d.

(cat. no. 151)

63. THREE WAYS TO SEND A MESSAGE:

TELEPHONE, TELEGRAM,

TELL-A-WOMAN

1980
(cat. no. 152)

64. MONDAY MORNING GOSSIP

1934

(cat. no. 153)

65. THE MONKEY FAMILY

1942
(cat. no. 154)

66. Grim Reaper

1974
(cat. no. 157)

67. Father Time Racing

1959

(cat. no. 159)

Saul on the Road to Damascus (detail, cat. no. 165)

PIERCE, THE UNIVERSAL MAN

Elijah Pierce's works reflect a single integrated vision. His oeuvre is a rich sermon in which his autobiographical, secular, moral, and religious carvings unite to preach one message. Just as he believed everything in life was connected, he believed all of his work was interrelated. His impulse to create visual relationships between his reliefs by joining them in assemblages dates from the earliest years of his serious work as a carver. Best known of the assemblages is his *Book of Wood*, which tells the story of Christ. Pierce also created a diptych consisting of four scenes from the life of Peter[1] and at least three other large-scale thematic diptychs. Unlike *Book of Wood*, these diptychs consist of reliefs of various dates, drawn from a range of subjects. Pierce's decision to unite the carvings on larger panels postdates the execution of certain individual panels by more than a decade.

It is unclear when Pierce created his diptychs. All four may date from as early as the late 1940s. It is known that some had been dismantled by the mid-seventies, soon after Pierce's discovery by a new audience of collectors. Responding to increased demands for his work, Pierce dismantled the large diptychs in order to sell the reliefs individually. At least one collector remembers being present when Pierce began to disassemble the diptych *Death on the Level. Book of Wood*, which was the centerpiece of the gallery he had established in his barbershop, remained intact, and the diptych *Bible Stories* was sold in its entirety to a collector.

Beginning in the 1970s, Pierce's work was increasingly removed from its original context and audience as examples of his work were included in major folk art exhibitions and entered important private collections. Another critical change in Pierce's relationship with his own community occurred in 1979 when Pierce accepted the young Leroy Almon as his aide and apprentice, one of the few known master-apprentice relationships to be established by a contemporary African American folk artist. Almon helped the aging Pierce continue to work, at first providing minor assistance and eventually executing works in full partnership with Pierce. Almon also assisted the Pierces by formally incorporating the Elijah Pierce Art Gallery and acting as Pierce's agent. Pierce's role as mentor for the young Almon offered him the opportunity to reintegrate his message into the African American community at a time when his work was being fragmented and dispersed through outside contact. Almon carried on the carving tradition of his mentor but in the manner and with the outlook of a younger generation of African Americans who had come of age during the civil rights movement. Almon, a recognized folk artist in his own right, today acknowledges his debt to Pierce:

> Elijah Pierce was a man of God who always demonstrated his love with actions. Elijah Pierce was my spiritual teacher. For one whole year I listened to him. I watched him. I believed him. I began to carve. Twelve years later I have found joy and peace in the Gospel of Jesus Christ. . . . The only difference in my work and the works of Pierce is that he created according to his time and experiences and I created according to my time and experiences. He was my spiritual teacher. My talent is a gift from God.[2]

1. The reliefs are *Peter Walking on the Water* (cat. no. 116), *Peter's Denial (And the Cock Did Crow)* (cat. no. 120), *The Transfiguration* (cat. no. 118), and *Christ's Charge to Peter: Feed My Sheep* (cat. no. 122). The reliefs range in date from 1932 to 1947.
2. Almon, 1991.

68. BEFORE DEATH ALL ARE EQUAL

(From *Death on the Level* diptych)

1946–1947

(cat. no. 160)

69. CRIME DON'T PAY

(From *Death on the Level* diptych)
ca. 1955
(cat. no. 162)

70. SAUL ON THE ROAD TO DAMASCUS

(From *Death on the Level* diptych)
1948
(cat. no. 165)

71. COMING OF CHRIST

(From *Redemption* diptych)

n.d.

(cat. no. 168)

72. BIBLE STORIES

n.d.

(cat. no. 169)

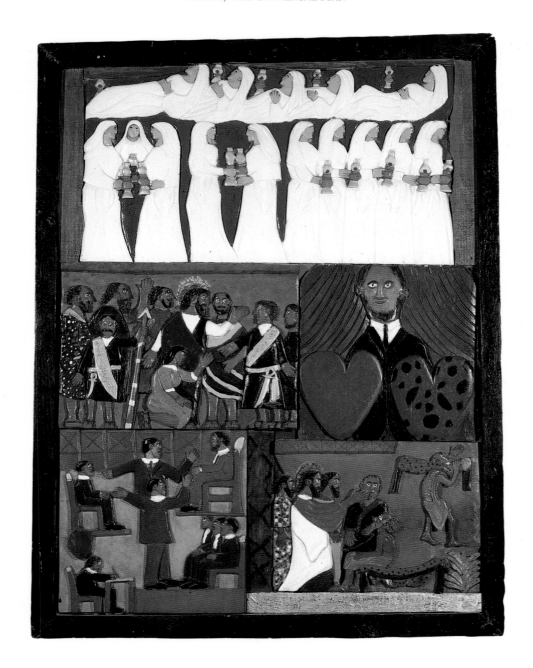

73. THE WISE AND FOOLISH VIRGINS AND

THE MAN WITH THE CLEAN AND

SOILED HEART

n.d.
(cat. no. 170)

74. UNIVERSAL MAN

1937

(cat. no. 173)

ANNOTATED CHECKLIST

E. JANE CONNELL

NANNETTE V. MACIEJUNES

Note: Dimensions are in inches and centimeters. Height precedes width and depth. Measurements include the frame in all framed works.

AUTOBIOGRAPHICAL WORKS

1.   **The Place of My Birth,** 1977   Colorplate 1
     Carved and painted wood relief
     29³/₈ × 26⁷/₈ (74.8 × 68.3)
     Columbus Museum of Art: Museum Purchase

Pierce was born in a log cabin, "right out almost in the cotton field," on a farm in Baldwyn, Mississippi.[1] A typical plantation structure derived from African architectural traditions,[2] the log "dog-trot" house, which is the focus of this work, is characterized by two rooms

flanking an open hallway.[3] The home is visually enframed by chimneys at both ends, and is shown nestled among cotton fields. In the background are the woods that provided a haven for the artist's youthful excursions and early carving. The house is surrounded with family members and animals of the household. Crowned with a sun, moon, and star—motifs representing a global realm found throughout Pierce's oeuvre—the house is portrayed as the center of his childhood universe.

1. Columbus Gallery of Fine Arts, unpaginated.
2. For an excellent discussion of African architecture as it was transplanted to the American South, see John Michael Vlach, *The Afro-American Tradition in Decorative Arts* (exh. cat., Cleveland Museum of Art, 1978), pp. 122–138.
3. An example is illustrated in ibid., p. 137.

2.   **My Home,** 1978
     Carved and painted wood relief
     16⁵/₁₆ × 33⁵/₈ (41.4 × 85.4)
     Columbus Museum of Art: Museum Purchase

Shown in front in this rendition of Pierce's log house in Baldwyn, Mississippi, are figures of Pierce's mother and father, a brother plowing the cotton field, and another driving a wagon. Above Pierce's father is the family's well; to its left stands young Elijah with Moscow, his beloved dog, friend, and protector.[1] The intimacy of the agrarian scene reveals the great nostalgia that Pierce felt toward his family and early environment.

1. Seibert interview, October 10, 1980.

---

3. **The Little White Church,** 1936   Colorplate 2
Carved and painted wood relief with glitter
25 × 25 (63.5 × 63.5)
Collection of Dr. and Mrs. Gerhard E. Martin[1]

The Little White Church, depicting the white clapboard church Pierce attended as a boy in Baldwyn, Mississippi, is a sophisticated union of childhood memories, biblical parables and proverbs, popular songs, literature, and 1930s cinema. As the church bell is rung, the congregation arrives by carriage, wagon, and on foot for Sunday services. Pierce himself stands with another boy beneath a tree behind the church; feigning a need to use the nearby outhouse, the mischievous Elijah and his young friend have sneaked away to play.

Directly below the church, four men stand next to a lighthouse and sing before a microphone. Pierce envisioned these seemingly illusory additions as a natural part of his memory landscape. The men were members of a gospel quartet—the most common form of singing group among black men in the early twentieth century. Pierce remembered listening to quartets on the radio. Indeed, by the mid-1930s, when Pierce carved *The Little White Church,* gospel music, commercially recorded or sung live on the radio, was a vital part of popular African American culture.[2] According to the present owners of the work, Pierce said he depicted the quartet singing "Shine on Me"—an old evangelical hymn represented by the lighthouse: "Oh, shine on me. Oh, shine on me. Let the light of the lighthouse shine on me."[3]

In front of the church, in the lower half of the composition, are farmlands, with men laboring in the fields. At the top, a sower disperses seed, watched by the birds beneath a bright sun. As the seed is scattered, some "fell by the wayside, and the fowls came and devoured them up. Some fell upon stony places,

. . . and when the sun was up, they were scorched; . . . but other fell into good ground and brought forth fruit" (Matt. 13:4–6, 8). Below the sower, a plowman sits idle beneath a tree while another plows an abundant field. This scene illustrates Proverbs 20:4: "The sluggard will not plow by reason of the cold; therefore shall he beg in harvest, and have nothing." Between the plowmen, Pierce inserted yet another reference to a proverb: beneath the tree is a buried hatchet, one of Pierce's favorite emblems of forgiveness (a buried hatchet also appears in *Pilgrim's Progress,* cat. no. 140).

At the lower right, surveying the fields and church of Pierce's world, is a distinguished bearded gentleman dressed like a country lawyer. This is "de Lawd"—the character of the Lord—from the play *The Green Pastures,* which was written for an all-black cast by Marc Connelly in 1929.[4] In 1930, Connelly won the Pulitzer prize for the play; in 1936—the year Pierce carved *The Little White Church*—Connelly wrote and directed *The Green Pastures* for Warner Brothers Pictures.[5]

The role of de Lawd was played 1,657 times by actor Richard Berry Harrison (1864–1935), a former Pullman porter and elocutionist whom Pierce also memorialized in *Bible Stories* (cat. no. 169).[6] In part 1, scene 7 of the play, de Lawd walks the earth along a fenced country road on a Sunday morning. He stops to admire a view of fields and a distant white church as does the character in Pierce's work. In fact, Pierce's depiction is nearly identical, in mirror image, to the movie version of the scene.[7]

Often in Pierce's works, childhood memories are enhanced by the vitality of gospel music, by mainstream American theater, and by Hollywood. This particular work is also a tribute to Pierce's African ancestry. In the upper left corner, Pierce has carved a head in profile—as beautifully formed and polished as any sub-Saharan mask. The symbolic associations of the mask with authority, religious ceremony, and initiation rites correspond with the social order imposed by church and home in Baldwyn. In this work, enduring African traditions join hands with popular American culture to form an integral part of the personal history of Elijah Pierce.

1. The Martins purchased *The Little White Church* directly from Pierce in the early 1970s. They have graciously shared with museum staff their conversations with Elijah Pierce concerning the carving.

2. For a survey of the early development of gospel music, including the histories of many popular quartets, see Anthony Heilbut, *The Gospel Sound: Good News and Bad Times* (New York: Limelight Editions, 1989; originally published by Simon and Schuster, 1971).

3. In 1930, Ernest Phipps and his Holiness Singers recorded "Shine on Me" on the Bluebird label. Blind Willie Johnson also recorded a version of the hymn for Columbia records. See Josh Dunson and Ethel Raim, eds., *Anthology of American Folk Music* (New York: Oak Publications, 1973), pp. 76–77.

4. *The Green Pastures* is counted among the masterpieces of American drama. Its original New York run, beginning February 26, 1930, totaled 640 performances. The all-black cast and choir, selected by Connelly, had a major impact on the acceptance of African American actors in commercial theater.

A biblical play performed in southern African American dialect, *The Green Pastures* is, according to its author, "an attempt to present certain aspects of a living religion in terms of its believers"; see Marc Connelly, *The Green Pastures: A Fable*, 2nd ed. (New York: Holt, Rinehart and Winston, 1958), p. xv. The main literary source for the play is the Old Testament. Connelly also acknowledges that Roark Bradford's *Ol' Man Adam an' His Chillun* (New York: Harper and Brothers, 1928) inspired him to write the play. For a study of the history of *The Green Pastures*, see Paul T. Nolan, *Marc Connelly* (New York: Twayne, 1969), pp. 79–91. Allen Woll's *Black Musical Theatre: From Coontown to Dreamgirls* (Baton Rouge: Louisiana State University Press, 1989), provides an excellent discussion of the play's critical acclaim by white as well as black writers and audiences. See pp. 136–141, 156ff.

5. The movie version was re-released in 1963 by United Artists Associated and is also available for viewing in video format. De Lawd was played by Rex Ingram.

6. For further biographical information on R. B. Harrison, see Woll, p. 138.

7. In addition, the dialogue of both play and movie— relaying biblical stories in terms of the humble, everyday experiences of rural African Americans in the South—is not unlike Pierce's own narratives. One can assume with some assurance that Pierce was familiar with *The Green Pastures* and felt an affinity with Connelly's storytelling as well as with his religious message.

4. **Slavery Time**, ca. 1965–1970   Colorplate 3
Carved and painted wood relief with glitter and pearl
28½ × 34⅞ (71.2 × 88.6)
Collection of Mr. and Mrs. Richard E. Guggenheim

My father, he was a slave born in a slave day. He was sold and he was taken away from his mother when he was four years old. After he growed up, he wouldn't stand for no whuppin' so the owner said, "We must get rid of this nigger because he'll ruin all the rest of 'em. Put him up on the auction block and the highest bidder would get him.[1]

Thus Pierce described his father's life as an enslaved person. He admired his father's pride and his fight for self-respect in the face of slavery. By illustrating slave life based upon his father's recollections, Pierce conveyed his admiration for his own family's history and connected it to that of many other African Americans.

A collage of slave life is presented here. Appearing clockwise from the upper left are scenes of slaves in a cottonfield; an overseer on horseback; a slave on the auction block, with three men bidding below; the slave master's white house with a pond, above which two slaves carry food on a pole; three slaves in chains standing before a trough of food from which they must eat with their hands; slaves washing clothes; a slave's log cabin; a slave being whipped; a slave confronting Uncle Sam; and freed slaves farming the land. Most prominent among the subjects is the scene in which a slave and his family demand of Uncle Sam a mule, forty acres of land, and fifty dollars—provisions which they were led to believe would be forthcoming from the government after emancipation.[2] Pierce carved these figures larger than the others and placed them in the center of the composition to emphasize the importance the promise held for the slaves' dream of independence.

1. Jones and Kook.
2. The saying "forty acres and a mule" was coined after the Civil War in 1866 during the Reconstruction period. When hungry freed slaves came to the war camps to find food, soldiers aroused extravagant hopes among them by jokingly saying that a benevolent U. S. government would provide them with forty acres of land and a mule. See Henry F. Woods, *American Sayings: Famous Phrases, Slogans, and Aphorisms* (New York: Duell, Sloan, and Pearce, 1945), p. 216.

5. **Slavery Time,** 1973   Colorplate 4
    Carved and painted wood relief with glitter
    35 × 37½ (88.9 × 95.3)
    Collection of Jerrold A. Basofin

In examining his own background, Pierce often returned to certain subjects, reworking or carving them anew. His working method reflects the style of the African American preacher who reinvents his messages and revises them over time. Pierce sometimes renewed his original creations simply with fresh paint or glitter (as in *Coming of Christ*, cat. no. 168), reconstructed them into entirely different compositional for-

mats (*Crucifixion*, cat. no. 99), or converted larger assemblages into smaller works (as in *Before Death All Are Equal*, cat. no. 160). In *Slavery Time*, Pierce carved variations on the theme. Different versions could be the consequence of his missing a work that he had sold or given away, of a special request from an individual, or of his perceived need to reintroduce the subject for the benefit of the community.

The subject of slavery had special meaning for Pierce in his role as family member and community historian. The two versions presented here were created relatively close in time and show subtle variations in content, style, and composition. Most notable is the addition of the words "slavery time," flanked by the sun and crescent moon, suggesting the universal suffering of all enslaved peoples.

6. **Obey God and Live (Vision of Heaven),**
    1956   Colorplate 5
    Carved and painted wood relief with glitter
    and marking-pen ink
    12⅞ × 29⁵⁄₁₆ (32.7 × 74.5)
    Columbus Museum of Art: Museum Purchase

Obey God and Live is a powerful story of worldly transgression, spiritual denial, and rebirth of faith. It is Pierce's account of an experience he had as a young man, when, during a family Bible reading at home in Baldwyn, he reached over the Bible for a Sears Roebuck catalogue, and God struck him down for his disobedience. Pierce recalled his conversion:

She [Mother] and I used to read in the evenings the Bible—different passages of scripture. And that day Sears and Roebuck sent a catalogue. . . . And I saw it on the table and I reached over the Bible with my left hand and picked up the catalogue to thumb through it. . . . And as I did so, the power from above—seems as though a hand touched my head. And when that happened, I began to fall out of the chair. . . . I heard a voice of God told you to read the Bible and you dis-obeyed Him and I'm just showing you my power.

So my mother and sister drug me into the bedroom and laid me on the bed. And I went out just like the sun going behind a cloud . . . and they pronounced me as being a dead man.

And Mother and Sister began to scream and cry and the neighbors heard them, came in to see what was the matter. And they said I was dead. . . . And they made preparations to get the doctor and the under-taker. . . . But finally I came back just like I went away: like the sun comin' from behind a cloud.

And I stood up and walked around and they all were looking. I didn't have any pain. . . . [God] was just showing me that it's bad to disobey.[1]

Obey God and Live is one of Pierce's most significant carvings. He frequently recounted the incident, but he carved it only once.[2] The story is told in narrative sequence—a technique common to traditional story-tellers and preachers and often used by Pierce. Here, the catastrophic and miraculous proportions of the event are emphasized. Pierce's inclusion of the com-manding word phrase "obey God and live" serves as both testimony and admonition and lends authority to the image. This work speaks of a time and place beyond that of Pierce's personal history. It illustrates, for example, the formidable worldly attraction that mail-order catalogues had in America in the teens and early 1920s. It also expresses the character of a close-knit, African American community that, with its emphasis on the power of religion, experiences together the joys and sorrows of daily life.

1. Hall interview, fall 1971.
2. Pierce added his name and dated the carving 1956, some twenty years after its creation. As late as 1977, it is illus-trated without name or date in Bridgman, November 13, 1977.

---

7.   **Home and Prayer (Obey God and Live)**, 1977[1]
     Carved and painted wood relief with
     glitter, marking-pen ink, graphite, and foil
     18 1/16 × 24 3/16 (45.8 × 61.5)
     Columbus Museum of Art: Museum Purchase

Home and Prayer may be considered a verbal counter-part to the essentially pictorial *Obey God and Live* (cat. no. 6). Like the preacher who uses stories and parables to convey a message, Pierce used words with images to

enliven his personal testimony. The word "prayer" (top, center) proclaims what was for Pierce the central means to establish a proper, moral life. To the left, the inscription "Elijah I am going to show you how a chris-tian die-siner [dies a sinner]" is written next to an open view of a two-story structure in which a figure in black (the sinner) squirms on his deathbed and a figure in white (the Christian believer) lies peacefully in a bright upper room. To the right, a sequence of three fleeing figures puts action to the words of Pierce's confession: "I ran 3 years before I told it and when I started to tell it my cup ran over, and I havnt [sic] told it yet." Below "Obey God and live" is "He talk to me/E. Pierce," which attests to his renewed faith and personal rela-tionship with God. Even on the corrugated cardboard backing of the picture Pierce continues, "E. Pierce in obideence [sic], What hapenen [sic] to me."

The energetic script, boldly incised wood surface, and sparkling gold paint and glitter raise the message of this work to an ecstatic pitch. Emotional impact is increased as Pierce depicts himself praising the Lord with outstretched arms at the lower left, his body undulating in spiritual surrender. The intense presen-tation is intended to inspire faith and to lead to the con-version of others.

1. This work is dated by Pierce February 13, 1977, on corru-gated cardboard attached to the reverse of the carving. The 1977 date is consistent with the technical and stylistic han-dling of other works from this period. The date 1970, inscribed at the lower right of the carving, was added later in another hand.

8. **Mother's Prayer,** 1972   Colorplate 6
Carved and painted wood relief with glitter
18³/₈ × 14¹/₄ (46.7 × 37.6)
Columbus Museum of Art: Museum Purchase

It was after I was a young man and had left home. I was up at a New Year's Eve dance—something I had never did. The bells was ringin' and we were on the floor dancin'. People was hollerin' 'n singin'; we were glidin' on the floor. In fact, I loved to dance.

But that night while I was dancin'—the hall was singin'—and I heard my mother prayin' just like she was in the dance hall. And when I heard her call my name—ask the Lord to take care of Elijah wherever he may be—I turned my girlfriend a-loose and ran and sit and cried like a baby.

This is something I'd never did: danced the New Year's in and old year out. And over all that noise I heard her praying just like she was right there in the room and saw her with my eyes. I said, "She is broadcastin' and televisin', too. And I'll never dance anymore if the Lord will forgive me.[1]

Pierce placed his mother at the center of his world. She was his spiritual mentor and the protector of his moral conscience during periods of personal turmoil. During this memorable New Year's Eve in an Illinois dance hall, Pierce said, he heard his mother's prayer and saw before him a picture of her kneeling in a bedroom. It is this vision that Pierce carved in *Mother's Prayer*, remembering that "at home, my mother always called the children . . . and she'd pray that every year 'I thank you, Lord, to see you have spared us, to see us to the New Year.'"[2]

In *Mother's Prayer* Pierce describes the fateful communication to heaven in a sweeping arc, crackling with the electricity of red dots and dashes and sparks of glitter. The power of his mother's prayer was matched in intensity by Pierce's heartfelt contrition. Even years later these emotions are evident in this portrayal.

1. From *Artists Among Us*.
2. Seibert interview, October 1980.

9. **Picking Wild Berries,** 1979   Colorplate 7
Carved and painted wood relief with glitter
and graphite, mounted on painted corrugated
cardboard
27¹/₄ × 20¹/₈ (69.2 × 51)
Columbus Museum of Art: Museum Purchase

Picking Wild Berries is based on the theme of salvation and refers to Pierce's return to the teachings of Christ. The story is built around the image of a mountain—a motif commonly found in the Bible and in African American folklore. Man atones for his sins—for falling into the pit, so to speak—by climbing up the mountain to salvation. As preacher and performer, Pierce used the technique of improvisation, telling the story in different versions and illustrating it in carved variations (such as *Picking Wild Berries*, cat. no. 166).[1] One version of the story is a personal narrative in which Pierce used himself as the model of a person who has risen above human failure:

> When I was a young boy, I was out in the woods picking wild berries when I came to a large cliff. And I fell over that cliff and down into what was like a large well. Down at the bottom of the opening the "hands of hope" came out to help me and I tried to climb up the other side to reach my guardian angel. But you know the devil was waiting down there for me. You know that he would give you anything to help you, tempt you. But I climbed up the other side of the crevice by myself and reached the angel.[2]

In another version, referring specifically to this carving, Pierce told the story in the third person as a preacher's narrative. It is a parable in which the temptation to reach for "forbidden fruit" often results in a fall from grace.

> That story was told by a preacher man, as a sermon—pickin' wild berries. And that man falling is on the cliff or mountain. And he's up on the top. Berries grow high on the mountainside.
>
> And there is Conscience [the angel at upper right] and the Good Word [the angel at lower left] down there. Sometimes we don't listen to conscience. We just get started and keep on talking.
>
> And over here, the devil [at lower right] wants him going down. "Come on down, we want him!" And the mercy of God caught him, just as he was falling down to the ground. That's life.
>
> Dangerous job, picking wild berries, which is sin, disobedience. Sometimes we go on and are not to do things. And we do it anyway, and the outcome is dangerous.[3]

Both the narrated and illustrated renditions emphasize man's dramatic struggle for salvation. In this illustrated version of the theme, Pierce devotes nearly a quarter of the composition to the angel representing God's mercy and the "good word"—a statuesque figure with powerful outstretched hands. In the central part of the scene, he depicts a double vision of the man

pulling himself up the mountainside. Pierce's metaphor for temptation as a vision of a man positioned precariously near or over a pit is consistent with that in other personal narratives (*Home and Prayer*, cat. no. 7, and *My Sayings*, cat. no. 20).

1. Yet another version of *Picking Wild Berries* was sold in 1991 at Sotheby's, New York; See *Important Americana*, lot no. 1060.
2. Moe (forthcoming).
3. Seibert interview, October 1980.

10. Answer to Prayer, 1976
Carved and painted wood relief with traces of marking-pen ink and small pieces of paper glued to wood surface
19½ × 24⅝ (49.5 × 62.7)
Columbus Museum of Art: Museum Purchase

As God saved, so did he provide, according to *Answer to Prayer*. This story took place in Danville, Illinois, where Pierce had settled temporarily after migrating from his southern home. Also called *Guidance Pays*, the carving shows Pierce being led by God to a supply of money so that he could pay a debt. Faithfully retracing a directive of the divine voice in this work, Pierce outlines the journey from his home at the top center down a back road that lay between two railroad tracks to a grassy field near a building variously identified by him as a church or a schoolhouse. At the lower right are bags marked with dollar signs. Bits of paper representing money, glued to the wood surface of the work, give tangible presence to the found treasure and heighten the impact of the narrative.

Very likely, Pierce related the divine subsidizing of his debt to the biblical story of the tribute money (Matt. 17:24–27), in which Jesus provided Peter with a silver coin from a fish's mouth sufficient to pay a tax. Recalling the experience, Pierce once again spoke of obedience and salvation:

> I had enough money to pay that bill off and quite a bit left. So God will take care of you. . . . That's true to life; that's a true story. . . . If you read your Bible you'll see, Jesus commands us to obey. . . . He put that money in the fish's mouth, didn't he? He said, "Ask and you shall receive." So I believe in Him. . . . I know he answered my prayer.[1]

1. Seibert interview, September 1980.

13.

12.   14.   11.

11.   **Masonic Plaque,** 1969   Colorplate 8
Carved and painted wood relief with glitter and brass tack
20 × 12½ (50.8 × 31.8)
Collection of Dewell Davis

12.   **Masonic Plaque,** 1969   Colorplate 8
Carved and painted wood relief with glitter, mounted on painted panel
19½ × 7¾ (49.5 × 19.7)
Columbus Museum of Art: Museum Purchase

13.   **Masonic Plaque,** 1974   Colorplate 8
Carved and painted wood with glitter
10⅞ × 14¼ (27.6 × 36.2)
Columbus Museum of Art: Museum Purchase

14.   **Masonic Plaque,** 1977   Colorplate 8
Carved and painted wood relief with glitter
11⅝ × 7¾ (29.6 × 19.7)
Columbus Museum of Art: Museum Purchase

Freemasonry is an important conduit for the advancement of personal and social conscience among many groups, including African Americans. Black Masons in Columbus have been fervent advocates of social, economical, and educational concerns, and they have been active at the local, state, and national levels.[1]

Pierce believed strongly in the moral tenets of Freemasonry. He was himself a Mason, a member of Master Lodge 62, Ancient Free and Accepted Masons, which he joined in 1947.[2] In the same spirit of community participation and acceptance that often inspired his gifts of carvings, Pierce created many Masonic plaques for his fellow lodge members to display in their homes. He also decorated an ark with symbols of the Royal Arch degree surmounted by a pair of winged cherubim. The ark is still used today by Master Lodge 62 for ceremonies related to the Royal Arch degree.

Among a number of plaques that are still treasured in Columbus's African American community is one made in 1969 for Dewell Davis (cat. no. 11). In the center is the universally recognized symbol of Freemasonry, the square (symbolizing morality, righteousness) and compasses (circumscribing desire and passion) surrounding the letter *G* (for God, or geometry). Arranged around the emblem of Freemasonry are, clockwise from upper left, an angel looking down upon a man taking a ceremonial oath before an altar; the burning bush (symbol of divine light and truth); a cross circumscribed by a heart (symbolizing Christ in one's heart); a sword pointing to the naked heart (justice); the word "love" flanked by two perennial plants, a sprig of acacia (faith) and a flowering evergreen (perpetuity, endurance); and a setting maul (ceremonial tool). The symbols were specially chosen by Pierce to honor Davis, who is a thirty-third degree Mason, the highest rank in Masonry.

Three Masonic plaques remained in Pierce's barbershop at the time of his death. One represents the standard square and compasses (cat. no. 13). Another (cat. no. 14) combines the square and compasses with the Rose of Sharon (a traditional symbol of Christ) and a star (an emblem associated with the women's Masonic counterpart, the Order of the Eastern Star). Another (cat. no. 12) is a six-emblem totemic plaque representing advanced degrees of the Master Mason, York Rite. Reading from the top, these are the square and compasses, the keystone of the Royal Arch degree, the Royal Arch motif of a trowel within a triangle, the Teutonic Cross of the Knights Templar degree, the double-headed eagle (without crown) of a thirty-second degree Mason, and the star of the Order of the Eastern Star.[3]

Many symbols in Pierce's work may be as much related to the ideology of Freemasonry as to religious or moral philosophy. Motifs such as the sun, moon, and stars (seen in *The Place of My Birth*, cat. no. 1); representations of the five senses, including the all-seeing eye (in *I Am the Door*, cat. no. 128); Jacob's Ladder (in *Climbing Jacob's Ladder*, cat. 106); and the names of virtuous goals (in *Bible Stories*, cat. no. 169) are all significantly related to Freemasonry.

1. See "Black Masons Promise Unity," *Columbus Call and Post*, March 17, 1979, and Nate Hobbs, "Masons Urged to Increase Involvement in Community," *Columbus Call and Post*, April 4, 1981.
2. Pierce left the lodge for personal reasons in 1967 and, at his request, was reinstated in 1979 as an honorary member.
3. For a general introduction to Freemasonry, see Allen E. Roberts, *The Craft and Its Symbols: Opening the Door to Masonic Symbolism* (Richmond, Virginia: Macoy Publishing and Masonic Supply, 1974). See also Albert G. Mackey, *Encyclopedia of Freemasonry*, 3 vols. (New York: Macoy Publishing and Masonic Supply, 1909).

15. **Preaching Stick,** ca. 1950   Colorplate 9
     Carved and painted wood with rhinestones
     H. 36, Dia. 1³/₈ (91.4 × 3.5)
     Collection of Alexis G. Pierce

I was working on this stick six years or more, and you find a little of everything on it to look at it close. It's a hard piece of wood; it's a cue stick. Represents every state except Hawaii and Alaska. As a customer would come in the shop I'd ask him his trade or his work or

his hobby or where he lived. And if he's from Massachusetts or anywhere I said, "What's your trade?" And he'd tell me and I'd put it on the stick. And as you look at this stick, the more you look the more you see.[1]

The walking stick is one of the primary expressions of African American woodcarving. Walking sticks related to ceremonial and authority staffs of African origin were first developed in the southeastern United States.[2] Pierce was fond of walking sticks, and he often carved them in his youth.[3] He also received them as gifts and carried them as objects of personal decoration.

When Pierce carved his own walking sticks, they often became part of his repertoire of storytelling and preaching devices. This preaching stick is perhaps the most memorable example of its kind by Pierce. It is carved with secular, religious, and Masonic motifs found throughout Pierce's oeuvre. Seen here are the sun, moon, stars, figures, animals, dice, cards, a handgun, and a cross. Those motifs represent elements of everyday life that would have been topics of conversation in the barbershop. Near the top of the preaching stick a man, a barber chair, and a comb are depicted. Above these, the inscription "1924/Col. Ohio/EP" records Pierce's establishment in the barber's trade in Columbus.

1. Jones and Kook.
2. See John Michael Vlach, *The Afro-American Tradition in Decorative Arts* (exh. cat., Cleveland Museum of Art, 1978), pp. 40–42.
3. See Horwitz, 1975, p. 86.

16. **Five Handled Vessels,** 1930s–1940s
     Carved and painted wood with glitter and
     aluminum foil
     H. 2¹/₂–5 (6.3–12.7)
     Collection of Gene Boughton, Columbus

17. **Four Handled Vessels,** 1930s–1940s
     Carved and painted wood with glitter
     H. 2³/₄–5 (6.9–12.7)
     Private Collection

During summers in the 1930s and 1940s, Pierce left his barbering trade in Columbus and served as an itinerant preacher. He traveled with his second wife, Cornelia, to other midwestern and southern towns and set up

knife. Both depended upon the creative talent centered in his hands. In one of his most unusual works, Pierce carved a life-size version of a right hand with all its lifelines and underlying structure delineated. While the carved hand is not the enormous size of Pierce's own, it is nevertheless a self-reference—summoning thoughts of the hand that barbered and carved, and the hand that gestured to tell a story or preach a sermon. The right hand is also associated with blessing, pledging, and oath taking. Thus references to moral uprightness and good citizenship are also implied. In fact, Pierce referred to this work as "the hand on the scale,"[1] symbolizing the weighing of moral and artistic integrity in his carvings. "I don't like to carve anything degrading," he said, "I wouldn't spoil the talent God gave me."[2]

1. Seibert interview, October 1980.
2. Cited in Foster. Once, however, Pierce digressed from his commitment to carve' good and "proper" works; see Almon, 1979, p. 11.

displays of his carvings for informal demonstrations at local churches, fairs, carnivals, and shops. At each site, Pierce would speak informally about the biblical meaning or moral message of each work.

The demonstrations were subsidized in part by the sale of small objects such as these handled vessels. Carved from a single piece of wood, with the body at least partially hollowed out, the vessels were frequently decorated with crosses and hearts in metallic paint; other examples were encased in aluminum foil painted with designs. This group of vessels sat on the living room mantel of Pierce's house on Margaret Street. They were apparently the first ones he carved, and he would not sell them.

18. Hand, 1974
Carved and painted wood
9¹⁄₈ × 5³⁄₈ × 8³⁄₄ (23.2 × 13.7 × 22.2)
Columbus Museum of Art: Museum Purchase

For Pierce, the perfect stroke of the barber's blade had much in common with the essential cut of the carving

19. Jonah and the Whale, 1978
Photographic color reproduction with glitter
17³⁄₈ × 17³⁄₄ (44.1 × 45.1)
Columbus Museum of Art: Museum Purchase

This is a photographic reproduction—possibly a calendar illustration—of Pierce's relief carving *Jonah and the Fish* (cat. no. 104). It reproduces the right half of the carving, which depicts Jonah's rescue from the bowels of the fish. Pierce added paint, glitter, and varnish to the image just as he did to the wood surfaces of his carvings.

Pierce strongly related to Jonah, the Old Testament hero who disobeyed God and refused to preach and was then shown God's power and mercy. The Jonah story parallels Pierce's image of himself as a penitent man restored to faith. By embellishing a reproduction of his *Jonah and the Fish*, Pierce recast something of his own creation in renewed form as a powerful reaffirmation of self.

20. **My Sayings,** n.d.   Colorplate 10
Carved and painted wood relief with marking-pen ink and graphite
25⁷⁄₈ × 40⁷⁄₈ (65.8 × 103.4)
Columbus Museum of Art: Museum Purchase

My Sayings is the largest and most complex of Pierce's message signs, or word carvings. It is autobiographical and introspective.

> God spoke to me one night and said/
> Elijah your life is a book and every day/
> is a page. God gives you a clean page ever[y]/
> day How do you give it back One day the book wi[ll]/
> be open and read before your eyes You/cant deny it
> You wrote it yourself and a recording angel/
> in heaven who see all you do and hear all you say./
> Go, tell your. Sister. Carrie. God [k]no[w] me. He.
> walks with me and talk/to me that I. am. his. own.
> The. joy. we. share. as. we. tarry. there. None/other.
> known. You go. tell. your. sister. Carrie this. I. was.
> sitting in a/rocking chair over a deep well and friends
> would tell me/to get up out off [*sic*] that chair and I
> would laugh at them but I got up.
> I am old

My Sayings was carved over a period of years. Pierce's decline in technical dexterity and his increasing age are evident in the change from more skillfully shaped and deeply cut words to phrases fervent in intent but crude and shallow in execution; marking pen was often used to emphasize the words. The carving remains unfinished. It ends with the stirring realization ''I am old,'' penciled onto the wood surface in the lower right corner.

Pierce has here created an epitaph that records his acknowledgment of God and asserts his belief that his life served a purpose. Urgent and commanding, the emotionally charged narrative begins with Pierce's testimony as he repeats his favorite saying in full, ''your life is a book.'' He then turns to the compelling rhythms of the popular hymn ''In the Garden'' to emphasize his spiritual union with God.

> And he walks with me, and He talks with me,
> And He tells me I am His own;
> And the joy we share as we tarry there,
> None other has ever known.[1]

Pierce proclaimed his salvation, when, as he put it, he struggled and rose from his chair over a well—his metaphor for the precariousness of disobedience (see *Picking Wild Berries,* cat. nos. 9 and 166). Pierce reinforced the words by adding a small sketch at the lower left depicting a man seated in a rocker. A nearly identical portrayal of Pierce appears in *Home and Prayer* (cat. no. 7).

1. ''In the Garden'' was composed by C. Austin Miles and copyrighted in 1912. The song appears in many standard hymnals and was made popular in recordings of the 1950s and 1960s by Tennessee Ernie Ford, Mahalia Jackson, Elvis Presley, and others.

FREESTANDING CARVINGS: ANIMALS AND FIGURES

21. **The Little Elephant,** ca. 1923
Carved and painted wood
2³⁄₄ × 4¹⁄₄ × 2¹⁄₄ (7.0 × 10.8 × 5.7);
base, Dia. 3 (7.8)
Columbus Museum of Art: Museum Purchase

The creation of *The Little Elephant* marked the beginning of Pierce's serious work as a carver. Dating from the mid-1920s, *The Little Elephant* is probably the earliest surviving carving by the artist; the small figure was still in his shop at the time of his death.

Pierce told the story of carving *The Little Elephant* many times. Though certain details of the story varied over the years, and he alternately described the little figure as a Christmas or birthday present, the role of his wife Cornelia always remained central to the tale:

> One day at home I saw this little piece of two-by-four and I picked it up and began to carve on it. It came out to be a little elephant. And I sandpapered it and showed it to my wife. And she looked at it and said "Oh, that is cute," and tied a little ribbon around its head and sat it up on the mantel. I said, "If you like that ugly thing that well, I'll carve you a zoo."[1]

The Little Elephant is one of the few figures that Pierce conceived fully in the round. Most of the later freestanding carved animals that came to populate his menagerie are presented in profile with only two distinct sides (see, for example, *Elephant*, cat. no. 22).

1. Jones and Kook. Though there are several sources that identify the carved elephant now in the permanent collection of the Columbus Museum of Art as the original *Little Elephant*, the indisputable source is the Jones and Kook documentary film *Sermons in Wood*, in which Pierce holds the figure and retells the story excerpted here.

---

22. Elephant, 1972   Colorplate 11
Carved and painted wood with glitter
and rhinestones
4¼ × 5¹¹/₁₆ × 2 (10.7 × 14.4 × 5.1)
Columbus Museum of Art: Gift of Mrs. Ursel
White Lewis

---

23. Long Bib Duck, 1978
Carved and painted wood with marking-pen ink
and rhinestones
9 × 19½ × 2¾ (22.8 × 49.6 × 7.0)
Private Collection

Though Pierce often discussed the meaning of his works with interested listeners, the fantastic spotted *Long Bib Duck* is the only known carving to which Pierce added a written commentary. The statement, which the artist wrote at the request of the owner, expresses the folk wisdom that invests many of Pierce's animal carvings: "One day when I was barbering, I had a customer in the chair. And someone was talking and he said nothing hurts a duck but his bill—one that talks too much."

Pierce's concern with gossip and its consequences is thus made explicit in this carving. The theme is also evident in several of his moralistic narrative works, particularly *Monday Morning Gossip* (cat. no. 153).

---

24. Dog, 1972   Colorplate 11
Carved and painted wood with rhinestones
4⅛ × 7⅝ × 2⅛ (10.3 × 19.3 × 5.4)
Columbus Museum of Art: Gift of Mrs. Ursel
White Lewis

25. Donkey, 1972
Carved and painted wood
7¼ × 2¼ × 6⅜ (18.3 × 5.7 × 16.1)
Columbus Museum of Art: Gift of Mrs. Ursel
White Lewis

26. **Giraffe,** 1980
Carved and painted wood with rhinestones
13³/₄ × 5¹/₂ × 3¹/₈ (34.8 × 14.0 × 7.9)
Columbus Museum of Art: Museum Purchase

27. **Tiger,** 1972   Colorplate 11
Carved and painted wood with rhinestones,
stones, and sawdust
7⁹/₁₆ × 1⁷/₈ × 21¹/₂ (19.2 × 4.8 × 54.6)
Columbus Museum of Art: Gift of Mrs. Ursel
White Lewis

28. **Dinosaur,** 1981   Colorplate 11
Carved and painted wood with glitter
and rhinestones
14 × 12¹/₄ × 3³/₈ (35.6 × 31.1 × 8.5)
Columbus Museum of Art: Museum Purchase

29. **Rhino,** 1981
Carved and painted wood with rhinestones
7¹/₂ × 14¹/₂ × 1³/₈ (19.1 × 36.8 × 3.4)
Columbus Museum of Art: Museum Purchase

30. **Monkey,** 1981   Colorplate 11
Carved and painted wood with glitter
5¹/₄ × 3³/₄ × 2³/₄ (13.0 × 9.5 × 7.2)
Columbus Museum of Art: Museum Purchase

This solitary image of a crouching monkey, who seems to peer inquisitively at the viewer, evokes meaningful associations with other works in Pierce's oeuvre and with a principal African American oral and literary tradition known as "signifying."[1] The monkey, in particular the "signifying monkey," is one of the animals most closely associated in African American stories and toasts with artful lies, verbal banter, and improvisational wit. In narrative works such as *The Monkey Family* (cat. no. 154) Pierce alludes to the antics of the

signifying monkey, who willfully stirs up the accepted order of things either for mischief's sake or for moral instruction. The monkey in other works by Pierce invokes a Christian moralizing tradition familiar to both black and white audiences. In *Card Players* (cat. no. 89) and *Seance* (cat. no. 90), the monkeys impersonate humans, their actions elucidating the follies and foibles of man.

1. The term "signifying" is a complex oral and literary strategy within the black community that uses language to test the limits of the conventional meaning of words, ideas, and actions. Acknowledging through this use of language the multiple—even contradictory—meanings implicit in any given word or event, the signifier employs wit and verbal nonsense (suggesting to an outsider that the speaker is merely playing around) to address serious concerns of community life. See *Afro-American Folktales: Stories from Black Traditions in the New World,* ed. Roger D. Abrahams (New York: Pantheon Books, 1985), pp. 5–7; and Henry Louis Gates, *The Signifying Monkey: A Theory of Afro-American Literary Criticism* (New York: Oxford University Press, 1988), pp. 44–88.

31.　**Gorilla,** 1981
Carved and painted wood with rhinestones
13⁷/₈ × 8³/₈ × 1¹¹/₁₆ (35.2 × 20.2 × 4.2)
Columbus Museum of Art: Museum Purchase

32.　**Penguin,** n.d.
Carved and painted wood with rhinestones
5¹/₂ × 3 × 1⁹/₁₆ (13.9 × 7.6 × 3.9)
Private Collection, Courtesy Keny Galleries, Inc.

33.　**Alligator,** ca. 1981
Carved and painted wood, with teeth from
a plastic comb
5 × 16¹/₄ × 5 (12.7 × 41.2 × 12.7)
Courtesy Janet Fleisher Gallery, Philadelphia

Though this carving has been identified as a dragon or a tiger, it is probably an alligator or a crocodile, two favorite subjects in Pierce's carvings. Part of the confusion over the figure's identity arises no doubt from how radically its appearance departs from Pierce's more familiar interpretation of an alligator as an upright, two-sided, profile figure with rows of sharp, dazzling white teeth lining gaping jaws (as in *Alligator,* cat. no.

35). Here, as in *Alligator* (cat. no. 34), Pierce shows his beast spread out on the ground. Seen from above, the alligator seems perfectly poised to race among the weeds of a riverbank and slip into the water. Here, our attention is drawn not to the huge jaws but to the elaborately carved scales, heightened with red paint, that cover the reptile's back and long serpentine tail.

34.　**Alligator,** 1974　　Colorplate 12
Carved and painted wood with rhinestones,
sawdust, and teeth from plastic comb
3¹/₈ × 18 × 3¹/₂ (7.9 × 45.8 × 8.9)
Private Collection

35.　**Alligator,** 1982
Carved and painted wood with rhinestones, with
teeth from a plastic comb
4⁵/₁₆ × 13⁹/₁₆ × 1³/₄ (11.0 × 34.4 × 4.4)
Columbus Museum of Art: Museum Purchase

In his role as a preacher and community elder, Pierce was a gifted storyteller. Many of the animals Pierce chose as subjects for his individual carvings are prominent characters in African American folktales with which Pierce was no doubt familiar. The moral issues and concerns expressed in these animal tales parallel those addressed directly in a number of the artist's narrative reliefs. It is possible, therefore, to consider many of Pierce's individual animals in the larger context of meaning which they held for Pierce and his original audience.

The carvings emphasize the alligators' rough scales and call to mind the African American folktale about the way the alligator got his unusual hide. A popular figure in folktales, Br'er Alligator is portrayed as a smug, self-satisfied creature who has little concern for other animals. At the opening of the tale, Br'er Alligator possesses a beautiful skin, "smooth and white as a catfish," of which he is inordinately proud. Tricked by a wily Br'er Rabbit and his own foolhardiness, the Alligator gets his skin scorched by fire until it is "just as black and crinkly as a burned log of wood, and as rough as a live oak bark."[1]

Like many African American folktales, this is both an explanatory tale, accounting for the "whys" of nature, and a cautionary tale. Often such stories teach the listener proper behavior by demonstrating how not to act. The issues touched on in the tale—the sin of pride, the importance of compassion for others, particularly the community at large, and the need to be always vigilant in one's dealings in the world—are pervasive themes in Pierce's oeuvre.

1. *Folktales: Stories from Black Traditions in the New World,* ed. Roger D. Abrahams (New York: Pantheon Books, 1985), pp. 153–155.

36. **Frog,** n.d.   Colorplate 11
Carved and painted wood with glitter and pearl
$5^3/_8 \times 6^1/_4 \times 3$ (13.6 × 15.9 × 7.6)
Private Collection

The frog, like many of Pierce's animal subjects, is a common creature. Pierce often recalled how, as a boy, he enjoyed capturing snakes and frogs.[1] The sophisticated pose of this frog—poised in a distinctive crouch ready to spring forward on its powerful hind legs—suggests that it may have been inspired by an illustration from a child's storybook or the comics, popular culture sources similar to those which inspired other works by Pierce (see, for example, cat. nos. 66, 79, and 81).

Pierce may have been attracted to the subject because of a popular southern folktale about how the frog came into being because of the disobedience of the tadpole.[2] In the story, when the newly created tadpoles decide to swim rather than pull weeds as God had instructed them to do, God cuts off their tails and gives

them legs as punishment for their misbehavior. The folktale not only explains an observable fact of nature but directly admonishes the listener that "when people don't do what they're told to do, they always get into trouble sooner or later."[3]

This moralistic explanation of the generation of frog from tadpole would certainly have appealed to Pierce, who addressed parables and fables directly in narrative carvings such as the *Parable of the Gnat and the Camel* (cat. no. 141) and *Crocodile and Unwary Cow* (cat. no. 142) and emphasized moralistic lessons in such autobiographical works as *Picking Wild Berries* (cat. nos. 9 and 166).

1. Jones and Kook.
2. *Afro-American Folktales: Stories from Black Traditions in the New World,* ed. Roger D. Abrahams (New York: Pantheon Books, 1985), pp. 65–66.
3. Ibid.

37. **Owl in Tree,** 1973   Colorplate 13
Carved and painted wood with glitter and rhinestones
$12^1/_4 \times 5^3/_4$ (31.1 × 14.6)
Collection of Mr. and Mrs. Richard E. Guggenheim

At first glance, the owl in this work appears to be yet another splendid inhabitant of Pierce's whimsical zoo. However, there is a strong suggestion of narrative implied in the relationship between the owl and the lizard that clings to the tree, which connects this carving more closely to Pierce's moralistic animal carvings such as *Crocodile and Unwary Cow* (cat. no. 142) and *You Can Lead a Horse to Water . . .* (cat. no. 147). The lizard as a symbol for the devil is nearly as ubiquitous in art and literature as the snake. In Pierce's carving the reptile is surely a reference to Old Nick, cunningly concealed from the owl's all-knowing eyes.

For the viewer familiar with the rich tradition of African American storytelling, Pierce's carving recalls the story of how the owl first acquired its nocturnal habits.[1] According to a tale from the American South, God originally created the owl like the other birds—"he had the same kind of eyes . . . and flew around and sang, in the daytime."[2] Worried about what mischievous things the devil might do at night during the first weeks of Creation, so the story goes, God asked the owl to stay up all night to act as his lookout. The owl foiled the devil, and his wide open stare and habit of remaining awake at night and sleeping in the daytime became permanent characteristics of the species.

In Pierce's work, the owl's huge, unblinking rhinestone eyes emphasize his role as a sentinel of the night. Pierce has given the owl majestic scale; he dwarfs not only his reptile adversary but the tree in which he is perched. The foliage surrounding the owl blends ambiguously with the bird's own plumage. The owl as a symbol of vigilance also appears in Pierce's narrative relief *Pilgrim's Progress* (cat. no. 140).

1. Retold in *Afro-American Folktales: Stories from Black Traditions in the New World,* ed. Roger D. Abrahams (New York: Pantheon Books, 1985), pp. 66–68.
2. Ibid.

38.　Scape Goat, n.d.
　　Carved and painted wood with bone, glitter,
　　marking-pen ink, and stones
　　9³/₄ × 11⁷/₈ × 10 (24.8 × 30.3 × 25.4)
　　Private Collection

The most distinctive feature of this work is its composition of wood and animal bone. The top of the head and the horns of Pierce's goat are in fact formed by the con-

necting skull plate and bony core of a ram's horns.[1] While this is the only known example of Pierce's use of animal bones, the incorporation of found objects into his works is consistent with other carvings (see cat. nos. 92, 93, and 96).

Pierce indicated the symbolic significance of his imposing goat by giving it the title *Scape Goat*. The biblical origins of the term "scapegoat," with which Pierce would certainly have been familiar, are found in Leviticus 16:7–22. On the Day of Atonement, the Jewish high priest chose two goats, one to sacrifice to the Lord, and the other, the scapegoat, to bear the confessed sins of the people and to be cast out into the wilderness to perish. Pierce's use of red paint, particularly in the scapegoat's red-rimmed eyes, heightens the sense of abandonment the forsaken animal suffers.

1. John Harder, associate professor of zoology, Ohio State University, in conversation with museum staff, June 9, 1992.

39.　Pinto Horse, 1972
　　Carved and painted wood
　　6³/₄ × 8¹/₈ × 1³/₈ (17.0 × 20.5 × 3.5)
　　Columbus Museum of Art: Gift of Mrs. Ursel
　　White Lewis

Pierce particularly enjoyed painting spotted horses in different color combinations. Spotted or pinto ponies, both with riders and alone, far outnumber his solid-colored horses, such as the one in *Sulky Driver* (cat. no. 43), which were inspired by the thoroughbreds of the racetrack.

40. **Pony and Chimp,** 1981
Carved and painted wood with glitter
4⁵/₈ × 7⁷/₈ × 3 (11.8 × 20.0 × 7.6)
Columbus Museum of Art: Museum Purchase

Pony and Chimp, which depicts a monkey perched like a small jockey on the back of a striding spotted pony, evokes strong associations with the common folktale about a small, wily animal tricking a larger, stronger animal into doing its bidding.[1] The trickster is a key character in many African American folktales. The importance of these tales in the black community is often attributed to the parallels between the wit and wile of the trickster and the inventiveness of American slaves who had to develop skills to survive in the hostile environment of the antebellum South. The trickster, however, is not just a symbol of the ability of the oppressed to transcend their powerless condition. In the African culture where the tales first originated, the trickster's inventiveness is valued for its own sake, "for the sheer joy in taking on the challenge" in a world that offers an eternal contest between wit and strength.[2] This broader significance of the trickster contributes to the vitality of the African American versions of tales with which Pierce would have been familiar.

The age-old tradition of the monkey as a symbol of man—an animal who mimics man's actions in order to point up his faults and foibles—is clearly alluded to in this as well as in other works by Pierce (see cat. nos. 89 and 90). In addition, *Pony and Chimp* bears a striking visual similarity to Pierce's carving of Paul Revere (cat. no. 41). Though Revere and his steed race at a full gallop in contrast to the loping gait of the pony in *Pony and Chimp,* the critical relationship between horse and rider is similar in both carvings.

1. The trickster is frequently portrayed as a rabbit or a spider. For a well-known version of a trickster tale in which a small animal tricks a larger animal into being his steed, see

"Anansi's Riding Horse, A Jamaican Folktale," in *Talk That Talk: An Anthology of African-American Storytelling,* ed. Linda Goss and Marian E. Barnes, (New York: Simon and Schuster, 1989), pp. 42–44.

2. For a discussion of the trickster in African and African American folktales, see Ivan Van Sertima, "Trickster, The Revolutionary Hero," in ibid., pp. 103–111; and *Afro-American Folktales: Stories from Black Traditions in the New World,* ed. Roger D. Abrahams (New York: Pantheon Books, 1985), pp. 3–35, 179–180.

41. **Horse and Rider (Paul Revere),**
ca. 1970s   Colorplate 14
Carved and painted wood with glitter
and rhinestones
8¹/₂ × 12¹/₄ × ⁷/₈ (21.6 × 31.2 × 2.3)
Collection of Harvey S. Shipley Miller and
J. Randall Plummer

The identity of this horse and rider is suggested by the horse's galloping stride and the resemblance of the man's black cap to a three-cornered colonial hat. A beloved revolutionary hero and a popular symbol of American patriotism, Paul Revere (1735–1818) is one of a number of legendary figures from American history that Pierce admired and carved. As with Pierce's image of Abraham Lincoln (cat. no. 78), there is some question about whether Revere is represented as an African American. The face is painted and seems to some viewers to indicate a black person. Pierce, however, was often casual or ambivalent in distinguishing the race of his subjects. He frequently left his carvings of African Americans unpainted (see, for example, *Joe Louis, World Champion,* cat. no. 66), allowing skin color to be determined by the shade of the varnished wood. Only occasionally did Pierce make a clear distinction between black and white figures, as in *Presidents and Convicts* (cat. no. 77).

42. **Horse and Rider**, n.d.
Carved and painted wood with chain
and thumb tacks
13 × 16⅞ × 3 (33.0 × 42.8 × 7.6)
Columbus Museum of Art: Museum Purchase

Horse and Rider is one of at least two similar works by Pierce in which the horse was not carved but cut out of thin plywood with a handsaw.[1] It is not known whether Pierce actually made the horses in the two works himself. The flat, even painting technique and the use of tacks for eyes are not found in any other known work by Pierce, suggesting that the horses may have been gifts, which Pierce later chose to manipulate by adding his own carved figure of a rider.[2]

In this work the rider is a small jockey grasping a beaded chain as he clings to the back of a giant black steed. Collectors who visited Pierce's shop beginning in the early 1970s distinctly remember that *Horse and Rider* was always there.[3] The importance of the work to Pierce is substantiated by the handwritten "Not for Sale" slip taped to its base. Pierce may have decided that *Horse and Rider* was not for sale after the other version of the work left his possession. *Horse and Rider* (dated 1975 and measuring 13⅜ × 16⅝ × 3 inches) in the collection of John Wiley Fenderick in 1982 is nearly identical to this one, with only slight variations in the silhouettes. Pierce, however, carved a saddle for the well-dressed upright rider in the Fenderick version rather than allowing a painted saddle to suffice as it does for the little jockey in the museum's work (the jockey is attached with soft green putty). In addition, the base on the Fenderick version is decorated with pebbles, whereas the base on the museum's work is simply painted green.

1. See Aschenbrand, pp. 24–25.
2. Pierce used manufactured objects in other works, for example *Jesus on the Cross* (cat. no. 96).
3. Michael Hall, communication with the author, summer 1991.

---

43. **Sulky Driver**, n.d.   Colorplate 17
Carved and painted wood with stones
and rhinestones
4 × 8 × 2 (10.2 × 20.3 × 5.1)
Collection of Mrs. Rose Chenfeld, Courtesy Keny Galleries, Inc.

Horses and horse racing are the subject of a number of Pierce's carvings. Though he enjoyed the racetrack as a young man, he considered himself uncommonly unlucky, commenting in his later years that whenever he bet, his horse "didn't act right. I'd pick out a horse that looked good, and he'd be the last horse to come in. I never did win."[1] He admired those who had the skill to pick winning horses, but he firmly believed that one should risk only a certain amount of money, and, "after that just be looking on."[2] The subject of *Sulky Driver* is treated in a comic manner in the relief *Ostrich Pulling Harness Racer* (cat. no. 65).

1. Seibert interview, July 1981.
2. Ibid. In the same interview Pierce also observed, "It's really a sport, playing the horses that are lucky to win." In her field research, Seibert notes how unusual it was for Pierce to use the phrase "lucky to win" in this context. Describing a horse as "lucky to win" is associated with British horse racing rather than American racing, where the horse is usually described as "a long shot."

44. **Silver,** 1982
    Carved and painted wood with glitter
    18⁷/₈ × 13³/₄ × 5³/₁₆ (47.8 × 35.0 × 13.1)
    Columbus Museum of Art: Museum Purchase

Outlaw heroes exist in both white and black cultural traditions. Suspicious of the law, which rarely defended them against the injustices inflicted by mainstream society, many African Americans have admired outlaws and embraced fugitive heroes who could outwit the law, at least for a time.[1] The subject of this carving is the pop-culture hero, the Lone Ranger, shown here riding his trusty horse Silver.

The fictional character of the Lone Ranger, a renegade lawman of the American West who fought for victims of injustice, originated as a radio show on WXYZ in Detroit in 1933, became a movie serial beginning in 1938, and moved to television in 1949, where it ran until 1958 and then became syndicated. The popularity of the character, who also appeared in countless books and comic strips, is indicated by the long run of the television show in syndication and by the production of a new Lone Ranger movie in 1980.[2]

It is not surprising that Pierce would choose to emphasize Silver in his portrayal of the Lone Ranger. Horses were among Pierce's favorite subjects. The identification of the Lone Ranger with his horse dates from the origins of the radio show, which was introduced with the masked man's memorable cry "Hi-yo Silver! Away!" Photographs of the Lone Ranger mounted on his horse were used for promotion from the very beginning of the radio show and throughout the television years. One of these innumerable photographs no doubt served as the visual source for Pierce's carving.

1. Prominent black outlaw heroes celebrated in ballads, songs, and folktales include Travelin' Man, Lost John, Railroad Bill, Roscoe Bill, Stackolee, Po' Lazarus, and Bad Leroy Brown. For a discussion of renegade heroes in African American culture, see Sterling Brown, "Negro Folk Expression: Spirituals, Seculars, Ballads and Work Songs," in *The Making of Black America: Essays in Negro Life and History,* vol. 1, ed. August Meier and Elliott Rudwick (New York: Atheneum, 1969), pp. 217–219.

2. For a detailed discussion of the Lone Ranger and his significance in popular culture, see David Rothel, *Who Was That Masked Man? The Story of the Lone Ranger* (San Diego and New York: A. S. Barnes and Company, 1981).

45. **Angel,** 1980   Colorplate 15
    Carved and painted wood with glitter
    11¹/₂ × 5¹/₂ (28.6 × 14)
    Arient Family Collection

This distinctive figure differs considerably from the other angels who appear throughout Pierce's work. The cross-legged pose and seemingly inexplicable blue sweatsuit strongly suggest the image of actor Warren Beatty that was used to publicize the Paramount film *Heaven Can Wait,* released in 1978. The movie was a remake of *Here Comes Mr. Jordan* from 1941. In the film, Beatty played an athlete whose soul was mistakenly taken to heaven before its time and had to be returned to fulfill its destiny on earth. The signature image of the film, used for most publicity, showed Beatty as a winged angel dressed in the running suit and athletic shoes he was wearing on his untimely arrival in heaven early in the movie. Pierce's interpretation is remarkably close to the original source. Even the color and style of the angel's hair is reminiscent of Beatty's. Pierce, however, eliminated the props (usually a watch or a clarinet) the character held. He also replaced the character's running shoes with sandals, which Pierce may have considered more appropriate for a heavenly messenger.

---

46. **Man (Sammy Davis, Jr.),** n.d.   Colorplate 17
Carved and painted wood with stones and
rhinestone
9⅝ × 6⅛ × 3¾ (24.5 × 15.5 × 9.6)
Columbus Museum of Art: Museum Purchase

This figure appears to many viewers to be a portrait of the entertainer Sammy Davis, Jr. (1925–1990), whom Pierce chose to immortalize along with other prominent African Americans such as Joe Louis, Hank Aaron, and Nancy Wilson.

A lifelong performer who debuted in his parents' vaudeville act at the age of two, Davis was a younger contemporary of Lena Horne (who is probably the subject of *Movie Star,* cat. no. 69). Like Horne, he was equally at home on the Broadway stage, in films, and in nightclubs. He was one of a handful of entertainers popular between the 1940s and the 1960s, among them (in addition to Lena Horne) Eartha Kitt and Harry Belafonte, who were able to break the racial barrier and become major stars. In 1964 Davis played the lead role in the critically successful Broadway play *Golden Boy,* one of the first plays on Broadway to address racial issues.[1] In 1966 Davis published his best-selling autobiography *Yes, I Can,* which had a broad appeal that transcended racial lines.

1. See Allen Woll, *Black Musical Theatre: From Coontown to Dreamgirls* (Baton Rouge: Louisiana State University Press, 1989), pp. 245–246.

---

47. **Archie Griffin,** 1976   Colorplate 16
Carved and painted wood
16⅛ × 14⅛ × 3⅝ (40.9 × 35.8 × 9.1)
Columbus Museum of Art: Museum Purchase

The subject of this carving is Archie Griffin, a star player for the Ohio State University football team from 1972 to 1975 and later a halfback for the Cincinnati Bengals. Griffin was the first athlete to be twice awarded college football's most coveted award, the Heisman Tro-

phy. A Columbus celebrity who was constantly heralded in the local press during his four years at the university, Griffin was admired not only as an outstanding player but as an upstanding student. His strong religious beliefs and the fact that he read the Bible regularly and prayed before each game were widely reported in the press, as was his "Three Ds" formula for success—desire, dedication, and determination. These all were qualities that would have made Griffin a particularly attractive subject for Pierce as an artist.

Though he carved the image in 1976, the year Griffin was drafted by the Bengals, Pierce depicted Griffin in the scarlet and gray uniform of his Ohio State team. The figure's pose imitates Griffin's distinctive running style. When he ran, Griffin's hips and shoulders seemed to move in opposite directions, and his legs appeared to churn out to one side as they do in Pierce's representation.[1] The image was captured in countless photographs and was certainly known to Pierce.

1. See Edward F. Dolan and Richard B. Lyttle, *Archie Griffin* (Garden City, New York: Doubleday, 1977), pp. 25–26.

---

48. **Baseball Game,** 1940s
Carved and painted wood figures (18 figures)
Height of tallest figure, 3 (7.6)
Collection of Brett and Vicci Jaffe

A devoted baseball fan and sometime player, Pierce grew up in the golden era of black professional baseball, from 1899 to 1938.[1] The subject of baseball in

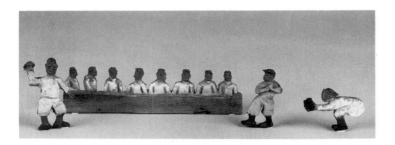

Pierce's work ranges from tributes to celebrated players such as Hank Aaron (see cat. no. 75) to simple depictions of moments of play. A baseball game even figures prominently in one of Pierce's most memorable autobiographic works, *Elijah Escapes the Mob* (whereabouts unknown).[2]

This set of two teams of nine players was carved by Pierce for two young boys from his neighborhood who came to Pierce's shop to have their hair cut.[3] As with the doll houses he made for his granddaughters, Pierce intended his baseball players to be used and enjoyed by their young owners. Friends of the two boys still remember playing with the figures in the basement of their home.[4] By the late 1940s, after Pierce carved his *Baseball Game*, major league baseball was finally becoming integrated. Pierce, however, did not choose to distinguish the races of his players.

1. For a discussion of African Americans in baseball, see Arthur Ashe, Jr., *A Hard Way to Glory: A History of the African American Athlete,* Vol. 1 (New York: Waumay Books, 1988), pp. 25–43, 69–88.

2. See discussion and illustration in *Elijah Pierce, Wood Carver* (exh. cat., Columbus Gallery of Fine Arts, 1973), unpaginated.

3. Aminah Robinson, in conversation with the author, October 1991.

4. Ibid.

---

49. Two Standing Figures, n.d.
Carved and painted wood
H. 6¼, 7½ (15.8, 19.1)
Collection of Roger McLane

The animated poses and gestures of these two figures—one bent over in excitement, hat in hand, with his mouth open wide in a cheer and the other reaching forward with one arm, his cap playfully reversed on his

head—suggest that they are spectators at one of Pierce's favorite sporting events, perhaps baseball, boxing, or horse racing.

50. Running Nude Woman on One Foot, ca. 1981
Carved and painted wood
8 × 7½ × 2½ (20.3 × 19.1 × 6.3)
Collection of Dennis and Martha Hayes

This small, fully painted figure, precariously balanced in a pose that suggests a gymnast or dancer, is a rare example of a nude in Pierce's work. With the exception of subjects such as *Adam and Eve* (cat. no. 101) that require the depiction of the nude, Pierce showed little interest in the nude figure.[1] Even with subjects that offered the latitude to explore the nude, Pierce rarely chose to do so. In *The Pickup* (cat. no. 146), a girl remains discreetly clad in a pink bikini, which the two men are about to hook with a fishing pole. Certainly this hesitancy on Pierce's part may be related to deep religious and moral convictions that made him consider certain subjects inappropriate. Pierce believed God once turned his right hand "black as soot" because he carved an unworthy subject.[2]

1. A reclining black female nude, which Pierce always referred to as "Black Beauty" is in a private collection. Those familiar with the carving regard it as Pierce's interpretation of the fine art theme of the reclining nude.
2. See Almon, 1979, p. 11.

51. **Dancing Couple,** 1978
Carved and painted wood
7½ × 3¾ × 2 (19.1 × 9.5 × 5.1)
Private Collection

52. **Jitterbug,** 1974   Colorplate 17
Carved and painted wood
4½ × 1⅝ × 3¼ (11.4 × 4.1 × 8.2)
Collection of Howard and Mimi Chenfeld

Pierce loved to dance as a young man. The years following the death of his first wife Pierce remembered especially as "a time of fast living, when he dressed well, played the piano, and liked to dance."[1] In fact, the moral penalty for his passion for dancing is the subject of his autobiographical relief *Mother's Prayer* (cat. no. 8). The two dancing couples in these works, however, seem more closely related to the jazz club spirit of *Music Box* (see cat. no. 87) than to the regrets expressed

in *Mother's Prayer*. In particular, the lively pair of dancers in *Jitterbug*, with their lips pressed together in a perpetual kiss, look as if they have just stepped out of *Music Box*.

1. Livingston and Beardsley, p. 117.

53. **Figure (Man with Purple Bottle),**
1982   Colorplate 17
Carved and painted wood with glitter
and rhinestones
8⅜ × 2⅛ × 2 (21.3 × 5.5 × 5.1)
Columbus Museum of Art: Museum Purchase

54. **Figure (Man with Cigarette),**
ca. 1982   Colorplate 17
Carved and painted wood with rhinestones
9⅛ × 1¾ × 2⅜ (23.2 × 4.5 × 6.0)
Columbus Museum of Art: Museum Purchase

55. **Seated Hunter,** n.d.
Carved and painted wood with glitter
8½ × 9½ × 8½ (21.6 × 24.2 × 21.6)
Collection of Roger McLane

56. **Two-Faced Man,** 1980
Carved and painted wood with glitter
8¼ × 5½ × 6 (21.0 × 14.0 × 15.3)
Private Collection

57. **Man in the Middle,** n.d.   Colorplate 18
Carved and painted wood
5½ × 6⅛ × 2½ (14.0 × 15.4 × 6.3)
Collection of Howard and Mimi Chenfeld

Both of these carvings are related to Pierce's moralistic reliefs that comment on human behavior through popular aphorisms such as "Don't bite the hand that feeds you" (the subject of cat. no. 148) and "You can lead a horse to water, but you can't make him drink" (the subject of cat. no. 147). Here Pierce seems to address the moral implications of everyday decision making by creating visual equivalents of the familiar notions of being two-faced or of being caught in the middle. The wonderful subtlety and humor of Pierce's artistic vision is readily apparent in the gestures of the three figures in *Man in the Middle.* The men on either side signal the extremes of their positions with the distinct open and closed gestures of their hands, while the seated man trapped between them keeps his hand firmly clasped in his lap, his face staring straight ahead.[1]

At another, more profound, level of meaning, both carvings can be interpreted as embodiments of Pierce's ideal of living life in balance.[2] *Two-Faced Man,* in particular, may be seen not as an image of duplicity but of wholeness, of opposites coexisting in harmony and balance. Such imagery has an ancient history that can be traced through both the Greco-Roman and African traditions.[3] In this broader interpretation, a man in the middle is not trapped but consciously chooses the middle path to achieve a balanced life.

1. The fact that the figure dressed in white and yellow seems to be reaching for his groin may also be a humorous reference to street gesture. Such sly, vernacular allusions are a frequent characteristic of black folk art. See Livingston and Beardsley, p. 13.

2. Suggested by Aminah Robinson in conversation with the author, October 1991.

3. Janus was a Roman deity represented by two joined faces that look in opposite directions. For a discussion of Janus imagery, see Juan E. Cirlot, *A Dictionary of Symbols* (New York: Philosophical Library, 1962), pp. 161–162. Esu, a figure similar to Janus, appears in the mythology of the Yoruba cultures of Nigeria, Benin, Brazil, Cuba, and Haiti. Esu is a symbol of wholeness; having the dual nature of both male and female, Esu signifies the potential of unreconciled opposites living in harmony. For further discussion, see Henry Louis Gates, Jr., *The Signifying Monkey: A Theory of Afro-American Literary Criticism* (New York: Oxford University Press, 1988), pp. 3–43. Also see Theodore Celenko, *A Treasury of African Art from the Harrison Eitel Jorg Collection* (Bloomington: Indiana University Press, 1983), pp. 150–151. It is possible that Pierce was familiar with one or both of these traditions in some form, for these were part of the broader cultural heritage that influenced his life philosophy.

58. **Knife with Totem Handle,** n.d.
Carved and painted wood
17½ × 1¾ × ¾ (44.4 × 4.4 × 1.8)
Collection of Mike and Cindy Noland

This carved knife, the blade of which has been painted silver to resemble steel, is closely related to Pierce's elaborately carved canes and preaching sticks. As such, it is more than simply a decorated object and probably has ritualistic significance comparable to that of the *Preaching Stick* (cat. no. 15). The work also may draw on the African American tradition of carving and embellishing utilitarian objects, which was originally brought from Africa and encouraged in the environment of the antebellum South.[1] Pierce's maternal uncle, Lewis Wallace, who had an important influence on Pierce, carved chairs and baskets.[2]

Carved on the handle of the knife is a two-faced man looking to the left and right, and the bust of another figure aligned with the knife blade and looking forward. This three-faced image reflects an ancient idea related to the principle of tri-unity.[3] In the context of the paired opposites of past and future, the third element represents the eternal present; in the pairing of life and death, it represents birth. The triform is a symbol of wholeness, a synthesis of co-existing opposites.[4] For Pierce the wholeness of life was intimately connected to the ideal of balancing the sacred and the secular, of acknowledging the laws of God and nature. In

this carving, the figure of the mustached man wearing a hat is literally balanced on top of the two-headed figure, and his upward glance seems to suggest how precarious the act of balancing can be.

1. See discussion in John Michael Vlach, *The Afro-American Tradition in Decorative Arts* (exh. cat., Cleveland Museum of Art, 1978), p. 31.
2. Moe, 1990, p. 14.
3. Juan E. Cirlot, *A Dictionary of Symbols* (New York: Philosophical Library, 1962), p. 352. For specifically African symbolic tradition, see Henry Louis Gates, Jr., *The Signifying Monkey: A Theory of Afro-American Literary Criticism* (New York: Oxford University Press, 1988), pp. 29–38.
4. In the mythology of ancient Yoruba cultures, the symbol for wholeness is Esu (see cat. nos. 56 and 57, n. 3). Though often represented as a two-headed figure, referring to Esu's dual nature as both male and female, Esu also signifies "the procreated element, the third principle." As messenger of the gods, Esu is the mediator, the one "who interrelates all the different and multiple parts" of the Yoruba mythological system.

59. **Migration North,** 1976 (man),
1977 (woman)   Colorplate 19
Carved and painted wood with fiber
and rhinestones
Man: 11¾ × 5⅜ × 7 (29.9 × 13.6 × 17.7);
Woman: 11 × 5 × 3⅞ (28.0 × 12.7 × 9.9)
Collection of Aminah and Sydney Robinson

Migration North is one of several versions of this subject that Pierce executed. The figures in all of the works, according to Pierce, represent his parents on their journey to freedom after Emancipation "with only the clothes on their back." Pierce's father, Richard, was a slave in the antebellum South, and Pierce had strong memories of the stories his father told about slavery. He was proud of the dignity with which his father had persevered in those years, recalling that his father had told him he had been "sold three times 'cause he would fight. . . . He would fight and they [sold him] for fear that it would learn some others to fight, protect themselves."[1]

This carving expresses the abiding love and respect that Pierce felt for his parents and his pride in his African American heritage. By extension Pierce's figures represent the quest of all black Americans for freedom and equality as symbolized by the act of migration. Pierce himself was part of the great migration of African Americans who left the South in the 1920s and migrated North in search of a better life.[2]

The various versions of *Migration North* differ slightly in the minimal possessions that the two figures carry, and only some of the versions feature the loyal dog that appears here. The most distinctive feature of this version is the full head of hair that has been glued onto each figure. The hair is actual human hair that Pierce gathered from the combs and brushes he used on his barbershop customers.[3]

1. Moe, 1990, p. 13.
2. Although Pierce's father did not move to the North after the Civil War, migrating instead from Raleigh, North Carolina, to Baldwyn, Mississippi, historians have hypothesized that the western movement of southern blacks in the decades following the war represents the same search for greater economic opportunity as the later massive migration north. For a recent discussion of migration patterns of African Americans, see Spencer R. Crew, *From Field to Factory: African American Migration, 1915–1940* (Washington, D.C.: Smithsonian Institution, 1992).
3. Aminah Robinson, in conversation with the author, October 1991.

---

60.   **Mother and Child,** n.d.   Colorplate 17
      Carved and painted wood with glitter
      5¹/₂ × 3³/₄ × 2³/₄ (14.0 × 9.5 × 7.0)
      Collection of Howard and Mimi Chenfeld

This tender portrayal of a young child held in an open-armed embrace on his mother's lap is believed to represent Pierce and his own mother.[1] Though Pierce felt a deep love and respect for both his parents, he was particularly close to his mother. The warmth of that love suffuses many of Pierce's idyllic representations of his childhood in Mississippi. His mother's influence at important moments in his life is epitomized in *Obey*

God and Live (cat. no. 6). And it was for his mother that Pierce created his elaborate *Doll House* (cat. no. 86), which includes a carved figure of his mother tended by a nurse. As an adult Pierce often spoke of his love for his mother: "I would do anything for my mother, 'cause she is the one who gave me life itself. I love my mother."[2]

1. The same is usually said of a pair of carved figures depicting a woman in a polka-dot dress seated in a large straight-back chair and accompanied by the small figure of a boy in a similar chair (see Moe, 1990, fig. 8). Pierce rarely sold works that pertained to his family, preferring to retain them for display in his shop. Both of these works left the artist's hands before his death.
2. Pierce, in interview with John F. Moe, n.d.

---

61.   **Seated Lady,** 1930   Colorplate 17
      Carved and painted wood
      6¹/₄ × 7³/₄ × 1¹/₄ (15.9 × 19.7 × 3.3)
      Collection of Aminah and Sydney Robinson

Seated Lady is a particularly beautiful example of the elegant simplicity of many of Pierce's early carvings. The placement of the figure's hands across her breast suggests that she may represent Mary, the mother of Christ. This gesture of supplication is found in many visual representations of the Annunciation and the Nativity.

SECULAR RELIEFS

---

62.   **Indians Hunting,** 1943   Colorplate 20
      Carved and painted wood relief with glitter,
      mounted on painted panel
      21³/₈ × 49¹/₂ (54.2 × 125.7)
      Columbus Museum of Art: Museum Purchase

The format of this work—carved reliefs mounted to two panels with painted background[1] in a hinged booklike presentation—is closely related to that of *Book of Wood* (cat. no. 100), Pierce's most ambitious work of the previous decade. The relief at the left, featuring a three-quarter-length brave who looks out at the viewer, seems to serve as an introduction to the three sequen-

the early 1970s show a calendar illustrated with images of hunting dogs, similar to the one that must have inspired this carving.[1]

1. The photographs were taken by Michael Hall.

tial narrative scenes at the right. Whether Pierce intended to add further "pages" to the work is unknown, but *Indians Hunting* is one of few assemblages—including *Book of Wood*—that survived dismemberment in the early 1970s.[2] The subject may have had autobiographical significance for Pierce. When Pierce was a boy, his father told him that he was partially of Indian descent.[3] Lee Prather's farm on which Pierce grew up was said to have been located on former Indian land.

1. According to the records of the Krannert Art Museum's exhibition of Pierce's work (December 12, 1971–January 2, 1972), the background in *Indians Hunting* was originally covered with paper. Apparently the material used was similar to that in *Bible Stories* (cat. no. 169) and the Redemption diptych (see cat. nos. 166–168).

2. *Indians Hunting* was not included in Pierce's 1971 Ohio State University exhibition but was included in the Peale House Galleries exhibition at the Pennsylvania Academy of the Fine Arts in late 1972.

3. Estelle Pierce, in interview with Seibert, September 12, 1991.

64. **Horse Racing,** 1928
Carved and painted wood relief
24 × 8³⁄₄ (61.0 × 22.2)
Collection of Jerrold A. Basofin

This relief celebrates Pierce's love of the sports of boxing and horse racing (see also cat. nos. 42, 65, 67, 68). The relationship of the four panels in the relief is not known, nor is the identity of the woman. It has been variously suggested that she represents Pierce's wife, or singer Marian Anderson, or, because of her somewhat equestrianlike attire, simply a beautiful horsewoman. There may be only the most tenuous relationship among the four panels. In discussing another seemingly incongruous multipanel relief, *Wild Horses and Barbershop,*[1] Pierce explained that the relationship among the images of the mustang ponies and the barbershop was serendipitous: "I was cutting a gentle-

63. **Pair of Pointers,** 1936
Carved and painted wood relief with glitter and rhinestones
9¹⁄₄ × 16 (23.5 × 40.6)
Columbus Museum of Art: Gift of Mrs. Ursel White Lewis

The subject and composition of this carved relief suggests an image appropriated from popular illustrations of hunting dogs. Photographs of Pierce's barbershop in

man's hair and my wife was painting a picture that I had just carved and this was all in the barbershop, and we just put them on the same board [as the two mustang pony carvings]."[2]

1. For an illustration of *Wild Horses and Barbershop,* also known as *Barbershop with Mustangs,* see Bašičević et al., p. 248.
2. Jones interview.

65. **Ostrich Pulling Harness Racer,** 1972
   Carved and painted wood relief with cotton
   14⁹/₁₆ × 20¼ (36.9 × 51.4)
   Collection of Mr. and Mrs. Richard E. Guggenheim

This is a humorous variation on the horseracing theme, which is treated in a straightforward manner by the artist in works such as *Sulky Driver* (cat. no. 43).

66. **Joe Louis, World Champion,** 1967
   Carved and painted wood relief mounted on
   painted panel
   21¼ × 10³/₈ (54.0 × 26.4)
   Columbus Museum of Art: Museum Purchase

Joe Louis, 1940.
UPI/Bettmann

Boxer Joe Louis (1914–1981) was the most famous African American athlete of the 1930s and 1940s, eclipsing even Jackie Robinson and Jesse Owens in the popular imagination. Louis, who was known as the "Brown Bomber," became in 1937 only the second African American ever to hold the world heavyweight title. His emergence as an American popular hero during the Depression had a significant impact on the aspirations of African Americans and contributed to the demise of many widely held racial stereotypes. An entire nation celebrated in 1938 when Louis knocked out German fighter Max Schmeling, who was being touted by Nazi sympathizers as proof of the supremacy of the white race. For African Americans, however, each of Louis's spectacular wins offered the hope that racial discrimination was crumbling in the United States.

Like many African Americans, Pierce was a great admirer of Louis. Commenting on Louis's wide appeal and significance to the black community, Pierce once observed, "Even my wife got interested when Joe was fighting."[1] This work is one of several tributes to Louis that Pierce carved. One relief from 1971, entitled *When Joe Became Champion* (private collection), depicts a crowned Louis sitting on top of the world under a canopy of roses while a tumble of figures representing all the boxers he defeated appears at his feet. *Joe Louis, World Champion* is a more straightforward presentation of Louis, based on a well-known, posed photograph taken at the height of his career. As in his relief of John Kennedy (cat. no. 81), which is also based on a popular photograph, Pierce followed his photographic source very closely, even replicating Louis's contrapposto pose. The relief, like the photograph, emphasizes the attributes for which Louis was best known as a fighter—his magnificent physique, his lightning-quick punches, and his stolid calm.

1. Seibert interview, November 21, 1980.

67. **Louis vs. Braddock,** n.d.   Colorplate 21
Carved and painted wood relief with glitter,
mounted on painted corrugated cardboard
21½ × 23 (54.6 × 58.4)
Collection of Jeffrey Wolf and Jeany
Nisenholz-Wolf

The subject of this relief is the world heavyweight championship fight between Joe Louis and James Braddock, held at Comiskey Park in Chicago on June 22, 1937. The twenty-three-year-old Louis was the first African American to fight for the coveted title since Jack Johnson in 1915.[1] Braddock, a thirty-two-year-old Irish fighter from New York, had held the title since 1935, and his fight with Louis was his first defense of his crown. Some 45,000 fans, 20,000 of them African Americans, the largest number ever to see a live bout, attended the fight, and tens of thousands more listened to the broadcast on radio. Louis's win in the eighth round was a jubilant moment for African Americans. Spontaneous street celebrations and parades occurred in black communities in most major cities, as they would again in 1938 when Louis knocked out Max Schmeling. Years later in an interview Braddock recalled, "What power that guy had! When he knocked me down, I could have stayed there for three weeks. But I'm glad I got to fight him because I made a good fight with him and he was one of the greatest fighters in history, maybe the greatest. That was some night."[2] Anyone who was alive and old enough to have seen or heard the fight never forgot it.

In Pierce's depiction of the fight, Louis wears the dark shorts and Braddock wears light blue. The center images of the two fighters allude to the back-and-forth struggle that characterized the early rounds of the fight. Louis's ultimate victory is indicated by the gold belt he wears at the right. The stop-action poses of the fighters are probably based on sequential, round-by-round photographs and descriptions of the fight that were readily available to fans through newspapers, magazines, and sports sheets. Details of historical accuracy, however, did not overly concern Pierce, who preferred his own palette. In the actual fight Braddock wore white trunks and Louis wore purple trunks.

It is somewhat surprising that in an event in which the race of the two fighters was so important to so many people Pierce did not clearly make racial distinctions in the figures. The skin of both fighters is unpainted, but dark, owing to the shade of the varnished wood.[3]

1. During this era in boxing, the best challengers did not always get the chance to compete for the title. The schedule of fights, particularly title fights, was strictly controlled by managers and promoters, many with organized crime connections, who were not always concerned with seeing the best fighters pitted against one another. Many talented black fighters never had the opportunity that Louis had to be a contender. Groomed by his promoter and trainer to be a champion, Louis was the antithesis of Jack Johnson, who had flaunted social convention and openly antagonized white boxing fans as well as his white opponents in the ring. When Jackson won the heavyweight championship, race riots broke out.

2. Quoted in Billy Libby, *Joe Louis: The Brown Bomber* (New York: Lothrop, Lee and Shepard Books, 1980), p. 109.

3. The subject of this relief has been traditionally identified as the Louis-Braddock fight, and the relief appeared under the current title in both the 1971 Ohio State University exhibition and the 1972 Peale House exhibition at the Pennsylvania Academy of the Fine Arts. Because of the lack of racial distinction between the two fighters, it has been suggested recently by William H. Wiggins, Indiana University, that the fight represented is the one between Louis and John Henry Lewis, the then-reigning lightweight champion. Though not memorable in itself, the fight, which took place on January 25, 1939, and lasted only one round, made history as the first time two African American fighters had competed for the heavyweight title. The relief bears no inscription in Pierce's hand identifying the subject. The current identification rests solely on the work's exhibition history while the artist was still alive, when the subjects were repeatedly identified as Louis and Braddock. It is known, however, that Pierce did not necessarily object to misidentification of the subjects of his reliefs and allowed them to be exhibited under titles given to them by others.

69. **Movie Star,** 1960
Carved and painted wood relief with glitter
10½ × 8½ (26.7 × 21.6)
Courtesy Janet Fleisher Gallery, Philadelphia

The identity of the woman in this strikingly elegant profile portrait is still in question. The figure has sometimes been identified as either the entertainer Lena Horne (b. 1917) or the singer Marian Anderson (b. 1902). Though the facial features are too generalized to determine with any certainty which woman is represented, the hairstyle strongly suggests it is Lena Horne. At the height of her fame, during the 1940s and 1950s, Horne almost always wore her long hair brushed away from her face, exposing her ears. Anderson, in contrast, usually wore a shorter hairstyle exposing the neck and covering the ears. As prominent African American performers, either one could have moved Pierce to create a tribute.

68. **Boxers,** n.d.
Carved and painted wood relief mounted
on masonite
6 × 12 (15.2 × 30.4)
Collection of Howard and Mimi Chenfeld

The use of stop-action shots in this relief is related to those in Pierce's well-known carving *Louis vs. Braddock* (cat. no. 67). In this continuous narrative, two fighters, watched by a referee, battle across the relief, their fight culminating in a knockout punch at the left. The carving is strongly reminiscent of, and was probably inspired by, the sequential photographs of fights that were available to fans from many printed sources.

70. **Popeye,** 1933   Colorplate 22
Carved and painted wood
13 × 10 (33.0 × 25.3)
Private Collection

Unlike *Jiggs and Maggie* (cat. no. 71) and the *Angel* (cat. no. 45), where the connection with popular culture can only be surmised, this figure is clearly identified. At its feet, Pierce has prominently inscribed in red and black paint the name "Popeye," with an image of the all-seeing eye inserted between the two syllables.

1. The other two dates, 1972 and 1977, are inscribed in black marking pen. They may refer to changes Pierce made in the carving during the seventies. It is also quite likely that the additional dates reflect Pierce's practice of inscribing works with new dates and signatures at the time he sold or made a gift of the carving.

2. *Thimble Theatre* lost much of its quirky originality after Segar's death in 1938, but Popeye's celebrity as a pop hero continued to flourish independently. In fact, Popeye's inseparable identification with spinach, the source of his strength, was more a result of Fleisher's cartoons than Segar's strip, where the idea was first introduced.

71.   **Jiggs and Maggie**, n.d.
      Carved and painted wood relief
      7½ × 11 (19.1 × 27.9)
      Private Collection

Pierce's carving bears three dates on the reverse, all seemingly in Pierce's own hand. The earliest, 1933,[1] is inscribed in pencil along with the artist's signature and the intials NFS, for "not for sale." This date places the making of the carving in the first years of Popeye's popularity, when the character had just begun to appear in animated cartoons. Popeye originated in 1929 as a bit character in E. C. Segar's comic strip *Thimble Theatre.* The scrappy sailor soon became a central character of the strip and one of the most widely merchandised comic strip characters of the 1930s. The first of Max Fleisher's many animated Popeye cartoons debuted in 1933.[2]

Pierce gives his Popeye the distinctive loping gait and body type of the original comic strip character, including the bulging muscles in his forearms, the small bump-shaped elbows and knees, and the wide bellbottoms. Although Pierce's Popeye retains the character's one-eyed squint and signature pipe clamped tightly in his mouth, the figure lacks the sailor cap that usually crowns Popeye's head, and the more familiar blue and white sailor suit of the comic strip has been replaced with "dress whites." Such alterations may have been conscious changes on Pierce's part or may reflect the specific depiction of Popeye that served as the visual source for Pierce's carving.

Popeye also provides an interesting insight into the source of Pierce's materials. Unlike other works in which Pierce regularly created a background for the carved image out of corrugated cardboard, *Popeye* is without a background. The wood used for the carving was originally part of a packing crate for lemons, and the paper label of the crate is still partially visible on the reverse of the work.

Although this relief has sometimes been called simply *Man and Woman*, the figures resemble Jiggs and Maggie, the central characters of the comic strip *Bringing Up Father.* The identification is in keeping with the growing evidence documenting Pierce's interest in popular culture (see cat. nos. 44 and 70).

Bringing Up Father is one of the longest running comic strips in history, having debuted in the *New York American* in 1913. Referred to by most readers as "Jiggs and Maggie" rather than by its formal title, the strip has achieved enduring popularity and through much of its history has appeared regularly in more than five hundred newspapers. The subject of the strip, which changed little over the years, centers on the antics of a nouveau riche Irish American couple who moved to Fifth Avenue. The conflicts between the two—the drink-loving Jiggs, who prefers his old cronies at the corner saloon, and the socially ambitious Maggie—are captured in Pierce's composition as the figures confront each other across a barrier.

72. **Anniversary Flowers,** 1970
Carved and painted wood relief with glitter
18 × 19¼ (45.8 × 48.9)
Private Collection, Courtesy Keny Galleries, Inc.

73. **Flowers,** 1972
Carved and painted wood relief with glitter
20⅞ × 12⅞ (52.9 × 32.7)
Columbus Museum of Art: Gift of Lucinda N.
Madden

Elijah Pierce enjoyed flowers. His wife Estelle kept a flower garden, and marigolds and irises grew wild in front of his Long Street barbershop. Throughout his work, flowers appear both as symbolic devices and as decorative motifs. The blooms in *Flowers* are related in appearance to the flowers found in the background of portraits such as *President Carter and His Sister* (cat. no. 75) from the same period.

Anniversary Flowers, from slightly earlier, had special significance for Pierce: "My wife was away, she was visiting her home, and our anniversary came, and I couldn't think what she'd like—and then I thought, she loves flowers, so I carved that for her, and she really loved it."[1]

Pierce's further comments about the carving elucidate the personal significance of the inscription "My Love/God/E.P./+":

> You can show affection, love, by what you do—you can make them flowers talk. If you just do something to be doing it, it don't amount to nothing, but if you put your mind, your heart and soul in it, there'll be a feeling. . . . So many people that came to my little studio said, "There's something I feel when I come in, something that makes me feel different." Well, because I put a portion of my life in everything that I carved. I tell people, everything that you have that these hands have carved with the help of the Good Lord, a portion of my life is in your home.[2]

1. Jones interview.
2. Ibid.

---

74. **The Kiss,** 1979
Carved and painted wood relief with rhinestones
19 × 15 (48.2 × 38.1)
Gitter-Yelen Folk Art Collection

This relief of two lovers fits into the broad category of portraits with flowers that Pierce executed in the 1970s. The flowers that bloom behind the two embracing figures may be an emblem of their love. Pierce certainly associated flowers directly with romantic love in works such as *Anniversary Flowers* (cat. no. 72).

The subject of a couple embracing in a kiss is not a common one in Pierce's body of work. However, a very similar image of a man and woman embraced in a near kiss occurs in the much earlier moralistic relief *Monday Morning Gossip* (cat. no. 153) of 1934, in which the

image of love is accompanied by two cranes, symbols of vigilance, loyalty, and eternal love.

75. **Mr. and Mrs. Hank Aaron,** 1974 Colorplate 23
Carved and painted wood relief
19½ × 14½ (49.5 × 36.8)
Collection of Mike and Cindy Noland

76. **President Carter and His Sister,** 1976
Carved and painted wood relief with glitter
17½ × 14¼ (44.5 × 36.2)
Collection of Mike and Cindy Noland

Both of these reliefs are part of a series of portraits executed by Pierce in the mid- to late 1970s. Many of these depict famous American couples and were inspired by photographs from popular magazines. The portraits frequently feature floral backgrounds, as in *President Carter and His Sister* and *The Kiss* (cat. no. 74),[1] though Pierce sometimes chose to retain the decorative background that appeared in the original photographic source, as in *Mr. and Mrs. Hank Aaron.*

President Carter and His Sister was carved the year that Jimmy Carter was elected the thirty-ninth president of the United States. Pierce's choice of Carter as a subject is in keeping with his interest in celebrating presidents who made significant contributions to the civil rights of black Americans. Carter was perceived by many as a leading spokesman for the New South's more moderate social and racial attitudes. He first gained national attention when he called for an end to racial discrimination in his 1970 inaugural address as governor of Georgia, declaring, "The time for racial discrimination is over. . . . No poor, rural, weak, or black person should ever have to bear the additional burden of being deprived of the opportunity of an education, a job, or simple justice." Carter's civil rights initiatives on the state level, which included a significant increase in the appointment of African Americans to state government posts, the equalization of state aid to schools, and the inclusion of portraits of important black Americans, such as Martin Luther King, Jr., among those that hung in the Georgia state capitol, held out great promise for civil rights accomplishments during his presidency. In Pierce's portrait of the two Carters, both flash the toothy grins that had already become a hallmark of the president's popular image.

Pierce's portrait of Atlanta Braves baseball player Hank Aaron and his wife Barbara dates from the year that Aaron surpassed Babe Ruth's lifetime record of major league home runs. Inscribed on Barbara Aaron's yellow and orange sweater is the number 715, representing the critical home run that Aaron hit on April 8, 1974, in Atlanta, making him the all-time top home run hitter in the history of American major league baseball. The relief was surely inspired by one of the countless publicity shots of Aaron taken to celebrate the ultimate achievement in a career that began in 1954, less than a decade after the ban on black players in the major leagues came to an end. Pierce's choice of Aaron as a subject reflects his interest in paying tribute to outstanding African American athletes.

1. In a conversation with the author (October 1991), Aminah Robinson mentioned that relief portraits of single individuals with a floral background from this period include a portrait of Aminah Robinson (private collection) and one of Martin Luther King, Jr., which is illustrated in Muller, p. 8.

Pierce. The military appearance of the armed guard in the top vignette suggests that the two men in stripes may be seen not just as convicts but as military prisoners, perhaps deserters. A strong believer in the importance of military service, Pierce believed the responsibilities of citizenship should be borne equally by all Americans. Thus the same fate befalls both the white man and the black man who have failed their country.[2] Pierce's own explanation of the relief's genesis is more straightforward:

> I was on a vacation trip down South, south of Atlanta, and I saw these convicts working on the road with picks. They had chains on their legs and there was a guard standing over them with a sawed-off shotgun and some bloodhounds near in case any of them would run away. I put the President on the same picture because he was the head of the country and it just flashed in my mind that that would be a good place to put the convicts—they were criminals and were out there doing their time—and it just impressed me so I put it on the same picture. That was near twenty years ago or more.[3]

Presidents and Convicts, a key work, was included in all exhibitions of Pierce's work in the early 1970s and is one of Pierce's best-known images.[4] Executed in 1941, *Presidents and Convicts* bears the inscription "Elijah

77. **Presidents and Convicts,** 1941   Colorplate 24
      Carved and painted wood relief mounted on
      painted corrugated cardboard
      33½ × 24¾ (85.1 × 62.9)
      Collection of Mr. and Mrs. André Previn

Carved in the same period as *Pearl Harbor and the African Queen* (cat. no. 155), *Presidents and Convicts* is another variation on the theme of patriotic duty. In the relief, vignettes of two convicts, one black and one white, working on a chain gang are juxtaposed with portraits of presidents Washington and Lincoln and a scene showing Uncle Sam shaking the hand of an African American serviceman beneath an unfurled American flag.[1] Here Pierce specifically alludes to the patriotism of black Americans. The image of Uncle Sam congratulating the duty-bound African American soldier is the quintessential symbol of that patriotism for

Pierce to Boris'' and the date 1971, the year Pierce gave the relief to Boris Gruenwald.

1. The portraits of both Washington and Lincoln seem to be based on the familiar images of the presidents that appear on U.S. currency. The choice of Washington and Lincoln, perennial favorites of folk artists and considered by many to be the fathers of American patriotism, is not surprising. Washington and Lincoln first appeared as a pair in popular imagery during Lincoln's political campaigns. After Lincoln's assassination, the link between the two figures became ingrained in the popular imagination. Uncle Sam also appears in the autobiographical reliefs *Slavery Time* (cat. no. 4 and cat. no. 5). For a discussion of Washington, Lincoln, and Uncle Sam in folk art, see Horwitz, 1976, pp. 92–106, 116–144.

2. When asked about how he chose the racial representation of his figures, Pierce often responded that race was not important, that his figures represent all people. According to Aminah Robinson, at times Pierce selected colors for his figures based simply on the paint he had available. Only in works such as *Presidents and Convicts,* when the race of the figures is critical to the work's meaning, did Pierce make a clear distinction in color.

3. Jones interview.

4. *Presidents and Convicts* is one of three works by Pierce chosen to be illustrated in Hemphill and Weissman, p. 101.

---

78. **Abraham Lincoln,** ca. 1975   Colorplate 25
Carved and painted wood relief
14½ × 9¼ (36.8 × 23.5)
Collection of the Museum of American Folk Art,
New York, Bequest of Robert Bishop

Unlike George Washington, who received nearly universal acclaim during his life, Abraham Lincoln was a controversial, highly criticized public figure. The first American president to be assassinated, Lincoln came to be seen as a martyred patriot. His humble beginnings, his ideals, his deep belief in the nation, and his wit, courage, and suffering inspired a vast body of American popular folk art.[1] The author of the Emancipation Proclamation, who led the nation through the horror of the Civil War, is a particularly favored subject of African American folk artists, some of whom chose to portray him as a black man. As is often the case in Pierce's work, it is unclear whether he intended to depict Lincoln as a black man. He may have preferred to present the figure as neither white nor black but as a symbol of all people. Pierce's patriotic intentions in this work are nonetheless quite clear, for he set his frontal portrait of Lincoln against a background of red, white, and blue stripes. Pierce used a similar device in his portrait of John Kennedy (cat. no. 81).

The figure's pose is based on a well-known photograph of the president taken by Alexander Gardner on November 8, 1863. The photograph has been reprinted countless times in both modern and historical publications.[2]

1. Horwitz, 1976, pp. 133–144.

2. Gardner took thirty photographs of Lincoln, more than any other single photographer. The photographic source of Pierce's carving is easily identified because it is one of the few full frontal bust photos of Lincoln ever taken. See Charles Hamilton and Lloyd Ostendorf, *Lincoln in Photographs: An Album of Every Known Pose* (Norman: University of Oklahoma Press, 1963), p. 145.

---

79. **Martin Luther King Jr. and the Kennedy Brothers,** 1977   Colorplate 26
Carved and painted wood relief with glitter
21⅛ × 26¼ (53.6 × 66.6)
Columbus Museum of Art: Museum Purchase

After the assassinations of John F. Kennedy, Martin Luther King, Jr., and Robert Kennedy, the three men who in life had been champions of the civil rights movement became linked in people's minds as a trio of martyred patriots.[1] Millions of Americans of all races mourned these irreparable losses to their country. The widely played song ''Abraham, Martin, and John,''[2] which connected King and the Kennedys with Abraham Lincoln, was recorded shortly after Robert Kennedy's death in 1968. Its refrain epitomized popular sentiment in the late 1960s: ''Didn't you love the things

Photograph from Pierce's home

2. "Abraham, Martin, and John" was written by Dick Holler and first recorded by Dion. Subsequent recordings of the song were made by Marvin Gaye and Mahalia Jackson. Robert Kennedy, who is not mentioned in the title, is mentioned in the last verse of the song.

80.   **Martin Luther King (Love)**, ca. 1968
Carved and painted wood relief with glitter
19 × 16 (48.3 × 40.6)
Courtesy Janet Fleisher Gallery, Philadelphia

they stood for?/Didn't they try to find some good for you and me?/And we'll be free/Someday soon it's gonna be one day."

Countless montages of King and the Kennedys appeared in popular art. Elijah Pierce owned one such print, which hung just inside the front door of his home. According to the artist's wife, this print directly inspired Pierce to carve *Martin Luther King Jr. and the Kennedy Brothers* as his own tribute to the three men. Pierce however, reworked his source to bring his own vision to the subject. In the relief, Pierce not only rearranged the figures but replaced the ethereal gold background of the print with a painted patriotic pattern of red, white, and blue. Above the head of each figure he placed a gold star to suggest the stature of the three men as American heroes.

1. For a discussion of folk and popular images of King and the Kennedys, see Horwitz, 1976, pp. 113–114, 148–154. A contemporary double portrait of King and Kennedy by Bob Mayhew is inscribed "United we stand! & Died for Freedom" (illus. in ibid., p. 114).

A great admirer of Martin Luther King, Jr., Pierce executed several carvings of the civil rights leader after his death in 1968.[1] Asked about King in 1981, Pierce responded: "He was a race man, a colored man. And he believed in justice. I did a work on him. Something I wanted to give for a dedication of his kind. I miss him."[2]

In this portrait King turns to face the viewer, while an angel with outstretched arms hovers behind him. To the left of the two figures floats a message sign bearing the single word "love." The message, like the presence of the angel, suggests layers of meaning in the relief. The word "love" may simultaneously refer to how beloved King was and is by those he influenced, and to the central idea of the nonviolent philosophy with which King led the civil rights movement. The angel may be a symbol not only of the Christian ministry to which King was committed but also of his martyrdom for his Christian ideals.

1. Pierce carved at least one other portrait of King alone, a bust-length portrait with a floral background probably dating from the mid-1970s; illustrated in Muller, p. 8. This portrait still hung next to the carving of *Martin Luther King Jr. and the Kennedy Brothers* (cat. no. 79) on the wall in Pierce's shop in photographs that date from the early 1980s.
2. Seibert interview, May 12, 1981.

81.   **Kennedy,** 1964
      Carved and painted wood relief with glitter
      20 × 15 (50.8 × 38.1)
      Collection of Lanford Wilson

Pierce executed this carving of President John F. Kennedy in the first months following his assassination, when the country was still in mourning.[1] A patriotic tribute to Kennedy, in which the President's head is framed by an unfurled American flag, Pierce's image of Kennedy is based on a widely published photograph taken by Ted Spiegel the first day of Kennedy's campaign for the presidency in September 1959 in Seattle,

Washington.[2] Pierce has even adopted Kennedy's upward glance in the photograph, giving his posthumous subject an appropriate heavenly gaze.

Although Kennedy was elected by the narrowest popular margin of any president in the twentieth century and was lampooned by critics while in office, in the years immediately following the assassination, he achieved the status of a popular icon.[3] Because of their irrepressible devotion to Kennedy, many Americans experienced his death as a profound personal loss. Few presidents other than Washington or Lincoln have cap-

John F. Kennedy, 1959.
Photograph by Ted Spiegel/Black Star

tured the public imagination as Kennedy did. A youthful, charismatic figure who embodied for many the vigor of a free nation on the horizon of what he called the New Frontier, Kennedy quickly became a favorite subject in popular as well as folk art. Because of his role in the civil rights movement and the hope he had given a generation of America's poor and oppressed, Kennedy became a particularly important subject for black folk artists such as Pierce and Josephus Farmer.[4]

1. Although there may be more than one portrait of Kennedy by Pierce, this portrait is the one referred to in most published writings on his work. It was included in both the 1971 Ohio State University exhibition and the Peale House exhibition at the Pennsylvania Academy of the Fine Arts in late 1972. The relief had left Pierce's hands by the time of the first Columbus Museum of Art exhibition in late 1973 and was not included in that exhibition.
2. Pierce would have had ample opportunity to see a copy of the photograph. It was first popularized by Kennedy himself as an autograph portrait. It later appeared in magazines and books on the Kennedy presidency and on commemorative postage stamps. A blowup of the photograph

was used as a backdrop in the 1964 Democratic National Convention.

3. For a discussion of Kennedy in folk and popular art, see Horwitz, 1976, pp. 150–154.

4. For a discussion of Josephus Farmer's images of Kennedy, see Cubbs.

82. **Nixon Being Driven from the White House,** 1975   Colorplate 27
Carved and painted wood relief with beads
14½ × 29¼ (36.8 × 74.3)
Collection of Joanne Buzzetta, Philadelphia

Pierce is known to have carved at least two reliefs of Richard Nixon: this one and *Nixon Being Chased by Inflation* (private collection). Both reliefs are wry commentaries on the crises that plagued the Nixon presidency. *Nixon Being Driven from the White House* is a continuous narrative, with the figure of Nixon repeated three times within the double row of running figures. He is being pursued by the press, most of whom hold what appear to be microphones in their outstretched hands as they run. The pair of running figures at the lower left may represent *Washington Post* reporters Bob Woodward and Carl Bernstein, who first publicly implicated high-ranking officials at the White House in the Watergate affair. It is difficult to tell what Nixon holds in his hand as he runs, perhaps the secret tapes he made of conversations in the White House, the public exposure of which ultimately led to his 1974 resignation. Pierce has placed the Capitol building at the far right of the relief to firmly establish the setting of his story.

83. **Police Dog,** 1971
Carved and painted wood relief with glitter
17 × 17¾ (43.2 × 45.1)
Collection Wexner Center for the Arts
The Ohio State University; Purchase 1985.6

In *Police Dog* Pierce directly addressed the subject of racial violence, a reality that shadowed the lives of African Americans throughout his lifetime. Pierce muted the stark power of his image by leaving both figures unpainted, their varnished surface leaving open, for some viewers, the question of race. It is possible to see in the confrontation echoes of fugitive heroes of popular black songs and ballads, such as "Travelin' Man," "Leroy Brown," and "Lost John," in which the hero is pursued by the sheriff and his bloodhounds. In the ballad "Long Gone, Lost John," for instance, the hero sings, "The hounds ain't caught me and they never will."[1] Given the date of the work it would be difficult not to link the image with the racial violence that plagued the civil rights movement in the sixties and beyond. By 1971 most Americans, black and white, were familiar with news photographs of civil rights activists being threatened or attacked by police dogs.

1. See Sterling Brown, "Negro Folk Expression: Spirituals, Seculars, Ballads and Work Songs," in *The Making of Black America: Essays in Negro Life and History,* Vol. 1, ed. August Meier and Elliott Budwick (New York: Atheneum, 1969), pp. 218–219.

84.   **The White House,** 1977   Colorplate 28
      Carved and painted wood relief with glitter,
      marking-pen ink, and rhinestones
      28³/₄ × 26⁷/₈ (73.1 × 68.3)
      Columbus Museum of Art: Museum Purchase

Carved in 1977, this relief may commemorate the cele-brations surrounding the nation's bicentennial the year before. The image has a jubilant verve appropriate to such a patriotic event; the planes, tank, helicopter, battleship, and cannons that are spread through the scene beneath a fluttering American flag seem to be the stuff of parades rather than war. The sea of faces that fills the narrow foreground space is similar to Pierce's depiction of the multitude in the 1978 carving *Prayers* (see cat. no. 131), and of the famous photographs of the 250,000 Americans who gathered on the Washington Mall in front of the Lincoln Memorial in August 1963 to hear Martin Luther King, Jr., speak during the March on Washington. The occasion of King's inspirational ''I have a dream'' speech was a moment of great hope and pride for black Americans during the civil rights struggle of the 1960s. The celebration of the bicenten-nial and memories of the March on Washington may have evoked in Pierce strong feelings about his country and motivated him to link the two events in his relief. Pierce's vision of the scene also includes images of the sun, moon, and stars, which he frequently incorpo-rated into his autobiographical and religious carvings as emblems of eternity.

The white house at the center of the composition seems to represent not the president's residence but the domed Capitol building, with the Washington Monu-ment positioned behind it. A solitary figure stands in the doorway, his arms raised, perhaps in a gesture of triumph. Pierce was an admirer of Jimmy Carter, and it is tempting to see this figure as representing the newly elected president, who took office in January 1977.

85.   **The Statue of Liberty,** 1973
      Carved and painted wood relief with glitter and
      commercial wood ornaments added to frame
      28 × 14 (71.0 × 35.5)
      Columbus Museum of Art: Museum Purchase

Of all the symbols of American patriotism, the Statue of Liberty, variously identified as ''Columbia,'' ''Miss Liberty,'' and the ''Goddess of Liberty,'' is the oldest. The Statue of Liberty has been the acknowledged sym-bol of American democracy since its completion in 1886. Officially titled *Liberty Enlightening the World,* the magnificent 151-foot copper figure that greets ships entering New York harbor was designed by Frederic-Auguste Barthold and was a gift from the people of France in honor of America's centennial. For more than a century a steady stream of souvenirs ranging from statuettes and postcards to commemorative salt shakers and thermometers has celebrated the Statue of Liberty. Advertisers have also contributed significantly to linking our national identity with the statue.[1] Folk artists in particular, beginning with the creators of nineteenth-century weathervanes, have often used the Statue of Liberty as a symbol of the nation.

Elijah Pierce is known to have executed several carvings of the Statue of Liberty, both as a relief and as a freestanding figure.[2] The theme of the light of freedom fascinated Pierce and appears in a much earlier related work from 1933 called *Spreading the Light* (cat. no. 164) from the diptych *Death on the Level*. The applied wood decoration on the frame of the museum's version is another example of Pierce's use of commercially produced objects in his carvings. This decorative element was probably sent to Pierce from his son in Chicago. Remembering it, Pierce said, ''It seemed like it was just made for that piece. I saw it in the wood.''[3]

1. The Statue of Liberty was particularly popular in tobacco advertisements as a symbol of quality. See Horwitz, 1976, pp. 86–90. Also see Ricco, Maresca, and Weissman, p. 276.

2. For a photograph of a 1971 freestanding version by Pierce, see Horwitz, 1976, p. 90.

3. Seibert interview, October 1980.

TABLEAUS

86. **Doll House,** before 1948   Colorplate 29
Carved and painted wood with fabric, plastic, and mirror
47 × 45½ × 25¾ (119.3 × 115.6 × 65.4)
Private Collection

I love my mother. . . . You know I made a house for my mother with all the furniture. Nice house. And we had a nurse in the house for my mother. I would give her anything. Of course, it was only a playhouse. But I would have given her anything she wanted.[1]

This is the doll house Pierce made for his mother.[2] It shows Pierce's love for his mother and the abiding love for family and home that he expressed in many of his autobiographical reliefs.

An open-faced, two-story structure with a gabled roof, Pierce's doll house has four rooms. On the first

floor are three rooms: from left to right, a bedroom, a sitting or dining room, and a kitchen. The second floor is a single large room occupied by the figures of Pierce's mother and her attending nurse.[3] Many of the fixtures and furnishings in the house are functional: the doors between the rooms open and close, as do the drawers and cupboard doors of all the furniture. The single most unusual feature of the house is the carved relief that covers the pediment on its facade. Flanking either side of a central structure inscribed with crosses, which may represent the Ark of the Covenant, are the images of horse-drawn chariots and Assyrian winged gate guardians. Though the meaning of this relief is not known, it was probably intended as more than mere decoration. Positioned directly above the room where Pierce's mother sits, the relief may have been meant to give spiritual protection to the house and its occupants.

Pierce has taken great care to create the ambience of a home, filling the rooms not just with furniture, wallpaper, and curtains but with countless individualized objects, including a myriad of shaped vases and lamps, radios, and knickknacks. Pierce even provided his mother with a dog for companionship. Mixed among Pierce's carved objects are bits of the real world, such as plastic figurines and animals. Two pink plastic rabbits crouch in the upstairs room, and a blue plastic Cracker Jack figurine of a man sits on the table in the first-floor bedroom.

1. Interview, Pierce and John F. Moe, n.d.

2. Pierce also created a doll house for his granddaughters, which he kept at his home for the children's visits. In addition, he carved the furnishings for a doll house owned by a folk art collector. See Gilmore.

3. The two floors are separate parts that stack on top of each other. The second story is twice as deep as the first story, making the room in which Pierce's mother sits nearly square and considerably larger than any of the rooms on

the first floor. A tableau of figures closely related to the figure group in this carving exists in a private collection and was included in the 1990 exhibition *Amazing Grace: The Life and Work of Elijah Pierce,* which was held at the Martin Luther King Jr. Center in Columbus. In this group the seated figure attended by a nurse is a man, and a third figure is present in addition to the dog.

87.   **Music Box,** n.d.   Colorplate 30
Carved and painted figures inside a commercial wood box
9¼ × 15¼ × 7¾ (23.5 × 38.7 × 19.7)
Collection of Sarah and John Freeman

Jazz emerged from the oral and musical performance traditions of the African American community, in which music played a key role in conveying history and values. The appeal of jazz spread during the wave of migration of African Americans to northern urban centers about the time of World War I.[1] In the 1920s jazz came to symbolize an era of change and coming of age in America.

In this enclosed tableau Pierce captures the spirit of the new nightclubs, cabarets, and ballrooms where jazz flourished in the teens and twenties. Pierce's small, dark, boxed space evokes the exotic, mysterious atmosphere of jazz clubs, which were often little more than transformed basements strung with tinted lights. The presence of five dancing couples and the absence of tables seem to suggest the popular ballrooms of the era, which for a small entrance fee provided a large open space in which to dance and an uninhibited jazz band, represented here by Pierce's fantastic stack of four horn players with their instruments intertwined. In keeping with the participatory character of African American oral performance, patrons and performers in the clubs and ballrooms engaged in improvisation and dynamic exchange. In this environment the lively and

often risque new dances of the era emerged. The jitterbug, or the lindy, as it was sometimes called, was born at the Manhattan Casino, one of New York's popular ballrooms. Pierce loved to play the piano and dance as a young man and must have been familiar with the jazz clubs and ballrooms of the cities he visited and lived in during the 1920s.

Music Box was included in the 1971 Ohio State University exhibition and was prominently featured in the 1976 documentary *Sermons in Wood.* The box, which is an integral part of the tableau's atmosphere, is a commercial display box adapted by Pierce to house his figures. The glass-covered front, slanting back so that the contents of the box are easily visible, makes the box particularly appropriate for Pierce's use. The jazz band is carved as a single relief at the rear of the open-backed box. The five couples are freestanding figure groups which have been placed inside the box.

1. For a discussion of the cultural environment of jazz and its relationship to African American culture, see Kathy J. Ogren, *The Jazz Revolution: Twenties America and the Meaning of Jazz* (New York: Oxford University Press, 1989), pp. 56–86.

88.   **Man in an Outhouse,** 1975
Carved and painted wood relief with paper
8¼ × 5⅛ × 7⅝ (21.0 × 13.0 × 19.3)
Collection of Howard and Mimi Chenfeld

This humorous tableau captures the bawdy side of Pierce's vernacular humor, which is often overlooked in discussions of his work. The carving even contains a peep-show element; the small wooden box that serves as the outhouse has a hinged door with a latch, which can be opened to reveal the seated occupant, in his long johns, reading a newspaper. Pierce even provided his little figure with a roll of toilet paper that unravels toward the floor.

The motif of the outhouse is repeated in *The Little White Church* (cat. no. 3), in which a feigned need to visit the outhouse was a ruse used by Pierce as a boy to sneak out of church.

89.   **Card Players,** 1940s–after 1964   Colorplate 31
      Carved and painted wood with glitter, on painted
      corrugated cardboard and painted wood base
      5¹/₂ × 15 × 10 (13.9 × 38.1 × 25.4)
      Collection of Edward V. Blanchard and
      M. Anne Hill

90.   **Seance,** n.d.
      Carved and painted wood
      4 × 6⁷/₈ × 3¹/₂ (10.2 × 17.5 × 8.9)
      Collection of Sarah and John Freeman

According to a Christian artistic tradition that dates from at least the Middle Ages, the monkey or ape symbolizes sin, malice, slyness, and lust, and accordingly the devil is sometimes portrayed as an ape.[1] More commonly, the ape personifies humankind's baser nature, or slothful soul. Pierce draws on this symbolism in both of these tableaus to provide humorous but insightful moral lessons about different aspects of human behavior.

Card Players depicts a group of whiskey-swilling, cigar-smoking simians engaged in a poker game.[2] The bottles, flasks, glasses, and plates strewn across the table point to gluttony and sloth and emphasize the dissolute nature of gambling, which corrupts not only the four card players but the three others who watch them. Pierce's belief in the sinful character of gambling and card playing is also reflected in other moralistic works such as *Pilgrim's Progress* (cat. no. 140) and *Devil Fishing* (cat. no. 145). Pierce heightens the emphasis on game playing by placing the entire group of players on a surface painted to resemble a game board. The monkeys are accompanied by a single human figure dressed in a blue uniform and holding a rifle. His presence, which may have been a later addition by the artist, may suggest a jail-house setting for the card players, implying that the monkeys are already paying the price for their wicked behavior.

Seance deals not with vice but with human gullibility. Three monkeys sit around a table with an empty fourth chair intended for the spirit of the dead they hope to conjure forth. This tableau may have been inspired by the popularity of Spiritualism in the teens and twenties when Pierce was a young man. A subject of public fascination throughout the period, Spiritualism was finally discredited through the efforts of Harry Houdini (1874–1926), America's most famous magician and escape artist and a fervid anti-Spiritualist who spent the last decade of his life exposing mediums and seances as fakes.

1. During the seventeenth century this practice was broadened by Dutch artists who used the symbol of the monkey in moralistic genre and still-life works.
2. Pierce depicts a similar subject in *Human Society* (see Bernard Danenberg Galleries, cat. no. 10, illus.), a tableau that was included in both of Pierce's early exhibitions at the Ohio State University and the Peale House Galleries at the Pennsylvania Academy of the Fine Arts. In this moralistic work, the card players are dogs rather than monkeys. Possibly inspired by a well-known popular image of card-playing dogs, the work, like *Card Players,* is displayed on a base that is like a game board.

91. **Three Fishermen,** 1975
Carved and painted wood with wire
9 × 13¼ × 3¼ (22.8 × 33.6 × 8.2)
Private Collection, Courtesy Keny Galleries, Inc.

The subject of this enigmatic tableau is still in question. Though the attire of the two fishermen seems to be contemporary, the garb and demeanor of the third figure, standing at the bow of the boat, has a biblical aura. The three are visually linked by the red of the fishermen's caps and the wide band of red in the robe of the third figure. Pierce may have intended the tableau to depict the calling of Peter and Andrew by Christ to become "fishers of men" (Matt. 4:18). This possibility is heightened by the fact that both fishermen have snagged fish which dangle on the ends of their rods. The fisherman facing the robed figure, seeming to acknowledge his presence, has caught the much larger fish, which he struggles to reel in, throwing his head back and arching his spine in the effort.

Whatever the subject, much of the tableau's charm is derived from Pierce's portrayal of the fishermen's reactions to their disproportionate catches and the artist's attention to details such as the two small oars and the carved fish that fill the bottom of the boat.

92. **Sacrifice of Isaac,** 1952   Colorplate 33
Carved and painted wood with glitter, plastic foliage, shells, and stones
8¾ × 11¼ × 7¼ (22.2 × 28.5 × 18.3)
Collection of George H. Meyer

93. **Abraham Sacrifices His Son,**
1979   Colorplate 34
Carved and painted wood with glitter, marking-pen ink, stones, plastic foliage, and aluminum foil
10 × 14 × 11 (25.5 × 35.5 × 27.9)
Columbus Museum of Art: Museum Purchase

For Elijah Pierce, as for most African Americans, the hope of salvation expressed in word, song, and image was at the heart of his religion and culture. One of the greatest of the salvation stories is that of the Old Testament patriarch Abraham and his son Isaac. According to the Book of Genesis (22:1–19), God tested Abraham's faith by commanding him to make an offering of his only son. In obedience, Abraham bound Isaac to a pyre, and drew his knife for the sacrifice. Seeing Abraham's great faith, an angel stayed his hand, and a ram appeared in a nearby thicket to be sacrificed instead.

Like many artists before him, Pierce depicted Abraham with his knife poised ready to fulfill the most painful and seemingly impossible of God's commands. The dreaded moment of truth is interpreted with subtle differences in these two tableaus, created perhaps twenty-five years apart. In the earlier version from 1952, Abraham draws his knife with one hand, yet shields Isaac's body with the other, dramatizing his parental dilemma of obedience and denial, destruction and preservation. At his feet, amid the vegetation, the ground is covered with seashells—believed in Kongo funerary custom to represent the presence of the immortal soul.[1] Abraham gazes heavenward in response to the angel's call, "Lay not thine hand upon the lad, neither do thou anything unto him" (Gen. 22:12), expanding the narrative space beyond the edges of the tableau itself.

The psychological impact of the later work is perhaps even greater. The setting is sparsely appointed—the ram's spots providing the only decorative patterning. Abraham holds a sword rather than a knife, and it is aimed directly at Isaac. No gesture is made to protect him. Abraham looks not heavenward, nor toward Isaac, but stares straight ahead, absorbed in determination to carry out his divine duty. The vertical folds of his garment seem to bind him, to ground him to his pain and suffering in this moment before divine intercession releases him. To the best of our knowledge, Pierce only illustrated this story in three-dimensional form. For all his genius in relief format, perhaps Pierce felt that this powerful narrative required a more literal approach. The subject of obedience must have particularly appealed to Pierce's personal experience (see *Obey God and Live*, cat. no. 6).

1. The African tradition of decorating tombs with shells continues today in parts of the midwestern and southern United States, Haiti, and elsewhere. See Robert Farris Thompson, *Flash of the Spirit: African and Afro-American Art and Philosophy* (New York: Vintage, 1984), pp. 135–138.

94. **Christ Entering Jerusalem,** 1942   Colorplate 32
Carved and painted wood with glitter, mounted
on wood panel
5 × 12½ × 10 (12.7 × 31.7 × 25.3)
Courtesy Janet Fleisher Gallery, Philadelphia

The story of Christ entering Jerusalem, cited in all four gospels, is the subject of one of the most regal and sensitive of Pierce's religious tableaus. It depicts the first scene of the Passion cycle, in which Christ makes his final visit to Jerusalem. Christ astride an ass enters the city gates, represented by a gabled and chimneyed brick house. Except for Zacchaeus—who sits in a tree at the right for a better view—Christ rises above the crowd at the center of the scene. As he blesses them, the crowd hails him in return, sounding trumpets and crying "Hosanna in the highest!" Its small scale notwithstanding, the tableau is monumental in effect. The solemn face of Christ, classical in its profile; his gesture of blessing, the narrative and psychological axis around which the story revolves; the vision of multitudes which yet accommodates individual gestures of homage—each of these elements is carefully conceived for maximum impact. Pierce's genius is perhaps best seen in his provision of space in the front row for the viewer's entry into the scene. Immediately we see Christ on the ass, a colt, and a woman in red with two children by her side. Notions of family and community, of protection and salvation, are evoked. Pierce's sensitivity toward his audience and his enlivening of the story with the appeal of personal experience and involvement give his art a memorable yet approachable grandeur and power.

95. Jesus on the Cross, 1942
Carved and painted wood with glitter
20¹/₂ × 9¹/₈ × 5⁵/₈ (52.1 × 23.0 × 14.2)
Columbus Museum of Art: Museum Purchase

97. Jesus on the Cross, ca. 1980
Carved and painted wood with stones
17⁵/₈ × 6 (44.7 × 15.2)
Columbus Museum of Art: Museum Purchase

96. Jesus on the Cross, 1975
Carved and painted wood with stones and
commercial plastic crucifix
14 × 11¹/₂ × 8¹/₄ (35.6 × 29.1 × 21.0)
Columbus Museum of Art: Museum Purchase

98. Paul and Silas in Jail, n.d.
Carved and painted wood with graphite and wire
9¹/₂ × 13⁵/₈ × 5⁷/₈ (24.1 × 34.6 × 14.9)
Columbus Museum of Art: Museum Purchase

Paul and Silas are popular biblical heroes frequently
mentioned in hymns and other forms of African American cultural expression. While preaching at the ancient

Macedonian city of Philippi, Paul and his companion Silas were beaten, chained together, and imprisoned by Roman magistrates. As Paul and Silas prayed, a great earthquake shook the foundations of the prison, opening the doors and loosing the prisoners from bondage. Though freed, Paul and Silas did not flee but instead baptized the jailer and his family (Acts 16:16–33).

As with his tableaus *Sacrifice of Isaac* (cat. no. 92) and *Abraham Sacrifices His Son* (cat. no. 93), Pierce apparently made only a three-dimensional version of the Paul and Silas story. A simple wooden box with a small window at the back represents the jail cell, which is barred across the front. Its grid is repeated in graphite on the floors and walls in the interior, as well as in black paint on the roof, intensifying the notion of captivity and repression in "the inner prison" (Acts 17:24). At the center, a hinged door stands partly open to reveal Paul and Silas kneeling in shackles and gesturing in prayer. Salvation by earthquake is implied by the open door. Instead of catastrophic forces, an angel looms like a specter in the shadowy background. Guardian angels of many kinds appear often in Pierce's works (see *Picking Wild Berries,* cat. no. 9; *Angel,* cat. no. 125; *Pride,* cat. no. 150). This angel is in fact the figure most easily observed through the barred facade. Its white wings and garments transcend the obscurity of the darkened interior in a compelling manifestation of divine release.

RELIGIOUS RELIEFS

99. **Crucifixion,** mid–1930s   Colorplate 35
Carved and painted wood with glitter, mounted on painted panel
47½ × 30½ (121.3 × 78.1)
Columbus Museum of Art: Museum Purchase

Crucifixion and *Book of Wood* (cat. no. 100) are among Pierce's greatest masterpieces. Both works were revised and modified over the years. Pierce made *Book of Wood* in the early 1930s, applying small reliefs to pieces of cardboard in a booklike assemblage, and remounting these in the seventies on a firmer support. In the early 1970s, he mounted on panel an extensive cast of 1930s figures to create the *Crucifixion* as we know it today.[1]

In its earliest form, *Crucifixion* was a tableau with figures arranged on five levels of narrow, steplike ledges.

Pierce with original *Crucifixion*

The present configuration of more than forty biblical and contemporary figures, as well as trees, flowers, and other objects, maintains the compositional integrity and dramatic impact of the earlier version. An event of cosmic proportions is proclaimed—from the march of Old Testament prophets along the lower tier upward to the image of the Crucifixion, crowned with a crescent moon raining blood and a blackened sun.

In the 1930s tableau, Satan was positioned off to one side among a group of sacred figures. Sporting horns, a pointed tail, and a modern suit, and brandishing a sword and pitchfork, he played the ultimate trickster, leaping above the crowd with sinister glee. In the present configuration, Satan takes center stage, his feet planted firmly in the red ground of hell-fire. In full, triumphant view, his outstretched arms now gesture, ironically, in imitation of Christ on the cross.

1. The present-day *Crucifixion* was assembled between October 1970, when Michael Hall saw it in its tableau form, and December 1971, when it was first exhibited at the Krannert Art Museum, University of Illinois at Urbana-Champaign. It is not clear whether the modifications were Pierce's own idea or whether these were made at the suggestion of others.

Elijah Pierce with *Book of Wood*

---

100. **Book of Wood,** ca. 1932   Colorplates 36–42a
Carved and painted wood reliefs with glitter,
mounted to painted commercial wood paneling
Four two-sided panels, each 27⅛ × 30¾
(68.8 × 78.0)
Columbus Museum of Art: Museum Purchase

I had carved up a lot of pictures, and my wife said, "Let's make a book, a book of wood," so we got together and started small pieces that we could put on a page: seven pages and thirty-three pictures representing the seven great churches of Asia Minor and the thirty and three years that Jesus Christ was here on earth. All the pictures represent some of the highlights of his life while he was here. I was working on this for about six months.[1]

Of all his works, whether religious or secular, *Book of Wood* was the most important to Pierce. "It's the onliest book of its kind in the world," he remarked, "Oh my, I love it."[2] He compared events of his own life to pages in a book. When reciting stories from the *Book of Wood* to visitors, he would often interject the words God spoke to him: "Elijah, your life is a book and every day is a page."

Book of Wood was assembled around 1932 on four large pieces of cardboard tied together with string. In the early 1980s, responding to concerns about the fragility of the cardboard, Pierce mounted the individual carvings on the present support of green-painted commercial wood paneling. Each panel is now edged with self-fashioned metal frames that can be hinged together with round metal loops. A large imitation

Panel 1 (recto): Nativity; Annunciation to the Shepherds; Flight into Egypt; First Meeting of Jesus and John the Baptist; Mary, Jesus, and John the Baptist; the Three Wise Men.

Panel 1 (verso): Marriage at Cana; Rose of Sharon; Baptism of Christ; Temptation of Christ by Satan on the Mountaintop.

Panel 2 (recto): Christ in the House of Martha and Mary; Christ Blesses the Little Children; Christ Meets the Woman at the Well; Christ Instructs Nicodemus; Lily of the Valley; Christ Gives Peter the Keys to the Kingdom of Heaven.

Panel 2 (verso): Christ Weeps over Jerusalem; Angel of Faith; The Bright and Morning Star; Christ in the Upper Room; Christ Heals.

Panel 3 (recto): Christ's Entry into Jerusalem; Zacchaeus Climbs the Sycamore Tree to Watch Christ's Entry; Christ Teaches Humility; "Behold, I Stand at the Door and Knock"; The Sower; The Sun Which Scorched Some of the Sower's Seed.

Panel 3 (verso): The Rose of Sharon; Woman with the Issue of Blood; Christ Prays in the Garden of Gethsemane; Angel Ministers to Christ in the Garden; The Kiss of Judas.

Panel 4 (recto): Angels of Grace, Mercy, and Truth; Crowing Cock; Angel at the Empty Tomb.
Panel 4 (verso): Title page; white paper taped and glued to panel. In black marking pen: *Book of Wood*.

In the 1930s and early 1940s, Pierce took *Book of Wood* with him on his summer preaching trips.[4] The work could also be viewed by appointment at Pierce's home. A period broadside announced: "The Mammoth

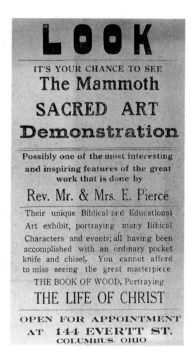

SACRED ART Demonstration . . . done by Rev. Mr. & Mrs. E. Pierce . . . You cannot afford to miss seeing the great masterpiece THE BOOK OF WOOD, Portraying THE LIFE OF CHRIST." In later years, *Book of Wood* was transferred to the barbershop, where it remained the centerpiece of Pierce's art displays until his death.

1. Columbus Gallery of Fine Arts, unpaginated.
2. Seibert interview, September 1980.
3. Interestingly, Pierce does not include the Crucifixion as one of the highlights of Christ's life, although several scenes from the Passion cycle are depicted. Pierce apparently preferred to treat the Crucifixion as a separate subject, frequently in the tableau format.
4. Pierce said, "I traveled with this work in a trailer." Seibert interview, September 1980.

101.   **Adam and Eve,** 1971   Colorplate 43
Carved and painted wood relief with glitter
21³/₄ × 31¹/₂ (55.3 × 80.0)
Private Collection

According to the Book of Genesis (1:26–31), God made Adam and Eve and all the plants and animals on the sixth day of creation. He prepared a garden for them, called Eden, and it is in this lush paradise that Pierce chose to depict them. Basking in innocent nakedness, the couple is surrounded by a multitude of colorful animals, birds, fish, and reptiles. All are affectionately portrayed with lively personalities—the signature of Pierce's animal carvings.

This is the Garden of Eden before the fall of man. Neither apple nor serpent foretells man's disobedience to God and the expulsion of Adam and Eve from paradise. The fruits beside Eve are many and suggest abundance and fertility; the serpent is still but a snake playing among reptilian friends. Beneath the sun and moon, the profusion of plant and animal life is a picture of bliss and tranquility.

102.   **God's Plenty,** 1973
Carved and painted wood relief with glitter
23 × 14³/₄ (58.4 × 37.5)
Courtesy Janet Fleisher Gallery, Philadelphia

God's Plenty recalls the bounties that God provided in the Garden of Eden and gives thankful recognition of the abundance that the earth yields. Pierce envisioned a land of plenty upon which an angel has bestowed a cornucopia overflowing with fruits. The rich color and

complex pattern of the array, heightened with the shimmer of metallic paint and glitter, endow this small work with a majestic sumptuousness.

animals two by two onto the ark in preparation for God's wrathful deluge (Gen. 6:18–21; 7:1–19).

To illustrate "two of every living thing" boarding the ark, Pierce portrayed more than forty-five pairs of beasts and birds. The procession covers every inch of the panel. Because the animals are unpainted, their carved forms take on an abundant visual intensity in contrast to the painted segments of the composition.

While there are two representatives of nearly everything, Pierce included only one tiny bedbug—not wishing it to reproduce![2] Like so many of Pierce's carvings, *Noah's Ark* is imbued with a sense of humor. Visitors to the barbershop relished the search for such unexpected undesirables as the lonely bedbug. Some found ants, houseflies, and mosquitoes in the ark and elsewhere on the panel. The intrigue of each new search kept the story of Noah and the ark alive.

1. Jones and Kook.
2. Seibert interview, July 1981.

103. **Noah's Ark,** 1944   Colorplate 44
Carved and painted wood relief
12¼ × 32 (31.1 × 81.2)
Collection of Mr. and Mrs. William Gilmore

Sometimes I'd carve something just to pass time or to satisfy my mind; little animals and other things. . . . And I did have in mind if I didn't sell these little animals and different birds and things and snakes that I'd carved, someday—if it was pleasing to God—I would make an ark.[1]

Like *Crucifixion* (cat. no. 99) and *Book of Wood* (cat. no. 100), *Noah's Ark* is a masterpiece that Pierce carved only once. He completed it in six intensive weeks, working at night and by day between haircuts. A parable of divine deliverance, the carving depicts the Old Testament patriarch Noah at the lower left, shepherding the

104. **Jonah and the Fish,** 1949   Colorplate 45
Carved and painted wood relief with glitter
15¼ × 28½ (38.7 × 72.4)
Private Collection, Courtesy Keny Galleries, Inc.

This story—I always did like it. You see, the Lord told Jonah to go down to preach in Nineveh, but Jonah didn't want to go, because that was a sinful place. So he took a ship in the other direction. A big storm came up, and the people were frightened; they didn't know what to do. They went to find Jonah; he was asleep in the hold of the ship. They throwed him overboard to save the rest of the people. This big fish swallowed him and he stayed in the belly of that fish for three days, and when the fish vomited him up, he was glad to go to Nineveh, or anywhere else that God wanted him to go.[1]

In this panel, whose narrative course undulates like the movement of the sea, Pierce illustrates key scenes from the Old Testament story of Jonah. The story unfolds in a circular path clockwise from the upper left: God, represented by a radiant hand, commands Jonah to preach at Nineveh; fleeing God's will, Jonah embarks on a ship for Tarshish; the ship is tossed by a turbulent sea; Jonah is thrown forth from the bowels of the fish onto dry land, where he sits under a tree; restored to life, Jonah walks toward the white church at Nineveh to preach.

In the lower right corner, at the turning point of the story, Pierce inscribed words from the Book of Jonah: "Take me up, and cast me forth into the sea: so shall the sea be calm unto you" (Jon. 1:12). Pierce knew that "you can't hide from God," and he strongly related to Jonah as a fellow transgressor (see *Jonah and the Whale*, cat. no. 19):

> I was a Jonah. I ran from the ministry twenty years. My wife said I carved every sermon that God made me preach. See, I was supposed to be a preacher since I was a little bitty kid. After I'm dead I'll still be preaching. Yes sirree.[2]

1. Columbus Gallery of Fine Arts, unpaginated.
2. Seibert interview, October 31, 1980.

105.   **Story of Job,** ca. 1936   Colorplate 46
Carved and painted wood relief
16 × 29 (40.7 × 73.6)
Milwaukee Art Museum, The Michael and Julie Hall
Collection of American Folk Art

The trials of Job epitomize the victory of faith over human suffering. Job was tormented with misfortune resulting from Satan's challenge to God that Job's faith could not withstand adversity. God allowed Satan to test the fidelity of Job, an upright man of great wealth. His livestock were stolen and destroyed, his servants were killed, and his sons and daughters perished when a hurricane razed their house. Job himself was afflicted with severe boils from head to toe, yet "in all this Job sinned not, nor charged God foolishly" (Job 1:22).

Pierce tells Job's story in a complex series of images punctuated with key biblical passages. The narrative is staged in three horizontal tiers: the top displays Job's wealth; the middle depicts the devastation that ensued from Satan's confrontation with God; and the lower portrays the exceeding misery that Job withstood.

Appearing in grand scale, crowned with the words "perfect and upright man" (Job 1:1), Job presides over the events of his fate at the center of the composition. Surrounding him are his extensive flocks of camels, sheep, and oxen, and his children, who are seen feasting and dancing in the house at the upper left. At the lower left, God is in discourse with Satan, whose pointed tail is exposed beneath a blazing red robe. The words "walking up and down seeking to and frow [*sic*]" (Job 1:7) describe Satan's search for someone to destroy. To the right of Satan is the story of Job's ruin, spread across the center of the panel. Reading from left to right, the children are crushed in the splintered and bloodstained remains of the house, servants plowing the fields are slain, and the sheep are consumed by fire. One man in a running position represents the four messengers who came before Job and in turn declared the terrible news: "I only am lef[t] to tell the[e]" (Job 1:15–17, 19).

Beneath the image of the upright Job lies the afflicted Job on hands and knees, naked, emaciated, and covered with sores. The words "ashes" and "sack cloth" symbolize the grief which overcame him. Twice more Pierce depicts Job—lying before the three friends who first consoled and then accused him, and being tormented by his wife, who said, "Dost thou still retain thine integrity: curse God and die" (Job 2:9).

Job's reply, "Th[o]ugh he slay me yet I will trust him" (Job 13:15), is inscribed in the lower right corner.

As the story goes, God finally released Job from his captivity and gave him "twice as much as he had before . . . and blessed the latter end of Job more than his beginning" (Job 42:10–12). The narrative has come full circle to the central figure of Job, at once God's perfect servant and the restored man. Wearing a white robe, he carries the staff of his spiritual pilgrimage. As with many African Americans who grew up in the troubled deep South of the post–Civil War period, Pierce found strength in Job's story.

106.   Climbing Jacob's Ladder, 1965
        Carved and painted wood relief with glitter
        17½ × 10⅝ (44.5 × 26.9)
        Private Collection

107.   Jacob Wrestling with the Angel, 1938
        Carved and painted wood relief mounted on
        painted paper on corrugated cardboard
        18¾ × 17 (47.7 × 43.2)
        Private Collection

Stories of the Old Testament patriarch Jacob, drawn from the Book of Genesis, have been a favored subject in art through the ages. In the story of Jacob's ladder, Jacob dreamed that angels ascended and descended a ladder reaching from earth to heaven. God appeared to Jacob from atop the ladder and promised to give him and his descendants, the Israelites, the land upon which he lay. When Jacob awoke, he took the stones which had been his pillow and built a pillar on the spot, calling the place Bethel—the house of God (Gen. 28:11–22).

While interpretations of Jacob's dream are many, it is perhaps the simplest and most direct meaning that Pierce envisioned: the ladder is the gateway to heaven, representing Christ who said, "I am the way" (John 14:6). Thus it is not so much Jacob or the angels that are portrayed, but an emblem of the divine way to the promised land so highly esteemed in African American religious tradition.

Pierce's image is heraldic in composition, majestic in effect. The ladder, placed diagonally from corner to corner, visually unites a show of hands and Jacob's crosslike pillar at the lower left with the radiant image of God at the upper right. Ascending the steps is a woman (perhaps Pierce's mother?) in glittering white. The hands applaud her ascent, recalling the strains of the hymn, "We are climbing Jacob's ladder . . . Soldiers of the Cross. Every rung goes higher, higher . . . Soldiers of the Cross."

In the story of Jacob wrestling with the angel, Pierce may have seen a parallel to his own struggles with the will of God. Jacob once had an encounter with an angel who wrestled him until dawn. When the angel could not defeat Jacob, he touched the hollow of Jacob's thigh, which withered. Jacob demanded to be blessed before letting the angel go. In further evidence of God's favor toward him, the angel did so. Jacob responded with words not unlike Pierce's own: "For I have seen God face to face, and my life is preserved" (Gen. 32:30).

Pierce depicted the wrestling match at the moment when the angel touched Jacob's thigh and rendered him lame. In this work he has concentrated on the stance, balance, and moves of the sport of wrestling. The struggle takes place on a rocky ledge that floats above a landscape of trees and flowers (probably later painted additions). By suspending the scene Pierce gave it a dreamlike quality that has an affinity with the mysterious biblical event.

108. **Samson,** 1942 Colorplate 47
Carved and painted wood relief with glitter
13¼ × 20¼ (33.6 × 54.1)
Collection of Michael D. Hall

109. **The Three Wise Men,** 1936
Carved and painted wood relief with glitter,
mounted to painted board with glitter and traces
of graphite
12¹³⁄₁₆ × 22¼ (32.1 × 56.5)
Columbus Museum of Art: Purchased with funds
from the Alfred L. Willson Fund of The Columbus
Foundation

Samson was an Old Testament judge best known for his swashbuckling adventures and his womanizing, Delilah being his most famous consort. In Pierce's depiction, Samson is frontally posed with hand on hip, proudly displaying a muscular torso and legs. Extravagant plaited locks, which were the source of his strength, frame Samson's face, and he carries the jawbone with which he slew a thousand Philistines (Judg. 15:15).

Behind Samson in contemporary dress is Delilah, the object of his desire and his undoing. She looks not at all like the alluring traitor who conspired with Philistine lords to emasculate Samson by cutting off his hair and blinding him (Judg. 16:4–21). To the right, Samson performs one of his Herculean feats of strength. Shown astride a young lion, his hair blowing behind him, Samson forces the lion's jaws apart with his bare hands and slays it, rendering it "as he would have rent a kid" (Judg. 14:5–6). The staglike animals leaping in series in the background evoke an exotic landscape in which unrestrained power and velocity reign.

In 1974, the Columbus Museum of Art acquired its first three carvings by Pierce: *Pride* (cat. no. 150), *Before Death All Are Equal* (cat. no. 160), and *Three Wise Men*. Scenes from the New Testament Nativity cycle, of which the story of the three wise men is a part, were Pierce's favorite subjects; he dedicated a whole panel of *Book of Wood* to the Birth of Christ (cat. no. 100, panel 1, recto). The majestic procession of the magi toward Bethlehem especially appealed to him, and he carved other versions of the story. Following the bright eastern star are Melchoir at the left with gold, Caspar in the center with frankincense, and Balthazar at the right with myrrh to offer to the infant Christ.[1]

Like other early works, including *Indians Hunting* (cat. no. 62) and *Crocodile and Unwary Cow* (cat. no. 142), *Three Wise Men* is a cutout relief mounted to a board on which the background detail is painted rather than carved. In this kind of presentation, the play of light and shadows cast against an essentially neutral background enhance three-dimensionality and produce a stagelike effect, whereas in fully carved surfaces, such as *Anniversary Flowers* (cat. no. 72) and *Noah's Ark* (cat. no. 103), overall decorative pattern and color prevail.

1. Seibert interview, September 19, 1980.

and Elizabeth, the mother of John, looking on. The complex poses of the figures and the unusual arch framing an exotically appointed interior strongly suggest that Pierce transcribed the image from a Bible illustration. The source is the same as that used for a nearly identical version of the scene in *Book of Wood* (cat. no. 100, panel 1, recto).

Christ Blessing also may have its origins in a book illustration. The exact subject is not clear. However, the presence of a kneeling man with a bandaged arm suggests Christ performing a healing miracle. This scene of man's humility before Christ is charged with solemnity.

110. **First Meeting of Jesus and John,**
1940   Colorplate 48
Carved and painted wood relief
18¼ × 18 (46.4 × 45.8)
Miami University Art Museum: Purchase through
the Cora Zemsky Folk Art Fund

112. **Suffer the Little Children,** n.d.   Colorplate 49
Carved and painted wood relief with glitter
21¼ × 19⅛ (54.0 × 48.4)
Private Collection, Courtesy Keny Galleries, Inc.

111. **Christ Blessing,** 1936
Carved and painted wood relief with glitter
26¼ × 22¾ (66.7 × 57.8)
Columbus Museum of Art: Museum Purchase

These works are examples of the rarer occasions when Pierce did not embellish his carvings with paint. The works are classical in their aesthetic, with the exposed grain and gold patina of the wood providing rich surfaces for intricate detail and subtle modeling.

The narrative of *First Meeting of Jesus and John* is taken from the story of the Nativity. The scene features the two infants in mutual adoration, with Joseph, Mary,

This tender scene of Christ blessing children illustrates his words to the disciples, "Suffer the little children, and forbid them not to come unto me; for of such is the kingdom of heaven" (Matt. 19:14, Mark 10:14, Luke 8:16). In an idyllic setting amidst palm trees and grand flowers, Christ is seated with a child on his lap as other children are brought before him. To the left, facing the viewer, stands a woman whose child is lifted up and framed by her white dress. Like this child who seemingly floats within her mother's aura, four trees hover in a blue sky as if ascending toward the glittering cross above. In this unusual expression of earthly transcendence, Pierce has created a dreamy paradise where peace reigns in Christ's presence.

113.   **Caught in the Act of Adultery,** 1979
       Carved and painted wood relief with glitter
       14 × 23⅞ (35.6 × 60.6)
       Columbus Museum of Art: Museum Purchase

In this depiction of a story from the Book of John (8:2–11), Christ stands before a kneeling woman, an adulteress, who has been brought before him. Scribes and Pharisees surround them gesturing accusingly and challenging Christ to pass judgment on the woman. His reply is, "He that is without sin among you, let him cast the first stone at her."

Pierce appeals to the conscience of his audience by placing Christ at the center of the composition, facing the viewer with a penetrating stare. Pierce relates his message to the concerns of the present time by depicting another woman—probably a contemporary adulteress—standing at the far right. Portrayed in a polka-dot dress of bright red—a color popularly associated with passion—she covers herself with crossed arms in the traditional posture of shame. The woman, too, faces the viewer directly, with brooding eyes of warning to others.

---

114.   **Christ Caused the Blind to See,** 1973
       Carved and painted wood relief with glitter
       14 × 24 (35.5 × 61.0)
       Courtesy Janet Fleisher Gallery, Philadelphia

He saw that man. He was born blind from his mother's womb. And he was crying by the wayside, and Jesus stopped and went out and takin' time out to heal him and give him sight. He made a drug out of spittle in the clay and anointed his eyes and told him to go to the pool and wash, that he may see.

Being obedient, he did what he was told to do, and he received his sight. He had been beggin' and had been seen by lots of people from his youth up. And after he was received of sight, he went rejoicing in the streets, and the people was amazed because they knew he was a blind man and now he sees. And they asked him who healed him. "Who give sight to the blind?" He said, "A man came along"—he didn't even know his name—but "a man came along and told me what to do. Made spittle, stooped down and made spittle in the clay and anointed my eyes."

"Ain't you the one born blind? Why? And how?" They went to his parents and asked about him. They told 'em, "Yes, he was born blind." "But how is it now that he see?" They said, "He is of age, ask him." One thing he said, "I was blind but now I see." [Pierce laughs] You know that's wonderful! I was blind but now I see! He went on his way rejoicing. It ain't no secret what God can do.[1]

In his explanation of this story from John 9:1–25, symbolizing man's restoration from spiritual blindness, Pierce invoked the well-known popular religious songs "Amazing Grace" and "It Is No Secret What God Can Do." He was speaking of his 1938 carving, *The Man That Was Born Blind Restored to Sight* (see fig. 1, p. 19), but his words of rejoicing speak as eloquently to this version created more than three decades later. In *Christ Caused the Blind to See*, the miracle is described in a three-part narrative sequence: Christ meets the blind man, he makes an ointment of clay and spittle, and he anoints the man's eyes. Complete trust is expressed in Pierce's placement of the blind man's hand on Christ's arm as he is healed.

1. Hall interview, fall 1971.

---

115.   **Jesus Feeds the Multitudes: He Fed 5000,** n.d.
       Carved and painted wood relief with glitter
       15¾ × 29 (40.0 × 73.7)
       Private Collection, Courtesy Keny Galleries, Inc.

In the story of the miracle of loaves and fishes (John 6:1–13), Christ fed a crowd of five thousand followers

from a small supply of fish and bread. The crowd had gathered near the Sea of Galilee—represented here by the blue circular area in the lower right corner—where a young boy delivered "five barley loaves and two small fishes" to Christ and his apostles. The image is iconic rather than narrative: Christ presents the food in a gesture of both blessing and offering. Pierce reinforced the image with the carved words "He Fed 5000."

The surrounding tree-filled landscape is a feast of decorative patterning, with eleven multicolored spheres and large leaf forms suggesting lush flora. The copious daubing of color on each sphere evokes notions of plenty. Perhaps the spheres represent the baskets of food that remained when all five thousand had eaten their fill.

117. Christ Walking on the Water,
ca. 1970   Colorplate 50
Carved and painted wood relief with glitter
16½ × 18½ (41.9 × 47.0)
Collection of George H. Meyer

After Christ performed the miracle of the loaves and fishes, he went into the mountains to pray and sent his disciples across the Sea of Galilee. A storm arose on the sea. The frightened disciples saw Christ walking toward them on the water and thought he was a ghost. Peter called to Christ and then stepped out of the boat to meet him. As Peter did so, he began to sink. Christ caught him and said,"Oh thou of little faith, wherefore didst thou doubt?" (Matt. 14:31).

Peter Walking on the Water is Pierce's iconic vision of the story. At the lower left, a partly submerged Peter reaches toward Christ, who stands in full majesty as the savior of the faithful. *Christ Walking on the Water* is the narrative counterpart to the iconic version. In this version, Peter is instantly consumed by the waters—his arms instinctively raised as is the hair on his head. Pierce's rendition of the terrified Peter is witty and seriously demonstrative, a dualism that is prevalent in the carvings of morality subjects. In contrast to Peter and his human limitations, Christ is shown in glorious surety, his pose resembling classic illustrations of the Ascension.

116. Peter Walking on the Water,[1] 1938
Carved and painted wood relief with glitter,
mounted to panel
32 × 17¾ (81.3 × 45.1)
Columbus Museum of Art: Museum Purchase

1. This work was once part of a diptych that included three other works from the Columbus Museum's collections: *The Transfiguration* (cat. no. 118), *Peter's Denial (And the Cock Did Crow)* (cat. no. 120), and *Jesus' Charge to Peter: Feed My Sheep* (cat. no. 122). The diptych is known only through its illustration on the cover of a photocopied brochure from the museum's archives which advertises "Pierce's Wood

Carving Exhibition, Over 1000 Carvings, Educational, Fascinating, Carved with a Pocket-Knife.'' The brochure lists Pierce's 144 Everett Street (North Everett Alley) address, where he lived from 1944 to 1969. Although the diptych may have been assembled in the mid-1940s, Pierce had dismantled it by the early 1970s, as evidenced in photographs of the four individually mounted reliefs taken in Pierce's barbershop at that time. The diptych is one of four known examples of similar scale and vertical format, only one of which now survives intact (see *Bible Stories*, cat. no. 169).

118.   **The Transfiguration**, 1936
Carved and painted wood relief with glitter, on painted board with glitter
38 × 24³/₁₆ (96.6 × 61.5)
Columbus Museum of Art: Museum Purchase

In the lower right corner of this carving is one of Pierce's perforated paper labels with the typed words, ''The Ascension/Act 1–1–12.'' The subject, however, is clearly not the Ascension but the Transfiguration—a revelation of Christ's divinity to three apostles. Here, Christ stands on a mountaintop and before Peter, James, and John is transfigured: ''His face did shine as the sun, and his raiment was white as the light'' (Matt. 17:2). The bearded patriarchs Elijah and Moses stand at his side, Elijah on the left and Moses on the right.

The figures of Christ and the Old Testament prophets are enhanced with paint and glitter, in sharp contrast to the articulation of the trio of apostles in varnished wood. The distinction reinforces the radiance of the sacred vision. The darkened appearance of the apostles may indicate that they have been over-shadowed by the bright cloud in the upper background, from whence the voice of God was heard to say, ''This is my beloved Son, in whom I am well pleased; hear ye him'' (Matt. 17:5).

119.   **Judas Betraying Christ**, 1966
Carved and painted wood relief with glitter
24 × 17 (61.0 × 43.2)
Collection of George H. Meyer

In some religious works by Pierce, the psychological intensity of a story is emphasized rather than the narrative content. In this work the feeling is contemplative, even ominous. Judas, one of the twelve apostles, betrayed Christ to the high priests and elders for thirty pieces of silver. The kiss of Judas (portrayed in *Book of Wood*, cat. no. 100, panel 3, verso), his remorse, and subsequent suicide are not illustrated. Instead Judas is represented as the personification of betrayal and is shown surrounded by his ill-gotten money. As he identifies Christ, Judas points not at the man about to be arrested and crucified. Instead he points to Christ as a divine vision rising out of the red rose of Sharon—Christ's personal symbol (''I am the rose of Sharon,'' Song of Sol. 2:1) and a traditional symbol of martyrdom.

120. Peter's Denial (And the Cock Did Crow), 1947
Carved and painted wood relief with glitter,
mounted on painted board
34³/₄ × 24³/₈ (88.3 × 62.1)
Columbus Museum of Art: Museum Purchase

After Christ was arrested, he was taken to Caiaphas, the high priest, for interrogation. Meanwhile, Peter warmed himself by the fire in the courtyard of the high priest's home, where he was questioned by a servant girl who recognized him as one of Christ's disciples. After three times denying any knowledge of Christ, "immediately the cock crew" (John 18:27), fulfilling Christ's prophecy, "The cock shall not crow, till thou hast denied me thrice" (John 13:38). Pierce depicted Peter as an imposing presence at the center of the composition. To the left, the cock crows in the treetops; to the right is a visionary portrait of Christ to remind Peter of the prophecy. In Peter's intense eyes, set jaw, and broad shoulders, Pierce has captured the bitterness and exceeding regret of this formidable disciple.

121. Jesus before Pilate, n.d.   Colorplate 51
Carved and painted wood relief with glitter
13 × 27¹/₂ (33.0 × 69.8)
Collection of George and Miriam van Walleghem

In all four gospels describing the events leading to the Crucifixion, Christ was brought before no fewer than

four judges—Annas, Caiaphas, Herod, and Pilate—to determine his innocence or guilt. Here Pierce has condensed into a single composition Christ's arrest by soldiers, who gesture accusingly toward him and his summons before the civil authorities. The figure on the right, crowned and enthroned on a raised platform, would be identified as King Herod in traditional Christian iconography. Pierce, however, referred to this figure as Pilate—the best-known figure and the one who passed final judgment on Christ and delivered him to be crucified.

Pierce had a genius for visually accommodating narrative sequence in abbreviated, easily recognizable form. To move from the arrest to the trial, Pierce literally turned the figures of Christ and a guard about-face for a scene before the king. The physical placement of the guard seems to hinge on the unyielding knot of wood located at the top of the panel and the small platform beneath the figure's feet. Christ, the protagonist, is depicted larger in scale than the other figures. He is clothed in brilliant white and bright blue, in contrast to the drab brown and gray dress of his accusers. The chevron created by the blue panel of Christ's robe as the figure is shown facing first in one direction then the other is a powerful visual device that unites the two scenes.

122. Jesus' Charge to Peter: Feed My Sheep, 1932
Carved and painted wood relief with glitter,
mounted on painted board
33³/₁₆ × 24¹/₄ (84.3 × 61.1)
Columbus Museum of Art: Museum Purchase

In his third and final appearance to the disciples after the Crucifixion, Christ gave his greatest charge to Peter. The two are shown in tender discourse beneath a lush canopy of leaves. Beside them are bread and fish, a reference to Christ's miraculous provision of the disciples' meal (John 21:5–9). The solemn import of Christ's pass-

ing of his ministry to Peter is expressed in the figures' intimate gazes and clasped hands. Pierce's depiction may have been drawn from a book illustration, but it is nevertheless true to his own vision. Pierce, like Peter, took up his mission after hearing the voice of the Lord.

124. **Jesus and John after the Resurrection**, 1979
Carved and painted wood relief with glitter
and plastic
32 × 15¹⁵/₁₆ (81.2 × 40.4)
Columbus Museum of Art: Museum Purchase

In the Book of Revelation, John records a series of fantastic visions concerning the Second Coming of Christ. In his first great vision, "one like unto the Son of Man," wearing a golden girdle, appeared amidst seven golden candlesticks representing the seven churches of Asia:

> His head and his hairs were white like wool, as
>   white as snow; and his eyes were as a flame of fire;
> And his feet like unto fine brass, as if they burned
>   in a furnace; and his voice as the sound of
>   many waters;
> And he had in his right hand seven stars; and out
>   of his mouth went a sharp two-edged sword: and
>   his countenance was as the sun shineth in his
>   strength. . . .
> I am he that liveth, and was dead; and, behold, I am
>   alive for evermore, Amen; and have the keys of hell
>   and of death. (Rev. 1:14–16, 18)

123. **Christ of the Apocalypse**, 1940s   Colorplate 52
Carved and painted wood relief with glitter
33½ × 15 (85.1 × 38.1)
Collection of George H. Meyer

In works created about forty years apart, Pierce carved John's vision in a literal transcription. From Christ's blazing eyes and his frothy white hair to the sparkling candlesticks, stars, and keys, Pierce gave substance to the words. The vision of Christ in the earlier carving has military, even patriotic overtones. Dressed in a blue coat with epaulets, Christ stands in the guise of a general—the great soldier who has come to destroy the wicked and overthrow Satan. Behind him the stars shining against a blue field and the candlesticks arranged in striped formation assume the character of an American flag. Perhaps Pierce intended to evoke in his imagery an equally apocalyptic sign of the uncertain destiny of a country at war.

The terrible splendor of Christ's appearance is made more believable by John's prostration before him ("And when I saw him, I fell at his feet as dead." [Rev. 1:17]). In the earlier version, he takes on a fetal position of fear and trembling; in the latter, a wide-eyed John hits the ground and, catching himself, projects his hand onto the picture frame with eye-catching immediacy. As he did with Jonah (see *Jonah and the Fish*, cat. no. 104), Pierce closely identified with John, and sometimes spoke of the prostrate figure as being himself. The prone John is comparable to the image of Pierce struck down in *Obey God and Live* (cat. no. 6). John's words, "And he laid his right hand upon me, saying unto me, Fear not; I am the first and the last" (Rev. 1:17), recall the story of Pierce's conversion: ". . . he just laid his hands on my head . . . and I heard a voice of God [tell me] I'm just showing you my power."[1]

1. Hall interview, fall 1971.

nos. 9 and 166); and a recording angel is referred to in *My Sayings* (cat. no. 20). Ultimately, to Pierce, angels embodied God's greatest gifts: hope and redemption.

---

125. **Angel**, ca. 1933
Carved and painted wood relief mounted
to painted panel
26⁷/₈ × 15³/₄ (68.3 × 40.1)
Columbus Museum of Art: Museum Purchase

In the Old and New Testaments, angels assume many roles. They are annunciators, protectors of good, punishers of evil, and mystic personifications of God. Pierce's angels manifest all of these functions. Yet, more than messengers of God, they are agents of man's preservation.

The angel in this work is nearly identical to the three angels in *Book of Wood* (cat. no. 100, panel 4, recto), and like them may represent grace, mercy, or truth. *Book of Wood* also includes an angel of faith (panel 2, verso). A guardian angel is present in *Pride* (cat. no. 150); an angel of conscience appears in *Picking Wild Berries* (cat.

126. **Madonna**, n.d.
Carved and painted wood relief with glitter
24 × 19¹/₄ (61.0 × 48.9)
Collection of Roger Brown

127. **Madonna**, 1980
Carved and painted wood relief with glitter and
marking-pen ink
30³/₄ × 21³/₈ (78.1 × 54.3)
Columbus Museum of Art: Museum Purchase

These are portrayals of the *Mater Dolorosa*, the mother
who mourns the death of her son. In each case she is
depicted bearing a flaming heart pierced with a sword
in fulfillment of Simeon's prophecy as told to Mary:
"Behold, this child is set for the fall and rising again of
many in Israel; and for a sign which shall be spoken
against; Yea a sword shall pierce through thy own soul
also" (Luke 2:34–35).

In the first version, the Madonna's heart is surrounded with the crown of thorns worn by Christ
when he was crucified. She carries in her hand a
flowering branch from the Tree of Jesse, the genealogi-
cal tree of Christ. This image is certainly derived from
a Bible illustration. It also has a strong affinity with
devotional statues of the Madonna, several of which
adorned the mantle of Pierce's Margaret Street home.

The 1980 carving is also to some extent derivative. Yet
it is more truly like Pierce in conception, even despite
his declining technical facility. The flowering branch is
made a full Tree of Jesse, not unlike those included in
Crucifixion (cat. no. 99) and other works. The vertical

folds of the Madonna's robes in the earlier version are
visually translated into fence posts in the later work
and her mesmerizing wide eyes are particularly haunt-
ing signs of sorrow and suffering.

128. **I Am the Door**, ca. 1940   Colorplate 53
Carved and painted wood relief with glitter,
mounted on painted panel
26 × 13 (66.0 × 33.0)
Collection of Dr. Siri von Reis

The representation of Christ as the door to salvation
occurs no fewer than four times in Pierce's oeuvre (see
also *Book of Wood*, cat. no. 100, panel 3, recto, and *Bible
Stories*, cat. no. 169). The subject is drawn from the
Book of Revelation (3:20): "Behold, I stand at the door
and knock: if any man hear my voice, and open the
door, I will come in to him, and will sup with him, and
he with me." These two versions, produced thirty to
forty years apart, represent iconic and vernacular variations on the theme.

130. **Power of Prayer**, 1960   Colorplate 54
Carved and painted wood relief with glitter
40⅝ × 19⅝ (103.2 × 49.7)
Collection of Julie Hall

129. **I Am the Door**, 1978
Carved and painted wood relief with collage
elements (foil and magazine illustrations), with
glitter and marking-pen ink
26¼ × 14⅞ (66.5 × 37.7)
Columbus Museum of Art: Museum Purchase

In the earlier work, Christ, in brilliant red and white,
stands in an archway suffused with vivid celestial blue.
Symbols ornament the framework: the fish, representing Christ, Jonah, and the miracles of feeding; the Rose
of Sharon and the palm of martyrdom; the yoke and
crutch of bondage; the vigilant all-seeing eye; the hand
of God and of creative power. Each symbol is imbued
with suffering and mercy, and each is a key to the gates
of heaven.

In the second carving, Pierce removes Christ from an
otherworldly realm and brings him to the entrance of a
house. Christ knocks at the door of this familiar white
clapboard house surrounded by flowers (cutouts from
popular magazines applied to the wood surface). By
appealing to notions of home, Pierce renders Christ
more man than mystic—a believable part of our everyday physical and psychological place.

For Pierce, prayer was the conduit to God and the
essential means to nurture faith and insure salvation.
From the message sign *Hear My Prayer* (cat. no. 135) to
narratives such as *Home and Prayer* (cat. no. 7), *Mother's
Prayer* (cat. no. 8), and *Answer to Prayer* (cat. no. 10),
Pierce's art is invested with the notion of divine communication. It is the sense of all-encompassing, all-
fulfilling prayer that is the subject of these carvings.

Power of Prayer is didactic and structural in concept.
With words and visual signs, Pierce tells us that prayer
is the key to faith in God and union with him. The vertical stacking of the word "faith" on the central axis of
the composition speeds the viewer's eye to the portrait
of Jesus as a young man, then onward via the outpour-
ing of God's bleeding heart to his patriarchal coun-
tenance in heaven. In totemic union, Father and Son
embrace the supplicants below with outstretched arms.
These representatives of the faithful form a human
chain to the star, a symbol of divine guidance, and the
cross, the symbol of suffering.

131.   **Prayers**, 1978
Carved and painted wood relief with marking-
pen ink
31⅝ × 16¾ (80.4 × 42.6)
Columbus Museum of Art: Museum Purchase

In *Prayers*, which was carved nearly two decades later, the power of prayer is felt more than it is described. The composition is all radiance, generated between the multitudes and the heavens. A resplendent Father and Son are spiritlike, their divine essence interpreted as hearts crowned by portrait heads and all-embracing arms. The wood surface resonates with the ecstatic charge of countless incised lines, painted daubs, and marking pen notations in a veritable broadcast of prayer.

MESSAGE SIGNS

132.   **Courage**, n.d.   Colorplate 55
Carved and painted wood relief with glitter
21³/₁₆ × 13 (54.4 × 33.0)
Collection of Mr. and Mrs. Richard E. Guggenheim

133.   **Your Life Is a Book**, 1978   Colorplate 55
Painted wood
11¼ × 29 (28.4 × 73.7)
Columbus Museum of Art: Museum Purchase

134.   **Love**, n.d.   Colorplate 55
Carved and painted wood relief
2 × 8⅞ (5.1 × 22.5)
Columbus Museum of Art: Museum Purchase

135.   **Hear My Prayer**, 1970   Colorplate 55
Carved and painted wood mounted on
commercial wood paneling
2⁹/₁₆ × 12⅛ (6.5 × 30.8)
Columbus Museum of Art: Museum Purchase

136.   **Put Your Trust in God and Not in Man**,
n.d.   Colorplate 55
Painted wood mounted on commercial wood
paneling
3⅜ × 23¼ (8.6 × 59.1)
Columbus Museum of Art: Museum Purchase

137.   **What the World Needs Now Is Love**,
n.d.   Colorplate 55
Carved and painted wood relief with glitter
3 × 8¾ (7.6 × 34.3)
Collection of Jeffrey Wolf and Jeany
Nisenholz-Wolf

138.   **Don't Lie**, n.d.   Colorplate 55
Carved and painted wood relief with glitter
3¾ × 19⅞ (9.5 × 50.5)
Columbus Museum of Art: Museum Purchase

139.   **God Is Love**, n.d.   Colorplate 55
Carved and painted wood relief with glitter
7¼ × 13⁷/₁₆ (18.0 × 34.1)
Columbus Museum of Art: Museum Purchase

MORAL LESSONS

140. **Pilgrim's Progress,** 1938   Colorplate 56
Carved and painted wood relief with glitter,
mounted on painted panel
26 × 14 (66.0 × 35.6)
Collection of Estelle E. Friedman

Pilgrim's Progress resonates with spiritual fervor and the vigorous realism of everyday life. Its message is simple: the true believer who follows the way of the cross will experience many trials in life's journey before heavenly salvation is reached. The carving is named after John Bunyan's book *The Pilgrim's Progress from This World to That Which Is to Come*, first published in 1678. An allegory recounting the pilgrimage of Christian and his wife Christiana from the City of Destruction to the Celestial City, this literary masterpiece that has perhaps been read more widely than any book except the Bible would have been known to Pierce.[1]

In Pierce's carving, the road of life is steep and fraught with danger, strife, and temptation—like the Hill of Difficulty which Christian climbed.[2] That each one must face such a journey is suggested by the portrait bust placed at the foot of the incline. A hatchet buried beneath the tree indicates the need to resolve differences with and ill-will toward others at the outset.

Pierce depicts a wayfarer with a wagonload of timber and rocks, representing the worldly burden which he must cast off to reach Christ at the summit. The wagon, guided by a preacher, is pulled by four oxen who strain and falter under the weight of their load. Above the travelers, a wide-eyed and wary owl is perched in a tree, probably to symbolize the vigilance that must accompany this heavenward mission.[3]

All the while the serpent is underfoot, lying in wait beneath the wagon, negotiating his way among travelers to champion life's easy pleasures. Appropriately, the viewer's attention is called to an array of dangers portrayed in the lower half of the panel: At the bottom left two men gossip; to the right a preacher and a woman tryst in a porchlike setting; beyond the couple are money, cards, dice, liquor, a fancy car, and an all-American woman, part beauty queen, part Dallas Cowboys cheerleader. All are seen by the artist as temptations. Among these are representatives of the animal kingdom evoking biblical and folkloric associations. The goat is a guilt offering (see *Scape Goat*, cat. no. 38).[4] The pig is also a sacrificial animal.[5] The lion, a ferocious and prideful character in many African American narratives, is contrasted with the elephant, who is ponderous and weak of mind; the surefooted lion seems better suited for this journey.

Crowning the work at the top center of the panel is an eagle with its wings outstretched as in several other three-dimensional representations of the bird carved by Pierce. With its strength of purpose, swiftness of flight, and accuracy of sight, the eagle conjures up images of God's power and omniscience. It may also be a metaphor for the soul, since its wings can seemingly bear it above earthly tribulations.

1. According to Erskine Peters, professor of English at the University of Notre Dame, there was a strong impulse toward moral education in public schools in the South during Pierce's youth. An edition of *Pilgrim's Progress*, in contemporary English was most likely on the required reading list for many elementary or junior high school students. In addition, Pierce was probably familiar with religious dramas such as *Heaven Bound* and *In the Rapture* that were performed in African American churches in the 1930s. Like *Pilgrim's Progress*, these dramas include characters named after their role in the narrative. Characters such as the Determined Soul, the Reformed Drunkard, and the Hypocrite are tempted by the Devil in their pilgrimage (in the play, they make their pilgrimage by walking down the church aisle) toward the gates of Heaven. See William H. Wiggins, Jr., "Pilgrims, Crosses, and Faith: The Folk Dimensions of *Heaven Bound*," in James V. Hatch and Michael S. Weaver, eds., "The Black Church and the Black Theater," a special edition of *Black American Literature Forum* 25 (Spring 1991): 93-100.

2. See John Bunyan, retold by James H. Thomas, *Pilgrim's Progress in Today's English* (Chicago: Moody Press, 1964), pp. 44ff.

3. The vigilant owl is the principal subject of Pierce's *Owl in Tree* (cat. no. 37). The owl may also symbolize misfortune or death in folk belief. See Iona Opie and Moira Tatem, *A Dictionary of Superstitions* (New York: Oxford University Press, 1989), pp. 295–296.

4. The goat as a sin offering is mentioned, for example, in Leviticus 16:7–22.

5. In Aesop's fable "The Pig and the Sheep," the sheep needs only to sacrifice its wool, but the farmer wants the whole pig for its bacon.

alents: a woman holds a strainer above which a gnat hovers; a man with a camel balanced on his knee consumes the animal head first. As in many African American folktales, humor is used to enhance the didactic purpose of the work. The pill of moral truth is more easily swallowed when one can laugh at the very seriousness of the message.[3]

1. Another version is illustrated in Bernard Danenberg Galleries, cover.

2. Jones and Kook.

3. The African American storyteller's technique of spinning elaborate fictions that simultaneously convey a serious message is explained in *Afro-American Folk Tales*, ed. Roger D. Abrahams (New York: Pantheon Books, 1985), pp. 5ff.

141. **Parable of the Gnat and the Camel,**
1974   Colorplate 58
Carved and painted wood relief
18¼ × 17⅝ (46.4 × 44.8)
Collection of Jeffrey Wolf and Jeany
Nisenholz-Wolf

In this carving, of which there are at least two versions,[1] Pierce depicts the parable of the gnat and the camel from Matthew 23:24–28: "Ye blind guides which strain at a gnat and swallow a camel! . . . Ye also outwardly appear righteous unto men, but within ye are full of hypocrisy and iniquity." Pierce told the story often, describing hypocrisy in contemporary terms:

> You've heard people say "I don't do this and I don't do that"—in the daytime. But let the sun go down and [people] get behind closed doors and they'll do almost anything; swallowing a camel at night, straining at a gnat in the nighttime.[2]

In this carved rendition of the parable, Pierce literally translates the biblical words into their visual equiv-

142.   **Crocodile and Unwary Cow,**
ca. 1945   Colorplate 59
Carved and painted wood relief with glitter
12¾ × 25¼ (32.4 × 64.1)
Private Collection

143.   **Man Being Chased by Lion and Rhino,** 1928
Carved and painted wood relief with glitter,
mounted on painted panel
14¼ × 24 (36.2 × 60)
Collection of Jeffrey Wolf and Jeany
Nisenholz-Wolf

144. Safari, 1940
Carved and painted wood relief mounted on
painted corrugated cardboard
13 × 22 (33.0 × 55.9)
Collection of Lee Garrett

The theme of the chase, or of being pursued, is one that threads throughout Pierce's work, occurring not only in his animal images but in autobiographical works such as *Elijah Escapes the Mob* (whereabouts unknown) and in moral reliefs such as *Nixon Chased by Inflation* (private collection) and *Nixon Being Driven from the White House* (cat. no. 82).

Images of pursuit are used in these three works to convey a moral lesson in vigilance, a popular theme in African American folktales.[1] In all three works a fleeing victim is chased by larger, swifter, or more dangerous animals.[2] As is so often the case in African American narratives, the reliefs show us how not to behave: don't be unwary, or you may not survive. A fact of life, according to many African American stories, is that the world is a dangerous place in which one survives only by one's wits. The wise are alert to enticements and traps that may lie ahead and never allow themselves to be seduced or caught off guard like the pursued figures in Pierce's reliefs.

Pierce seems to have intended the figure in *Man Chased by Lion and Rhino* (cat. no. 143) to represent a white man. In the context of the African American folktale tradition, the relief may allude to the Master John stories of the Old South which specifically parodied the curious, and often foolish, behavior of whites as seen from a black perspective.[3]

1. Pierce was also aware of the biblical injunction (Matt. 25:1–13) to always be vigilant for the Second Coming of the Lord, which is the subject of his carving *The Wise and Foolish Virgins and the Man with the Clean and Soiled Heart* (cat. no. 170).

2. The image of a horse being pursued in *Safari* is related to Pierce's carving *Wild Horses and the Barbershop* (or *Barbershop with Mustangs*); see illus. in Bašičević et al., p. 248. The bottom relief shows a mustang pony being attacked from behind by another animal.

3. For a discussion and examples of Master John stories, see *Afro-American Folktales: Stories from Black Traditions in the New World*, ed. Roger D. Abrahams (New York: Pantheon Books, 1985), pp. 265–295.

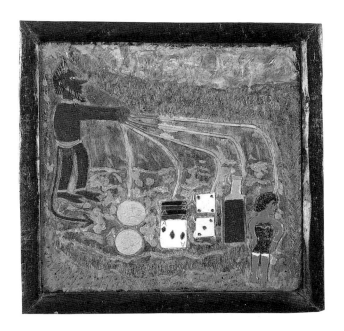

145. Devil Fishing, n.d.   Colorplate 60
Carved and painted wood relief with glitter
18 × 18 (45.7 × 45.7)
Collection of Mr. and Mrs. Meyer P. Potamkin

Pierce alternately credits a barbershop customer or a preacher as sources for this story. As frequently occurs in his telling of a tale, Pierce validates the story by relating it to his own life experience:

> Devil decided to go fishing. And he knew within himself to have luck—success—fishing, he had to have good bait. So he decided he'd bait his hook with money, cards, dice, whiskey, and a woman. And he knew he would catch some or all of us. I got caught, and a whole lot of others.[1]

In Pierce's carved translation of the story, the vices of lust for money, gambling, drinking, and womanizing are used as enticements by a fiery red Satan. His pointed extremities, from peaked hair and long nose to cloven hoof and arrow-headed tail, embody his sinister, bestial nature. Satan has cast his line without benefit of a real fishing pole. Instead, the lines to money, cards, dice, liquor, and a bathing beauty are brought forth from his fingertips—as though he were conjuring from devilish powers the bait of human weakness.

Pierce's presentation is bold, bright, and glittering; the lesson is self-evident. This is one of two known versions of the devil-fishing theme;[2] a work with a similar concept is *The Pickup* (cat. no. 146). The devil also appears in such works as *Picking Wild Berries* (cat. no. 9) and *Crucifixion* (cat. no. 99). Money, cards, and other symbols of human vulnerability are seen in such works as *Pilgrim's Progress* (cat. no. 140), *Father Time Racing* (cat. no. 156), and *Preaching Stick* (cat. no. 15).

1. From *Artists Among Us.*
2. Another version is reproduced in *Elijah Pierce, Wood Carver,* unpaginated.

146.   **The Pickup,** 1973   Colorplate 61
Carved and painted wood relief with glitter
15³/₈ × 23¹/₂ (39 × 59.7)
Collection of Margot Wolf

In *The Pickup,* Pierce has improvised on the devil-fishing theme (see *Devil Fishing,* cat. no. 145). Instead of showing the cunning devil baiting his hook with a woman, Pierce portrayed two merry menfolk who have hooked one by means of a huge fishing pole. The great flowering bush that separates the bikini-clad beauty from these gallivanters only entices them with thoughts of hidden delights and expectations.

The woman, standing behind the bushes, is at once demure and coquettish as she strikes a bathing-suit-contest pose. The tall rose beside her is suggestive of

passion, and it appears in other lustier works (for example, *The Kiss,* cat. no. 74). As the object of desire, the woman is the pickup. Visual and word punning are favorite narrative devices used by Pierce. The catchy phrase coupled with humorous presentation points a firm yet genial finger at lascivious behavior.

147.   **You Can Lead a Horse to Water But You Can't Make Him Drink,** 1973
Carved and painted wood relief with graphite and rhinestones
10¹/₂ × 20 (26.7 × 50.7)
Collection of Dr. and Mrs. Gerhard E. Martin

The popular proverb "you can lead a horse to water but you can't make him drink" is here presented in pictorial translation. The idea for the subject came from a newspaper illustration.[1] Man and horse, with their jaws set, are pitted against one another. Small strains against large, plaid competes with polka dots, concentrated effort meets smug resistance. The absurdity of the poses and the antics of the struggle recall the prankishness of African American folktales. The work also shows an affinity with cartoon animation and comedy routines from television and film—mass-media sources from which Pierce would freely draw to convey a message. Pierce's interpretation of the proverb is full of good-natured humor. He delights in the storytelling itself and charms his audience with the vitality of the action.

1. Wolf interview.

148. **Don't Bite the Hand that Feeds You,** 1960s
Carved wood relief
5 × 6 (12.8 × 15.2)
Collection of Howard and Mimi Chenfeld

In this small carving, the saying "don't bite the hand that feeds you" is described with monumental feeling. Instead of color, Pierce used gesture and silhouette as the expressive means to evoke the drama of ingratitude: the snarls and growls of the biting dogs are frightful; the sizable bat is believably aggressive. Likewise, the gift-giving gesture of hands offering sustenance is forthright and deliberate. The man and his dogs are dwarfed by the large hands, as if the humbling experience of the admonition has made them feel small. In pose and purpose, the outstretched hands recall the hands of mercy in Pierce's *Picking Wild Berries* (cat. nos. 9 and 166).

149. **Hear No, See No, Speak No Evil,** 1972
Carved and painted wood relief
9½ × 11⅛ (24 × 28.1)
Private Collection

The monkey figures prominently in both African American and Western European narrative and visual traditions. As a medium of amusement, ridicule, and ultimately of moralizing, the monkey often serves as a surrogate human. The animal's mischievous powers of imitation mirror man's actions, making the lessons of his foibles more palatable.

In *Hear No, See No, Speak No Evil,* three monkeys mimic the familiar phrase in a cameo appearance from the larger, more complex work, *The Monkey Family* (cat.

no. 154). Below the trio, the gesture of each monkey is paired with a depiction of its sensory source—ear, eye, and mouth—which, isolated from the face, strongly delineated and brightly painted, are impressive theatrical devices. In a dynamic delivery, Pierce's simultaneous presentation of action and sensory symbol makes the message doubly understood and enjoyed.

150. **Pride,** ca. 1925
Carved and painted wood figures and plastic greenery mounted on corrugated cardboard outlined in graphite with collage additions (color magazine illustrations)
19⅞ × 23⅞ (50.4 × 60.8)
Columbus Museum of Art: Gift of the Artist

Pride was Pierce's single gift to the Columbus Museum of Art, presented in 1974. The word "pride" tops a scene of animals and people tumbling downward to a catastrophic end, represented by the figure of a man lying prostrate on the lower edge of the frame. This precarious assemblage of figures illustrates Proverbs 16:18, ''Pride goeth before destruction, and an haughty spirit before a fall.''[1] Visible among the toppling creatures are a peacock at the lower left, a symbol of pride (''proud as a peacock''), and two goats butting heads at the upper center, a symbol of rudeness (''always butting in''). Two gossiping women seated above the fallen man symbolize Pierce's belief that gossip, often provoked by jealousy, is especially evil. A guardian angel—perhaps Pierce's angel of conscience (which appears in *Picking Wild Berries*, cat. no. 9)—stands over the scene.[2]

While it depicts Pierce's interpretation of the biblical proverb, *Pride* is also a personal admission of Pierce's own undoing from prideful behavior. Below the word ''pride'' Pierce depicted a pair of hands—his own—placing the right hand next to a knot in the wood.[3] To Pierce, the darkness of the knot approximated the color his right hand once turned when he carved an unworthy subject.[4] Only when he was sorry, he said, did his hand—pure black from fingertip to wrist—return to its normal color.

1. The use of biblical sayings is especially prevalent in the South. See Charles Joyner, ''Proverbs,'' in Charles Reagan Wilson and William Ferris, eds., *Encyclopedia of Southern Culture* (Chapel Hill: The University of North Carolina Press, 1989), p. 516.

2. The meaning of *Pride* was explained by the Pierces during a visit to the Columbus Museum of Art on September 19, 1980 (Seibert notes, Columbus Museum of Art archives).

3. Pierce also used knots in wood in a symbolic way in *Book of Wood* (cat. no. 100, panel 2, verso), where he described the healing of the sick. At the upper right, a man with crutches, who does not believe in Christ's healing powers, has a knot of doubt before his eyes. In the opposite corner at the upper left, a woman with faith has put doubt behind her (the knot appears behind her head) and casts away her crutch (from Seibert interview, October 31, 1980).

4. See Almon, 1979, p. 11.

151. **Three Ways to Send a Message: Telephone, Telegram, Tell-a-Woman,** n.d.   Colorplate 62
Carved and painted wood relief
15¹⁄₂ × 18 (39.4 × 45.8)
Collection of Julie Hall

152. **Three Ways to Send a Message: Telephone, Telegram, Tell-a-Woman,** 1980   Colorplate 63
Carved and painted wood relief with glitter
11³⁄₄ × 33 (29.8 × 83.8)
Collection of Robert M. Greenberg

Pierce again turned to the subject of gossip in his *Telephone, Telegram, Tell-a-Woman* carvings. The earliest known version (cat. no. 151) combines the main theme with a portrait and a message sign. The left panel illustrates ways to communicate messages—and by implication gossip—by means of a bicycling messenger, a woman talking on the telephone, and a man and a woman conversing. In the right panel is a portrait of George Washington Carver (ca. 1864–1943), the renowned African American educator, surrounded by the peanuts and sweet potatoes of his famed agricultural experiments. The sign ''Home,'' evoking thoughts of family and security, adorns the top of the panel. The trio of images is compositionally satisfying, yet contextually less interrelated than works with similar subject matter, such as *Monday Morning Gossip* (cat. no. 153).

In the later version of the subject (cat. no. 152), Pierce concentrated fully on visualizing the old saying that there are "three ways to get a message: telephone, telegram, and the third—the best—is to tell a woman."[1] The panel is divided into three equal parts, each illustrating a portion of the saying.

1. Jones and Kook.

153. **Monday Morning Gossip,** 1934   Colorplate 64
Carved and painted wood relief with glitter,
mounted on painted panel
33½ × 24⅛ (85.1 × 61.2)
Collection of Michael D. Hall

Pierce saw habitual gossip as indiscretion and wrongdoing. He turned to the theme often and communicated its message with varying degrees of warning in works such as *Pilgrim's Progress* (cat. no. 140), *Pride* (cat. no. 150), and *Three Ways to Send a Message: Telephone, Telegram, Tell-a-Woman* (cat. nos. 151 and 152). In *Monday Morning Gossip* Pierce concerned himself with the

effects of various kinds of behaviors involving speech, among these idle gossip.

At the top of the carving, in a rare interior setting, two maids prattle on the job, leaving a bed unmade and food on the kitchen stove. It is the memorable stance of a particular gossiper that he has depicted in this scene, as he recalled a gossiping woman from his neighborhood who stood across the street with one hand on her hip and one hand raised, "giving the lowdown."[1]

Below the gossipers stands a man with his hand locked in the mouth of a lion. The entrapment illustrates an adage used by one of Pierce's barbershop customers, who said, "When you get your hand in the lion's mouth you have to work easy." Pierce moralized, "Be careful and slow with life. Talk things out and work them out."[2] Talk here becomes a positive endeavor rather than a meddlesome pastime.

At the lower right, a well-dressed man is portrayed with a piece of wood lodged in his eye. Like *Parable of the Gnat and the Camel* (cat. no. 141), this segment gives a direct visual translation of a biblical passage as a reminder about hypocrisy: "Judge not, that ye be not judged. . . . Why beholdest thou the mote that is in thy brother's eye, but considerest not the beam that is in thine own eye?" (Matt. 7:1–3). The man points to the eye of his companion with a gesture that mirrors that of the gossiping maid above. Action and talk at the expense of others are thus compared.

The three commentaries on behavior are arranged beside two images of love—one of a monkey who raised a human baby as its own, the other an embracing couple flanked by cranes, which are known to mate for life. Five individual reliefs inform one another as collages of Pierce's own thoughts. Like a storyteller or preacher, he strings pearls of wisdom together with parables and anecdotes, alternating the familiar with the extraordinary and making his message felt with a good measure of sentiment and gentle exhortation.

1. Wolf interview.
2. Ibid.

154. **The Monkey Family,** 1942   Colorplate 65
Carved and painted wood relief with glitter,
mounted on painted corrugated cardboard
31⅞ × 25⅜ (80.9 × 64.5)
Columbus Museum of Art: Museum Purchase

The Monkey Family hung for many years alongside *Monday Morning Gossip* (cat. no. 153) on a wall of Pierce's

independent of conventional moral meanings. The monkey is a trickster, a creature who loves to stir up mischief for its own sake. At the upper right, a mother's satisfied, after-meal nap will soon come to an end as her young prepare to swat the fly on her head with a large club. Above her, a monkey grabs for his companion's drinking cup as he and his friends partake of a tasty meal. At the upper left, two monkeys engage the assistance of an elephant to spray water from its trunk for a baby monkey's bath. The resourceful monkey is often paired with the elephant in African American folktales. Portrayed as physically strong but mentally weak, the elephant is easily manipulated to do the monkey's bidding.[5]

1. Seibert interview, October 31, 1980.
2. See discussion of "signifying," cat. no. 30, n. 1.
3. Seibert interview, October 31, 1980.
4. Ibid.
5. Numerous toasts which feature the monkey and elephant are found in Bruce A. Jackson, *"Get Your Ass in the Water and Swim Like Me": Narrative Poetry from Black Oral Tradition* (Cambridge, Massachusetts: Harvard University Press, 1974), pp. 161–179; and Roger D. Abrahams, *Deep Down in the Jungle . . . Negro Narrative Folklore from the Streets of Philadelphia* (Chicago: Aldine Publishing Company, 1970), pp. 113–119.

barbershop. It is, like its pendant, a collage of smaller relief carvings illustrating humorous, often moralizing, anecdotes from the animal kingdom. "It's good to lecture from," Pierce said of this work,[1] which he sometimes called *Monkey See, Monkey Do*. His elaborate narratives, enacted by animals personifying human characters, were a special delight to the children who visited him.

The nineteen monkeys portrayed in this work are endowed with the same craftiness, wit, and resourcefulness frequently attributed to them in African American folktales, toasts, and signifying narratives, in which serious concerns are addressed in mainly humorous terms.[2] At the lower left, for example, two monkeys are jealous of a third, who has a longer tail. As the two jealous monkeys prepare to sever the envied long tail, the owner of it bites off the tail of the ax-wielding opportunist. The moral of the story is, in Pierce's words, "Sometimes you get your own tail cut off trying to cut off somebody else's. So you got to watch."[3] In a scene at the lower right, another trio of monkeys mimes the old adage "hear no evil, see no evil, speak no evil," which Pierce expressed as "see nothin', hear nothin', say nothin'."[4] In Pierce's version, the monkeys feign lack of awareness and thereby relieve themselves of any burden of accountability or responsibility. Thus do the artful simians embody plain truths with simplicity and candor.

On the other hand, monkeys are a vehicle by which the artist can describe a nonsensical virtuosity that is

155. **Pearl Harbor and the African Queen,**
1941   Colorplate 57
Carved and painted wood relief with glitter
23¼ × 27 (59.1 × 68.6)
Milwaukee Art Museum, The Michael and Julie Hall
Collection of American Folk Art

Four individual relief carvings are joined together in *Pearl Harbor and the African Queen,* one of Pierce's most iconographically complex works. The carving was completed after the surprise attack by the Japanese on Pearl Harbor, December 7, 1941, which brought the United States into World War II.[1] At the upper right, a Japanese diplomatic envoy, having the assault already in mind, has lulled Uncle Sam into complacency, promising him that Japan has no hostile intentions. Utterly deceived, Uncle Sam points an angry finger at the envoy and gestures skyward as the bombs drop on the anchored fleet. To the left, a man and woman flanking a portrait of President Franklin D. Roosevelt represent the youth of America.[2] They respond to Uncle Sam's call and enlist, against the backdrop of an American flag.

At the lower left, Pierce illustrated the Aesop fable "The Dog and the Shadow." The dog holding a bone sees a larger bone in the stream and opens his mouth to grasp it. As a result he loses both bones, recalling Aesop's moral, "Greed begets nothing." By means of this illustration, Pierce commented on Japan's greed for control of the South Pacific islands. The fable is also paired with another story of a tempting reflection, the tale of the African queen who looked in a mirror for the first time and "saw herself as she was and not as she wanted [to be]."[3] The story alludes to the pride and vanity of the Japanese aggressors.

The carving, with its prominent message "duty," speaks eloquently of Pierce's belief in the moral obligations of people and nations. In a well-informed commentary, highly charged with historical, folk, and literary references, Pierce pleads for political vigilance and deplores the vagaries of war begotten of power, vainglory, and self-importance. He saw loyalty to one's country as an essential aspect of citizenship, a subject he treated in *Presidents and Convicts* (cat. no. 67), carved about the same time.[4]

1. Although the work is dated 1941, the aftershock of the attack was not felt by the U.S. public until the first months of 1942. It is possible, therefore, that Pierce actually carved the work in 1942 or thereafter.

2. Pierce identified the figure in the center of the panel as Roosevelt in interviews with Michael Hall in the early 1970s. Some scholars, unaware of Pierce's identification of the portrait, have interpreted the figure as an Everyman symbol.

3. Seibert interview, October 29, 1980.

4. There was a feeling among some African Americans that their support should be given to Japan, a "colored empire." John Oliver Killens discusses this belief in his World War II novel *And Then We Heard the Thunder* (Washington, D.C.: Howard University Press, 1983). Whether or not Pierce was aware of this belief is unknown. But the fable of the dog and the bone may suggest that African Americans must not be tempted to "drop the bone" of democracy for the promise of a better life. It was the patriotic duty of all African Americans to remain loyal to their country in wartime. Such was the message of countless political cartoons and editorials in African American weekly newspapers during World War II.

Pearl Harbor and the African Queen has inspired yet other interpretations, in addition to those which Pierce spoke of in interviews. To William H. Wiggins, Indiana University, for example, the word "duty" underscores a plea for racial and patriotic unity in America, calling to mind the Double V Campaign—victory against fascism abroad and racism at home—conducted by the National Association for the Advancement of Colored People and the *Pittsburgh Courier.*

156.　**African Queen and the Mirror,** 1980
Carved and painted wood relief with glitter, rhinestones, and gold reflective plastic
$17^{3}/_{8} \times 22^{15}/_{16}$ (44.2 × 58.3)
Columbus Museum of Art: Museum Purchase

There was a queen in Africa who had thousands of subjects. And there was a missionary lady who had a little mirror she used to tidy up. Now the queen didn't know about this mirror; she thought she was the greatest and most beautiful woman in the world with all her fine dressing and gold earrings, but she had never seen herself as others saw her. She saw one of the girls looking in the mirror and wanted to know what it was; so they carried it to her. And she looked in it and saw that others were more beautiful than she was—and issued a law that if anyone else was caught with a mirror they would be punished to death. . . . If only some people could see themselves as others see them.[1]

The story of the vain African queen who discovers her true self in her own reflection was a favorite of Pierce's. Pierce said of the African queen story, "It's true to life. A lot of people think they look better than they do. . . . I've lectured on that so much. That's a wonderful lesson."[2] The lesson was carved more than once, the most notable example being *Pearl Harbor and the African Queen* (cat. no. 155).

In this late version, however, the crowned and bejeweled queen of grand proportions is enthroned before her mirror reflection. Upon her are the eyes of all her subjects, whom Pierce envisioned being dressed in choir robes. The visual potency of Pierce's gridlike, repetitive patterning raises the narrative pitch of the story. In a crescendo of eyes and mouths framed by white collars, the chorus of faces seems to sing the queen's praises and yet mock her newfound uncomeliness.[3]

1. Columbus Gallery of Fine Arts, unpaginated.

2. Seibert interview, October 29, 1980.

3. The story of the African queen certainly recalls, and may be related to, the Euro-American *Snow White and the Seven Dwarfs*. We are reminded of the "Mirror, mirror on the wall" refrain from the fairy tale.

157. **Grim Reaper,** 1974   Colorplate 66
Carved and painted wood relief with glitter
15 × 11 (38.1 × 28.0)
Collection of Roger McLane

158. **Father Time,** 1975
Carved and painted wood relief
14⅝ × 10⅛ (37.0 × 25.9)
Columbus Museum of Art: Museum Purchase

159.   **Father Time Racing,** 1959   Colorplate 67
Carved and painted wood relief with glitter
13 × 29 (33.0 × 73.7)
Collection of Julie Hall

With his heart and mind set on a virtuous life and the glories of salvation, Pierce was rarely preoccupied with the inevitability of death. Yet when he did take up the subject, death's knock clearly resonated in his carvings. *Grim Reaper* is one of Pierce's most unnerving works. Death stands cloaked and hooded, not as a skeleton but as man's ghostly reflection. He holds up a great scythe with which to cut life short. Transfixed by his large eyes and the vacant stares of twenty-six skulls that line his doorway, the viewer is reminded that there is no avoiding Death. Time, Death's messenger, is also hooded in *Father Time* and has wings to indicate life's fleeting passage. Presented in the context of the Ages of Man, Time, bearded and leaning heavily on a walking stick, personifies Old Age.

In *Father Time Racing,* Pierce favors the vitality and improvisation of narrative, and he again turns to contemporary life for inspiration. Father Time dispenses with wings and walking stick, dons sporting attire, and takes up his scythe. He challenges man to a marathon race of life, running from sin to a heavenly finish line. Speed is gauged by no less than five images of Father Time dashing fleet of foot past the crowd of runners. His frequent appearance illustrates the adage, "time repeats itself." The passage of time is measured historically by the written names, left to right, of biblical characters from Adam, the first man, to John, who foretold the climactic events of the future Apocalypse. As Pierce tells the story, Father Time challenges a champion runner to race him.[1] The contest between Father Time and the champion drives home Pierce's message that Father Time is not to be outdone by anyone.

There was a champion who'd won every race he'd ever run. One day an old man came along; he heard about this champion and wanted to run a race with him. The champion said he thought it was ridiculous: "An old man wants to run a race with me, and I am the champion." But the old man just insisted. So finally they decided to run the race; the champion just dashed off and went about his business. The old man came on behind; but as they got closer to the end, the old man began to creep up. As they continued, the champion looked around, and the old man was right behind him. And just before they got to the end of the line, the old man went on past, and won the race. And the champion was so undone, he went to the old man and asked him "Who are you? Where did you come from?" And the old man said, "Why son, don't you know who I am? My name is Father Time. I've been running for a long time, and I've never had nobody outrun me."[2]

1. It is possible that the champion—probably the black runner depicted at the upper right near the star—was meant to be Jesse Owens. Owens was the greatest track and field athlete of the first half of the twentieth century and a gold medalist at the 1936 Olympics in Berlin.
2. Columbus Gallery of Fine Arts, unpaginated.

PIERCE, THE UNIVERSAL MAN

160.   **Before Death All Are Equal,**
1946–1947   Colorplate 68
Carved and painted wood relief
13½ × 13⁵/₁₆ (34.3 × 33.8)
Columbus Museum of Art: Gift of Mr. and
Mrs. Boris Gruenwald

162.   **Crime Don't Pay,** ca. 1955   Colorplate 69
Carved and painted wood relief
13½ × 11 (34.3 × 28.0)
Collection of Dr. Alan Jay Ominsky

161.   **Buzzard,** 1948
Carved and painted wood relief mounted
on painted corrugated cardboard
16 × 12⅞ (40.1 × 32.8)
Collection of Mr. and Mrs. Meyer P. Potamkin

163.   **Angel,** 1948
Carved and painted wood relief mounted
on painted corrugated cardboard
18 × 11¾ (45.7 × 29.8)
Collection of Jill and Sheldon Bonovitz

164.   **Spreading the Light,** 1933
Carved and painted wood relief mounted
on painted panel
16 × 7³/₈ (40.7 × 18.7)
Private Collection

165.   **Saul on the Road to Damascus,**
1948   Colorplate 70
Carved and painted wood relief mounted
on painted board
25¹/₈ × 13¹/₄ (63.7 × 33.6)
The Schumacher Gallery, Capital University,
Columbus, Ohio

These six works were components of the diptych *Death on the Level,* which once included nineteen relief carvings. After appearing in early exhibitions of Pierce's work in 1971 and 1972, this diptych was dismantled by November 1973, when *Before Death All Are Equal* appeared as an independent relief in the first exhibition of Pierce's work at the Columbus Museum of Art. A photograph of the diptych shows that Pierce did not disassemble the diptych all at once, but only as the need arose. *Spreading the Light* and other reliefs are missing in the photograph, leaving only the outline where they once were placed. All the reliefs in the original diptych individually and in loose association with one another elucidate the twin themes of death and judgment. In keeping with Pierce's integrated approach to his diptychs, the subjects of the reliefs range from biblical stories and moralistic advice to symbolic animals.

The power of death is epitomized in the diptych by *Before Death All Are Equal,* in which a skeleton standing atop a coffin in a cemetery welcomes four men balanced on a scale, whom Pierce identified as ranging from the richest to the poorest.[1] *Buzzard,* depicting the scavenger bird associated with death in popular folklore, originally appeared below this relief. On the opposite panel were carvings of the Grim Reaper and a scene of one animal being attacked by another, continuing the theme of death.

The association of death with judgment is represented by the relief *Crime Don't Pay,* which shows

Death on the Level diptych.
Photograph by Jeffrey Wolf

below its painted message a man in the electric chair and other criminals peering out from behind bars. Pierce originally juxtaposed *Crime Don't Pay* with a scene of Blind Justice weighing someone on a scale, and he placed these two reliefs near a sword-bearing angel of vengeance and *Spreading the Light,* an image of a figure who upholds what is no doubt meant to be the light of truth and justice.

The idea of judgment leading to the death of one way of life and the birth of a new one is expressed in the biblical subjects in the diptych. *Saul on the Road to Damascus* relates the dramatic story of Saul's conversion (Acts 9:1–18); in particular it focuses on the moment in the story when Saul (Paul's name before he became a Christian) is struck blind by God. In Pierce's version of the story, a bolt of lightning is accompanied by a witnessing angel, who demands to know why Saul is persecuting Christ. Below this relief in the original diptych Pierce placed the image of Christ praying in the Garden of Gethsemane, just before Judas betrayed him.

1. Seibert interview, September 19, 1980.

167. **Flowers,** 1948
Carved and painted wood relief with glitter, mounted on panel
16½ × 13½ (41.9 × 34.3)
Private Collection, Courtesy Keny Galleries, Inc.

166. **Picking Wild Berries,** n.d.
Carved and painted wood with glitter, mounted on painted corrugated cardboard
37¼ × 17⅝ (94.6 × 44.7)
Collection of Jeffrey Wolf and Jeany Nisenholz-Wolf

168. **Coming of Christ,** n.d.   Colorplate 71
Carved and painted wood relief with glitter
27⅛ × 18½ (68.9 × 47.0)
Columbus Museum of Art: Museum Purchase

These three works (cat. nos. 166–168) were components of the diptych *Redemption,* which was still intact in early 1973 when it appeared in the Peale House exhibition at the Pennsylvania Academy of the Fine Arts. It is considerably less ambitious than the diptych *Death on the Level* (cat. nos. 160–165). *Redemption* originally included six reliefs, most of which exist in other versions in Pierce's work. In this diptych Pierce explores

Redemption diptych

169.   **Bible Stories,** n.d.   Colorplate 72
Carved and painted wood relief with glitter,
mounted on board faced with painted crepe
paper
Each panel 58¼ × 23¼ (148.0 × 59.0)
Private Collection

the theme of redemption in several ways. In addition to the religious subjects, as in *Coming of Christ* and *God's Plenty* (private collection), Pierce includes a carving of flowers. Taking into account Pierce's explanation of the meaning of *Anniversary Flowers* (cat. no. 72), it is possible to see these flowers as a personal emblem symbolizing redemption through love. A definite autobiographical reference is included in *Picking Wild Berries,* which depicts Pierce being saved from temptation by the "hands of hope" (which also appear in *Picking Wild Berries,* cat. no. 9) as he tries to reach his guardian angel on the far side of the cliff. The subject and present location of the relief that was originally placed below *Picking Wild Berries* in the diptych are unknown. However, a surviving photograph of the complete diptych indicates it has either an autobiographical or a moralizing subject, for it features figures in front of a little white house accompanied by symbols of vice such as liquor and money.

Bible Stories is the only surviving large-scale diptych known to have been assembled by Pierce. Like *Death on the Level* (cat. nos. 160–165), it is composed of nineteen reliefs. Its dominant subject matter ranges from Old Testament scenes such as David playing his harp, David slaying Goliath, Noah's ark, and Daniel in the lion's den to New Testament scenes such as the three wise men, Christ among the doctors, Christ washing the feet of the apostles, and Christ as the door to salvation (from the Book of Revelation). A unifying theme seems less apparent in this work than in the other diptychs. Like the other two diptychs, this includes loosely related scenes from varied contexts, thus asserting once again the power of Pierce's integrated vision.

The image in the upper right corner of the right panel depicts African American actor Richard B. Harrison in his role as "de Lawd" in the play *Green Pastures,* a subject that Pierce also incorporated into his autobiographical relief *The Little White Church* (cat. no. 3). Pierce depicts Harrison in the costume he wore in the play, on a stage strewn with bouquets of flowers, being applauded by a multitude of hands.

Pierce also includes in the diptych an elaborate moral commentary on the joys and sorrows of marriage in a relief at the left. Under the spreading branches of a tree, its trunk inscribed with a heart and its crown topped by an all-seeing eye, stand two couples. The man and woman at the left struggle with their backs to each other, determined to escape the chain that binds them together, while the couple at the right embrace and move forward together. On the branches of the tree Pierce inscribed the virtues and corresponding vices that relate to these opposing views of marital life.

At least two of the reliefs have autobiographical significance for the artist. Below and slightly to the left of the marriage relief, Pierce carved a birds-eye view of a landscape which he identified as a revival meeting that took place in Ohio. Pierce also identified the mother and child as his own mother and himself.[1]

1. Communication (April 1, 1992) from the owner, who purchased the work from Pierce.

170. **The Wise and Foolish Virgins and the Man with the Clean and Soiled Heart,** n.d.   Colorplate 73
Carved and painted wood relief with glitter
39³/₈ × 28⁷/₈ (100.0 × 73.3)
Collection of Sarah and John Freeman

The theme of this multiple relief panel is the just rewards of faith and vigilance. As in the diptychs, Pierce has created a subtle dynamic among the reliefs, which enriches their individual meanings within the context of the panel. The upper relief depicts the par-

able of the wise and foolish virgins (Matt. 25:1–13), who symbolize the importance of being constantly vigilant and always prepared for the coming of the Lord. According to the parable, ten virgins went out with their lamps to meet the bridegroom. Five of the virgins wisely brought extra oil for their lamps; five did not. The bridegroom was delayed and the virgins laid down and slept while they waited. When the cry went forth at midnight to announce the groom's approach, the five foolish virgins had no oil and left in search of more. Upon their return they found the door barred with the wise virgins already inside. When the foolish virgins asked to enter, the bridegroom responded that he did not know them.

Pierce depicts the story in two registers. The virgins in the upper register are seen slumbering as they wait for the bridegroom. Below them at the left are the five wise virgins preparing their lamps for the approaching bridegroom while the five foolish virgins are shown setting out in search of oil.

In the sections below the wise and foolish virgins, Pierce has paired two reliefs. At left is a depiction of the woman taken in adultery (John 8:3-12), who is seen kneeling at Christ's feet. Next to this is an image of a man holding a clean heart and a spotted heart. There are several references in Psalms and Proverbs to having one's heart cleansed of sin. The juxtaposition of these images stresses the need to be vigilant in the face of the sins of one's own heart. According to John, the people accusing the adulteress are "convicted by their own conscience" when Christ tells them that he who is without sin must cast the first stone. The theme of justice is again brought forth in an unidentified court scene depicted in the lower left panel. Paired with it, at the right, is an image of Christ raising Lazarus from his tomb. Here the vigilant faith of Martha and Mary brings their brother back to life.

Leroy Almon (b. 1938), in partnership with
Elijah Pierce

171. **Cruelty of Slavery,** n.d.
Carved and painted wood relief
27 × 27⁵/₈ (68.6 × 70.2)
Columbus Museum of Art: Museum Purchase

This carving is from the late period of Pierce's career when he acted as mentor for the aspiring young artist Leroy Almon and executed works in full partnership with Almon. Although this work is inscribed on the

back with the names of both Pierce and Almon, most scholars now attribute the majority of the carving to Almon, who was working under Pierce's influence.[1] The conception, tone, and carving technique all point to Almon as the primary artist. A child of the civil rights struggle of the 1960s, Almon had a view of slavery that was quite different from Pierce's. In works such as *Slavery Time* (cat. nos. 4 and 5), Pierce emphasized the promise of life after slavery. *Cruelty of Slavery* has a sharper, political edge, focusing on the cruel abuses of slavery and admonishing in the upper right-hand corner, "God is watching." Like Pierce, Almon seems to have drawn on popular culture for visual source material. The depiction of the slave being whipped and the image of the slave kneeling in chains bear strong resemblance to scenes in the 1977 television miniseries *Roots*, featuring Kunta Kinte, the character played by actor Levar Burton. Almon's carving style is more aggressive and schematic than Pierce's. On the whole, the surface of the relief is flatter—unlike Pierce's surfaces, which feature rounded forms—and the background is roughly carved away to accommodate the figures. Almon also makes extensive use of pencil outlines as a guide for incising details.

1. Another work, dating from 1980, *God Said Let Us Make Man* (private collection), which is carved in a style consistent with Almon's, is inscribed on the reverse "Elijah Pierce Teacher."

172. **The Image of Man,** n.d.
Carved and painted wood relief
24 × 9 (61.0 × 22.8)
Collection of Dr. and Mrs. Gerhard E. Martin

Totemic images of man occur in a number of Pierce's works, including *The Image of Man* and the very late work *The Whole Man* (Columbus Museum of Art). In both works Pierce stresses the role of the five senses in the "whole man," whose head appears at the top of the arrangement. Below the head, arranged in seemingly hierarchical order, are images of a heart, an eye, a hand, an ear, a nose, a mouth, and a foot. The totemic device is also used in Pierce's carved canes and ritualistic knife (cat. no. 58).

173. **Universal Man,** 1937   Colorplate 74
Carved and painted wood relief with glitter
16¾ × 28¾ (42.4 × 73.1)
Collection of Michael D. Hall

According to Pierce this haloed figure represents not Christ but the image of Everyman. Flanked by trees and a wall (perhaps meant to signify an enclosed garden setting) and surrounded by the eternal symbols of the sun, the moon, and the stars, the figure faces us with arms outstretched, seemingly embracing the universe. Pierce's firm belief that everything in life is connected makes the image of the universal man a particularly important symbol in his work. The concept of the "universal man" is central to Pierce's ambivalent attitude toward race in his reliefs. Pierce often said his figures were neither black nor white but represented all people.

CHRONOLOGY

MARGARET ARMBRUST SEIBERT

ca. 1863 — Richard Pierce, slave, is freed in Raleigh, North Carolina, and travels to Baldwyn, Mississippi. There he marries a woman named Mattie and has four children: Tom, Richard, Ella, and Carrie.

After Mattie's death, Richard Pierce marries Nellie Wallace.
(Seibert, conversation with Adeline Gilbert, artist's descendant, July 1991)

Richard Pierce is a farmer and church deacon.
(Columbus Gallery of Fine Arts, unpaginated)

1892 — March 5. Elijah Pierce is born in a log cabin on a farm on Lee Prather's plantation in Baldwyn, Mississippi. He is the third of four children (Willie, Jesse, Elijah, and Minnie) born to Richard and Nellie Wallace Pierce.
(Columbus Gallery of Fine Arts, unpaginated; Jones and Kook; *Artists Among Us;* Probate Court, Franklin County, Ohio, Marriage License Application, no. 65976, Sept. 8, 1923)

Early 1900s — Starts to carve.
(Crome, unpaginated; Garrett, 1972, p.17)

1908–1916 — Works as assistant to an elderly barber in Baldwyn. Manages the shop after the man's death. Also works in nearby Corinth at various establishments, including a hotel, a department store, and a barbershop.
(Livingston and Beardsley, p.117; Wolf interview; Wolf, notes from conversations with Pierce family members, 1981)

1911 — April 14. Born to Elijah Pierce and Carrie Beene, a son, Arthur, in Baldwyn, Mississippi.
(Seibert, conversations with Zetta Pierce and Adeline Gilbert, artist's descendants, July 1991)

ca. 1912 — Carves a walking stick from a piece of hickory—the first thing he remembered carving as a boy besides pictures of animals on tree trunks.
(Garrett and Lentz, p. 123)

ca. 1913 — July 4. Arrested in Tupelo, Mississippi, and falsely accused of murdering a white man; records event in well-known carving *Elijah Escapes the Mob* (location unknown).
(Fennessy)

ca. 1914 — Converted in Mt. Zion Baptist Church in Baldwyn, Mississippi.
(Wolf interview)

ca. 1915   Marries Zetta Palm.
> (Probate Court, Franklin County, Ohio, Marriage License Application, no. 73044, May 28, 1952)

1915   November 14. Born to Elijah Pierce and Zetta Pierce a son, Willie Aaron, in Meridian, Mississippi.
> (Seibert, conversations with Alexis, Dana, Dorothy, and Zetta Pierce, artist's descendants, July 1991)

Death of Zetta Pierce soon after childbirth. Willie is raised by Zetta's mother.
> (Seibert, conversations with Dana and Dorothy Pierce, artist's descendants, July 1991)

1917   January 10. Death of Richard Pierce, Elijah Pierce's father.
> (Seibert, conversation with Adeline Gilbert, artist's descendant, July 1991)

ca. 1917–1920   Period of itinerant living; works on bridge gangs for the railroad, receives passes and travels to Memphis, St. Louis, and other cities.
> (Livingston and Beardsley, p. 117)

1920   September 26, 1920. Issued preacher's license from Mt. Zion Baptist Church, Baldwyn, Mississippi.

early 1920s   Lives in Champaign, then in Danville, Illinois, where he meets Cornelia West Houeston (born April 2, 1886).
> (Columbus Gallery of Fine Arts, unpaginated)

1923   Follows Cornelia Houeston from Danville, Illinois, to Columbus, Ohio.

Marries Cornelia West Houeston. Pierce's occupation listed as barber; Cornelia's occupation listed as domestic.
> (Probate Court, Franklin County, Ohio, Marriage License Application and Marriage Certificate no. 65976, September 8, 1923)

September 9. Begins work as a barber for John T. Dixon.
> (Columbus Gallery of Fine Arts, unpaginated)

ca. 1923   Carves *The Little Elephant* (cat. no. 21) for his wife Cornelia.
> (Columbus Gallery of Fine Arts, unpaginated; Muller, p. 10)

1924   Works as a barber; resides at 1312 Hawthorn St.
> (*Columbus City Directory*, 1924).

1929   Works as a barber for John T. Dixon at 239 E. Naghten St., Columbus; resides at 239 St. Clair Ave.
> (*Columbus City Directory*, 1929)

1930–1931   Works as a barber at 390 E. Naghten St.; resides at 467 Galloway Ave.
> (*Columbus City Directory*, 1930, 1931)

ca. 1932   Completes *Book of Wood* (cat. no. 100).

1932–1938   Works as a barber at 395 E. Naghten St.; resides at 393 E. Naghten.
> (*Columbus City Directory*, 1932–1938)

1930s–1940s   Period of itinerant preaching; during summers displays his carvings at fairs, churches, and shops in Kentucky, Tennessee, Alabama, Mississippi, Kansas, Nebraska, Illinois, and Ohio.
> (Crome, unpaginated; Columbus Gallery of Fine Arts, unpaginated)

1940   Works as a barber for D. Ransome Jones at 518 Mt. Vernon Ave., site of John T. Dixon's shop in 1931–1932; resides at 71 N. Washington Ave.
(*Columbus City Directory,* 1940)

1941   Works as a barber for D. Ransome Jones at 520 Mt. Vernon Ave.; resides at 518 Mt. Vernon Ave.
(*Columbus City Directory,* 1941)

1943   Works as a barber for Willis Whaley at 518 E. Long St.; resides at 186 Jefferson Ave.
(*Columbus City Directory,* 1943)

ca. 1944–1947   Elijah and Cornelia Pierce hold "sacred art demonstrations" to explain the meaning of *Book of Wood* (cat. no. 100), by appointment at their home, 144 Everett St.
(Archives, Columbus Museum of Art)

1947   Joins Master Lodge 62, Ancient Free and Accepted Masons, Columbus.
(Archives, Master Lodge 62)

1948   February 8. Death of Cornelia Houeston Pierce, 61 years old, of cervical cancer in Columbus.
(Ohio Department of Health, Columbus; Certificate of Death, state file no. 8721)

ca. 1948   Death of Nellie Pierce, Elijah's mother.
(Seibert, conversation with Nellie Brookins, artist's descendant, July 1991)

1949   Works as a barber at 144 N. Everett Alley, which is also his residence.
(*Columbus City Directory,* 1949)

1950   Works as a barber for Elijah Eirack at 483 E. Long St.; Pierce and Eirack reside at 144 N. Everett Alley.
(*Columbus City Directory,* 1950)

1951–1969   Self-employed as a barber at 483 E. Long St.; resides at 144 N. Everett Alley.
(*Columbus City Directory,* 1951–1969)

Marries Estelle Greene, age 46.
(Probate Court, Franklin County, Ohio, Marriage License Application and Marriage Certificate no. 73044, June 2, 1952)

1967   Leaves Master Lodge 62, Ancient Free and Accepted Masons, Columbus.
(Archives, Master Lodge 62)

October 26. Ben Hayes publishes the first of many articles on Pierce's art in a local newspaper, *Columbus Citizen-Journal.*
(Hayes, 1967)

1968   Represented in exhibition, *Columbus Folk Art,* at YMCA, Columbus. Represented in exhibition, *International Art Festival,* at YWCA, Columbus.

1969   Begins to use a part of his shop as an art gallery and calls it Elijah Pierce Wood Studio, 536 E. Long St. Works as a barber at 534 E. Long St.
(*Columbus City Directory,* 1969)

1970   Summer. Meets Boris Gruenwald, a graduate student in the art department at Ohio State University, when Gruenwald sees Pierce's work at a Columbus YMCA exhibition.
(Seibert, interview with Gruenwald in Los Angeles, December 30, 1980; confirmed by artists Michael Sweeney and Michael Hall, August 1991)

1971   Resides at 2290 Margaret Ave.
       (*Columbus City Directory,* 1971)

Represented in exhibition, *The Citizen-Journal's Golden Age Hobby Show,* Martin Janis Senior Center, Ohio State Fairgrounds, Columbus.
       (Garrett and Lentz, p. 123)

October 18–29. Exhibition, *Elijah Pierce Carvings,* Hopkins Hall Gallery, Ohio State University, Columbus.

October 27. Boris Gruenwald agrees to act as agent for Pierce with no commission or pay.
       (Seibert archive, copies of Boris Gruenwald papers)

November 9, 1971–January 2, 1972. Represented in exhibition, *American Folk Sculpture: The Personal and the Eccentric,* Cranbrook Academy of Art Galleries, Bloomfield Hills, Michigan.

December 12, 1971–January 2, 1972. Exhibition, *Elijah Pierce,* Krannert Art Museum, University of Illinois, Urbana-Champaign.

1972   January 25–March 13. One-artist exhibition, *Untitled III,* Penthouse, Museum of Modern Art, New York.

June 6–24. Exhibition, *Elijah Pierce: Painted Carvings,* Bernard Danenberg Galleries, New York.

December 21, 1972–January 28, 1973. Exhibition, *Elijah Pierce,* Peale House Galleries, Pennsylvania Academy of the Fine Arts, Philadelphia.

December 28. Exhibition, Yule Art Fair, Beatty Recreation Center, Columbus; featured with Robert J. Stull.
       ("Yule Art Fair . . .")

1973   February 4–22. Represented in exhibition, *Jim Dupree, Elijah Pierce, Brenda Robinson,* The Huntington Trust Gallery, Columbus.

Summer. Represented in exhibition, *Naivi '73,* International Meeting of Naive Art, Zagreb, Yugoslavia. Receives first prize.

October 12. Interviews with Aminah Robinson and Robert Stull, on *Afromation,* produced and hosted by Dr. Mary Ann Williams, Department of Black Studies, Ohio State University, for WOSU-TV, Columbus.

November 23. First known film on Pierce aired on WBNS-TV, Columbus.
       ("Pierce Story on TV")

November 30–December 30. Exhibition, *Elijah Pierce, Wood Carver,* Columbus Gallery of Fine Arts.

1974   January 1. Pierce named as one of *Columbus Citizen-Journal's* top ten men of 1973.
       ("C-J's Top 10 . . .")

January. Columbus Gallery of Fine Arts acquires first three works by Pierce for its permanent collections.

February 17–March 10. Represented in exhibition, *American Folk Sculpture from the Hall Collection,* University of Kentucky Art Gallery, Lexington.

April 2. Elijah and Estelle Pierce receive commendation from the Ohio House of Representatives, House Resolution no. 351.

June 14. Receives Ohio Governor's Award for Community Action from Governor John J. Gilligan.

July. Featured in *Ebony Magazine*, the first national magazine to publish an article on the artist.
> (Treadwell, 1974)

August 16. Receives first Honorary Life Membership, International Wood Collectors Society.

September 27. Receives the Award for Outstanding Contributions to the Community, from Paul Laurence Dunbar Afro-American Cultural Arts Center, Columbus.

1975   Receives award from Gay Tabernacle Baptist Church, Columbus, from the Reverend Odell Waller, minister.

The Black Hall of Respect, Community Extension Center, Ohio State University, is dedicated to the artist.

April 20. Receives Appreciation Award for Outstanding Contributions to the Art Profession and the Black Community, from the Office of Minority Affairs, Ohio State University.

September 26. Receives Ohio Arts Council Award for Folk Art.

1976   January 15. Documentary film, *Elijah Pierce, Woodcarver,* produced by Dr. Mary Ann Williams, is presented as part of the series *Afromation,* WOSU-TV, Columbus.

March 6–May 31. Represented in exhibition, *Folk Sculpture U.S.A.,* organized and toured nationally by the Brooklyn Museum, New York.

March 14–28. Exhibition, *Elijah Pierce, Wood Carver*, Columbus Jewish Center.

March 21. Exhibition, *Elijah Pierce,* Bethel A.M.E. Church, Columbus.

March 21–April 17. Represented in exhibition, Fendrick Gallery, Washington, D.C.
> (Kernan)

May 2. Documentary film, *Sermons in Wood,* produced by Carolyn Jones and Raymond Kook, is shown at Columbus Gallery of Fine Arts.

September 18–December 5. Represented in exhibition, *American Folk Art in Ohio Collections,* Akron Art Institute, Ohio.

October 16–November 6. Exhibition, *Elijah Pierce,* Phyllis Kind Gallery, New York.

1977   Featured with folk sculptors Edgar Tolson and Miles Carpenter in the television documentary *Artists Among Us,* produced by WNET/Thirteen, New York.

December 31. Receives second Life Membership, International Wood Collectors Society.

1978   Represented in exhibition, *Reviews and Previews,* Phyllis Kind Gallery, New York.

Retires from barbering after hip injury.
> ("Smithsonian Exhibits . . ."; Foster)

Meets Leroy Almon.
(Regenia Perry, conversation with Leroy Almon, August 1991)

June. Presents two carvings, *The All-Seeing Eye* and *Dr. Martin Luther King, Jr.*, to the Martin Luther King, Jr., Branch of the Public Library of Columbus and Franklin County.
("Pierce Carving Given to Branch")

July 9–22. Exhibition, Kojo Art Studio, Columbus.
("To Exhibit Carvings . . .")

September 23. Exhibition features artist at Members Day, Columbus Zoo.
("Zoo Event . . .")

1979   Rejoins Master Lodge 62, Ancient Free and Accepted Masons, as an honorary member.
(Archives, Master Lodge 62)

Accepts Leroy Almon as an aide and apprentice at his gallery.
(Schwindler, 1986, p.18)

March 4–25. Exhibition, works from the permanent collection of Schumacher Gallery, Capital University, Columbus.

July 13. Elijah Pierce Art Gallery is incorporated under Section 1702.01 revised Code of Ohio for purposes of display and exhibition of art as a nonprofit corporation. Elijah Pierce, Estelle Pierce, and Leroy Almon are trustees. Leroy Almon is also listed as agent.
(Certificate 53885. Roll E621, frame 0473, Office of the Secretary of State of Ohio)

August 6–27. Represented in exhibition, *Marjorie Bender/Elijah Pierce*, Cultural Arts Center, Columbus.

August 26. Featured in *New York Times Magazine*.
(Moore)

September 14–16. Honored artist exhibition, *Golden Age Hobby Show*, Martin Janis Senior Center, Ohio State Fairgrounds, Columbus.

October 14–November 6. Represented in exhibition, *A Tribute to Elijah Pierce*, Gallery 200, Columbus. Works by Pierce and local artists Joe Cieslewski, Gary Schwindler, and James Wiese are included.

1980   January 11–13. Official opening of Elijah Pierce Art Gallery.
("Opens Gallery")

February 29. Receives Pioneer for Human Dignity Award, Ethnic Student Community of Ohio Dominican College, Columbus.

April 20. Receives Honorary Doctorate of Fine Arts, Franklin University, Columbus.

Receives Outstanding Achievement Award, Franklin University.

May 2–4. Exhibition, *Golden Age Hobby Show*, Martin Janis Senior Center, Ohio State Fairgrounds, Columbus.
(Heinke, April 1, 1980)

May 25–September 14. Represented in exhibition, *Folk Art USA since 1900*, Abby Aldrich Rockefeller Folk Art Center, Williamsburg, Virginia.

June. Featured in *Life*.
    (Brewster)

June 1. Receives Distinguished Achievement Award, Office of Minority Affairs, Ohio State University, for Superior Contribution to the Arts, and the Promotion and Advancement of Afro-American Culture.

August 12–24. Represented in group exhibition, *American Folk Art from Ohio Collections,* James M. Cox Art Center, Ohio State Fairgrounds, Columbus.

October 22. Inducted into Ohio Senior Citizens Hall of Fame, Martin Janis Senior Center, Ohio State Fairgrounds, Columbus.

December 12. Annual auction for the benefit of the Metropolitan School of Columbus includes sculpture by Pierce, photos by Kojo Kamau, and ceramics by Jenny Floch.
    ("Pierce Sculpture, Kojo Photos . . .")

1981   January 9–February 16. Represented in exhibition, *Afro-American Art from the Collection of Ursel White Lewis,* Franklin University Gallery, Columbus.

March 3–June 7. Represented in exhibition, *Woodworks II: Folk Traditions in Ohio and Kentucky,* Dayton Art Institute, Ohio.

March 6–April 8. Represented in exhibition, *Transmitters: The Isolate Artist in America,* Philadelphia College of Art Gallery, Pennsylvania.

April 5–26. Exhibition, *The Painted Woodcarvings of Elijah Pierce,* Zanesville Art Center, Ohio.

April 6–May 13. Represented in exhibition, *Primitives . . . and Beyond,* with Morris Newman and Lee Garrett, Nationwide Gallery, Columbus.

April 13–April 17. Represented in exhibition, *Food for Thought,* St. Stephen's Church, Black Community Festival, Columbus.
    ("Festival to Feature . . .")

August 4–21. Represented in exhibition, *Holidays,* Ohio Expositions Center, Ohio State Fair, Columbus.

September 17–November 1. Represented in exhibition, *American Folk Art: The Herbert Waide Hemphill Jr. Collection,* organized and toured nationally by the Milwaukee Art Museum.

Autumn. Third room added to the Elijah Pierce Art Gallery.
    (Edwards, 1981)

Autumn–Winter. Featured in the Ohio Arts Council's 1981–1982 programs calendar.

December 1, 1981–February 28, 1982. Exhibition, *Elijah Pierce: Messages in Wood,* Renwick Gallery of the National Museum of American Art, Smithsonian Institution, Washington, D.C.

December 13. Exhibits with Leroy Almon at the Art for Community Expression Gallery, Kojo Photo Art Studio, Columbus.
    ("Carvings on Exhibit")

1982   January 14. Meets First Lady Nancy Reagan when she previews the exhibition, *Black Folk Art in America 1930–1980*, at the Corcoran Gallery of Art, Washington, D.C.
> ("Folk Artist Elijah Pierce Weeps . . ."; Taylor)

January 15–March 28. Represented in exhibition, *Black Folk Art in America, 1930–1980*, organized and toured nationally by the Corcoran Gallery of Art, Washington, D.C.

January 24–March 7. Represented in exhibition, *Touching Wood*, Southern Ohio Museum and Cultural Center, Portsmouth.

February 12. Receives Ohio Governor's Award for Excellence of Achievement Benefiting Mankind and Improving the Quality of Life for All Ohioans.

Spring. Picture of one of Pierce's carved crocodiles is featured on billboard at High Street and Frank Road, Columbus; sponsored by the Greater Columbus Arts Council, Franklin University Art Gallery, and Donray Outdoor Advertising Company.
> (Herban and Herban, 1982)

June 12–13. Columbus "AfroFair '82" salutes black artists, including Pierce.

July 3. Receives National Heritage Fellowship, from National Endowment for the Arts, Washington, D.C.

September 19. Honored with a reception by the Ohio Arts Council and Ephesus Seventh-Day Adventist Church, at Ephesus Elementary School. Receives Distinguished Humanitarian Arts Award.

October 2. Receives tributes from members of the Ohio Arts Council, the Ohio House of Representatives, the vice provost of Minority Affairs of Ohio State University, and Columbus artist Aminah Robinson at Ephesus Seventh-Day Adventist Church.

October 8. Inducted as 24th member, Columbus Hall of Fame, Columbus City Hall.

November 1. Receives citation for distinguished service, at the 12th Annual Graduate and Professional Schools Visitation Days, Ohio State University.

1983   Receives Columbus Art League Distinguished Service Award.

January 8–29. Represented in exhibition, *Visions from the Elders*, Garrat Gallery, Public Library, Lancaster, Ohio.

March 30. Judges Southside Artists competition for children ages 9–15.
> ("Best Young Southside Artist . . .")

Spring. Celebration in honor of artist's 91st birthday at Shepard Branch Library with presentations from the Governor's office, Office of the Adjunct General of Ohio, Ohio Senator Richard Pfeiffer, Jr., Columbus Area Chamber of Commerce, and Ephesus Seventh-Day Adventist Church.
> (Hamlet, 1983)

May 20–June 10. Exhibition, *Elijah Pierce*, Office of Minority Affairs, Ohio State University, Columbus.

October. Elijah Pierce Art Gallery and the artist's former residence on Everett Alley designated as National Historic Site in the National Register of Historic Places.
> (Edwards, Oct. 4, 1983)

October 7. Featured at Folk Crafts Festival, Nationwide Plaza Park, as part of third Columbus U.S.A. festivities.

    ("Woodcarver Pierce to Be Featured . . .")

October 7–November 2. Exhibition, *Sermons in Wood: Ohio Folk Artist Elijah Pierce*, Firelands Association for the Visual Arts Gallery, Oberlin, Ohio.

October 15. Receives 11th Ohioana Library Association Pegasus Award, 54th annual meeting.

October 17. Death of son Willie in Chicago, Illinois.

    (Seibert, conversation with Alexis Pierce, artist's descendant, July 1991)

1983–1984   Represented in exhibition, *New Epiphanies: Religious Contemporary Art*, organized by the Gallery of Contemporary Art, University of Colorado, Colorado Springs, and the Ohio Foundation on the Arts, Columbus; circulated by the Statewide Arts Touring Exhibitions Service.

1984   May 7. Dies in Columbus of a heart attack.

    (Kehres; "Master Carver Meets Master . . .")

May 10. Obituary appears in *New York Times*.

May 11. Master Lodge 62, Ancient Free and Accepted Masons, holds memorial service. Funeral service held at Wayne T. Lee Funeral Chapel. Services conducted by the Reverend S. T. Lewis, pastor, Ephesus Seventh-Day Adventist Church, and the Reverend Odell Waller, Tabernacle Baptist Church. Burial, Evergreen Cemetery, Columbus.

    ("Elijah Pierce," Obituary, *Columbus Dispatch*; Ellis; "Master Carver Meets Master . . .")

August. Estelle Pierce, 78, and her 100-year-old mother, Ina Gentry, reopen the Elijah Pierce Art Gallery to the public.

    (McMurray, p. 16)

August 4–September 2. Represented in exhibition, *Folk Art*, Parkersburg Art Center, Parkersburg, West Virginia.

Columbus U.S.A. Celebration of the Arts is dedicated to the memory of Elijah Pierce.

    (Edwards, Sept. 14, 1984)

November 7. Carving *Judas Betraying Christ*, dated 1966, auctioned at Butterfield and Butterfield, San Francisco, for $4,400. First known sale of work at nationally recognized auction house.

    ("Elijah Pierce Carvings at Auction . . .")

1985   February 13–March 8. Represented in exhibition, *Black History Month*, Bricker Hall and Main Library, Ohio State University, Office of Minority Affairs.

    (Smith, 1985)

March 28. Columbus Museum of Art acquires more than one hundred carvings and archival materials from the artist's estate, establishing the largest public collection of works by Pierce in the country.

May 29–July 14. Represented in exhibition, *Visionary Constructions*, Hoyt L. Sherman Gallery, Sullivant Hall, Ohio State University.

July 2–December 31. Special exhibition of newly acquired Pierce collection, entitled *Elijah Pierce, Woodcarver*, is installed at the Columbus Museum of Art.

November 7–30. Exhibition, *Elijah Pierce,* Keny and Johnson Gallery, Columbus.

1986   January 30–March 15. Represented in exhibition, *Naivety in Art*; organized and toured in Japan by Setagaya Art Museum, Tokyo.

November 9, 1986–January 4, 1987. Represented in exhibition, *Choice by Choice: Celebrating Notable Acquisitions, 1976–1986*, Columbus Museum of Art.

November 21, 1986–January 10, 1987. Represented in exhibition, *The Ties That Bind: Folk Art in Contemporary American Culture*; organized and toured nationally by the Contemporary Arts Center, Cincinnati, Ohio.

1987   June 13–August 16. Exhibition, *On Earth as It Is in Heaven: The Carvings of Elijah Pierce,* Akron Art Museum, Ohio.

September 19–20. Represented in exhibition, *Grove City Arts in the Alley Festival,* Huntington National Bank, Grove City, Ohio.

October 11–November 29. Represented in exhibition, *Accent on Sculpture,* Columbus Museum of Art.

Represented in exhibition, *The Grand Generation: Memory, Mastery, and Legacy,* organized and toured nationally by the Smithsonian Institution Traveling Exhibition Service, Washington, D.C.

Marvin Callif, Columbus Time Recorder Co., purchases the former Elijah Pierce Art Gallery building at 534 E. Long St. and the residence behind it on Everett Alley.
    (Smith, 1988)

1988   February 12–March 13. Exhibition, *Elijah Pierce: Woodcarver,* Southern Ohio Museum and Cultural Center, Portsmouth; organized from Columbus Museum of Art collection.

1989   February 3–March 12. Exhibition, *Elijah Pierce, Woodcarver,* South Bend Art Center, South Bend, Indiana; organized from Columbus Museum of Art collection.

November 6–December 30. Exhibition, *Elijah Pierce Woodcarvings,* Massillon Museum, Ohio; organized from Columbus Museum of Art collection.

November 13, 1989–April 1990. Represented in exhibition, *America's Living Folk Traditions,* organized and toured nationally by the Museum of International Folk Art, Santa Fe, New Mexico.

December 2, 1989–January 2, 1990. Represented in exhibition, *New Traditions/Non-Traditions: Contemporary Folk Art in Ohio,* Riffe Gallery, Columbus.

1990   January 15–March 15. Exhibition, *Amazing Grace: The Life and Work of Elijah Pierce,* Martin Luther King Jr. Center for Performing and Cultural Arts, Columbus.

January 15. Artist's memory honored in "A Night of Remembrance: Words for the Future," opening ceremonies for the exhibition *Amazing Grace: The Life and Work of Elijah Pierce*, Martin Luther King Jr. Center for Performing and Cultural Arts.
    ("Gallery Will Display . . .")

February 6–August 5. Represented in exhibition, *Contemporary American Folk, Naive, and Outsider Art: Into the Mainstream?*, Miami University Art Museum, Oxford, Ohio.

July 31. Death of son Arthur Beene in Chicago, Illinois.
> (Seibert, conversations with Zetta and Alexis Pierce, artist's descendants, July 1991)

August 2–25. Represented in exhibition, *Columbus Art in the 1930s and 1940s*, in conjunction with the Festival of American Culture, Columbus Cultural Arts Center.

May 11–September 2. Represented in exhibition, *The Fine Art of Folk Art*, Cincinnati Art Museum, Ohio.

October 21–November 30. Represented in exhibition, *A Presentation of Woodcarving*, William H. Thomas Gallery, Columbus.

1991   January 31–February 2. Artist's carving *Picking Wild Berries*, dated 1979, sells at Sotheby's, New York, for $1,100.
> (*Important Americana*, lot no. 1060)

February 24–May 5. Represented in exhibition, *Spirits: Selections from the Collection of Geoffrey Holder and Carmen de Lavallade*; organized and toured nationally by Katonah Museum of Art, Katonah, New York.

November 8–December 22. Represented in exhibition, *Personal Intensity: Artists in Spite of the Mainstream*, Art Museum, University of Wisconsin, Milwaukee.

1992   Publication of children's book, *Elijah's Angel*, by Michael Rosen, with illustrations by Aminah Robinson.

1993   January 24. Opening of exhibition and national tour of *Elijah Pierce, Woodcarver*; organized and toured nationally by the Columbus Museum of Art.

BIBLIOGRAPHY

MARGARET ARMBRUST SEIBERT

Abercrombie, Sharon. "Art Community Saddened by Death of Master Carver." *Columbus Citizen-Journal* (May 9, 1984).

"African Culture Celebrated in Black Expressions Show." *Columbus Call and Post* (March 15, 1980).

"'AfroFair '82' Weekend Headliner at Mt. Vernon Plaza Focal Point." *Columbus Call and Post* (June 12, 1982).

Almon, Leroy. "Elijah Pierce Story." *Maccabeus* (August–September 1979): 9–11.

———. "Speakeasy." *New Art Examiner* 19 (September 1991): 13–14.

American Folk Sculpture from the Hall Collection (exh. cat.). Lexington, Kentucky: University of Kentucky Press, 1974.

"Aminah Robinson." *Folk Art Finder* 11 (July–October 1990): 5.

"Antique Folk Art on Display." *Massillon Evening Independent,* 1989 [date unknown, from the Archives of the Massillon Museum, Massillon, Ohio. Show held from November 6–December 30, 1989].

"Area Artist Honored." *Columbus Dispatch* (April 27, 1976).

"Art Gallery Carves Spot for Pierce." *Columbus Dispatch, Capitol Magazine* (November 10, 1985): 20.

"Art Gallery Guide." *Art Gallery Magazine* (April 1972).

"Art Gallery Guide." *Art Gallery Magazine* (December 1972).

"Art Gallery Scene." *Art Gallery Magazine* (October 1976).

"Art Gallery Scene." *Art Gallery Magazine* (November 1976).

"Art Gallery to Air Elijah Pierce Film." *Columbus Call and Post* (May 1, 1976).

The Art of Education. Columbus, Ohio: Franklin University 1983 President's Report/1984 Appointment Calendar.

Artists Among Us (television documentary film). New York: WNET/Thirteen, 1977.

Aschenbrand, Richard A. "Elijah Pierce: Preacher in Wood." *American Craft Magazine* 42 (June–July 1982): 24–25, cover 3.

Ayle, Fritzi. "Artist's Life Changes Little after Fame." *Columbus Citizen-Journal* (April 18, 1977).

Bašičević, Dimitrije, et al, *Primitive Painting: An Anthology of the World's Naive Painters.* Zagreb, Yugoslavia: Spektar, GZH Frankopanska, 1981.

Bernard Danenberg Galleries. *Elijah Pierce: Painted Carvings.* New York, 1972.

Berry, Steve. "Artist Carved Niche in World." *Columbus Dispatch* (May 8, 1984).

"Best Young Southside Artist to Win $100 in Competition." *Columbus Call and Post* (March 17, 1983).

Bihalji-Merin, Oto, and Nebojša-Bato Tomašević, eds. *World Encyclopedia of Naive Art.* Belgrade: Jugoslovenska Revija, 1984; Scranton, Pennsylvania: Scala/Philip Wilson in association with Harper & Row, 1985.

Bishop, Robert. *American Folk Sculpture.* New York: E. P. Dutton, 1974.

———. "Much Current Folk Art Depicts Life of the Past." *Antique Monthly* (May 1975): 10C.

Bishop, Robert, Judith Reiter Weissman, Michael McManus, and Henry Neimann. *Folk Art: Paintings, Sculpture, and Country Objects.* New York: Alfred A. Knopf, 1983.

"Black Art." Elyria, Ohio: *Elyria Chronicle Telegram* (September 23, 1983).

"Black Folk Art in America: Elijah Pierce." *Folk Art Finder* (January–February 1982): 5.

"A Book of Wood: The Art and Words of Elijah Pierce." *Columbus Art* (Fall 1982): 7.

Bowman-Richards, Deborah. "Elijah Pierce." *Artspace* (September–October 1981): 19.

Brewster, Todd. "Fanciful Art of Plain Folk." *Life* (June 1980): 112–118, 120, 122.

Bridgman, Mary. "Primitives Keep Pierce Perking." *Columbus Dispatch* (November 13, 1977).

———. "Proxmire Says Economy Won't Turn Around Soon." *Columbus Dispatch* (April 21, 1980).

Bronner, Simon J. *American Folk Art: A Guide to Sources*. New York and London: Garland Publishing, 1984.

Browning, D. L. "Major Elijah Pierce Exhibit at the King Center." Columbus: *Westside Messenger* (January 22, 1990).

Burris, Tom. Interview with Elijah Pierce. Channel 6 Television News, WSYX, Columbus, Ohio, July 7, 1981.

Burstein, J. "Intimate Records." *Art Week* (August 28, 1982): 3.

Carroll, Sara. "1981 Launched with Varied Exhibitions." *Columbus Dispatch* (December 28, 1980).

"Carvings on Exhibit." *Columbus Dispatch Weekend Planner* (December 10, 1981).

Cederholm, Theresa Dickason. *Afro-American Artists: Bio-bibliographical Directory*. Boston: Trustees of the Boston Public Library, 1973.

Chafetz, Sidney. "A Show of Good Choices." *Columbus Monthly* (November 1986): 157–163.

Clark, Sharon Minor. "The Gossip We Label Primitive Art." *Artspace* (May–June 1985): 10.

Columbus City Directory. Columbus, Ohio: R.L. Polk, 1924, 1929–1938, 1940–1941, 1943, 1949–1969, 1971.

"C-J's Top 10 Men of 1973." *Columbus Citizen-Journal* (January 1, 1974).

Columbus Gallery of Fine Arts. *Elijah Pierce, Wood Carver* (exh. cat.). Columbus, Ohio, 1973.

"Columbus Is Represented in Washington D.C. at the Renwick Gallery." *Columbus Citizen-Journal* (December 7, 1981).

Columbus Jewish Center. *Elijah Pierce, Wood Carver* (exh. bro.). Columbus, Ohio, 1976.

Columbus Museum of Art. *The American Collections*. Columbus, Ohio, 1988.

Columbus Museum of Art and Ohio Arts Council. *New Traditions/Non-Traditions: Contemporary Folk Art in Ohio* (exh. bro.). Columbus, 1989.

"Concerned Citizens Bring Community Center to Life." *Columbus Call and Post* (January 8, 1980).

Constable, Leslie. "Amazing Grace: The Life and Times of Elijah Pierce." *Dialogue: An Art Journal* (May–June 1990): 28–29.

———. "Artists Bring Life to Wood." *Columbus Dispatch* (November 11, 1990).

Contemporary Arts Center. *The Ties That Bind: Folk Art in Contemporary American Culture* (exh. cat.). Cincinnati, Ohio, 1986.

"Continuing Exhibitions—Elijah Pierce: Messages in Wood." Renwick Gallery of the National Museum of American Art, *Smithsonian Institution Calendar* (February 1982).

Crome, Nicholas. *Elijah Pierce Carvings* (exh. cat.). Columbus, Ohio: Ohio State University, 1971.

Cubbs, Joanne. *The Gift of Josephus Farmer* (exh. cat.). Milwaukee, Wisconsin: University of Wisconsin Art History Gallery, 1982.

Dayton Art Institute. *Woodworks II: Folk Traditions in Ohio and Kentucky* (exh. cat.). Dayton, Ohio, 1981.

"Death of Two Folk Artists: Elijah Pierce and Edgar Tolson." *Folk Art Finder* (January–February 1985): 2, 17.

Derbeck, Jeanne. "Pierce's Folk Artistry Reflects His Religion." South Bend, Indiana: *South Bend Tribune* (February 5, 1989).

Detroit Institute of Art. *Black Folk Art in America 1930–1980* (exh. bro.), 1983.

Dewhurst, Kurt C., Marsha MacDowell, and Betty MacDowell. *Religious Folk Art in America: Reflections of Faith*. New York: E. P. Dutton, 1983.

"Dominican College Begins Awards for Human Dignity." *Columbus Call and Post* (March 22, 1980).

Donmoyer, June. "Columbus Museum of Art: Elijah Pierce, Woodcarver." *Antique Review Preview* (August 1985): 1, 7–8, 10–11.

Donohoe, Victoria. "Pierce and McCarthy: Old and Brightly New." *Philadelphia Inquirer* (December 29, 1972).

Doty, Robert. *American Folk Art in Ohio Collections* (exh. cat.). Akron, Ohio, and New York: Akron Art Institute in association with Dodd, Mead & Co., 1976.

"Dual Art Exhibition Pairs Octogenarians." Oreland, Pennsylvania: *Springfield Sun* (January 4, 1973).

"Eastside Woodcarver Chosen for 1st Honorary Doctorate." *Columbus Call and Post* (April 19, 1980).

Edwards, Larrilyn. "Elijah P. Posing for 'Life.'" *Columbus Citizen-Journal* (June 2, 1980).

———. "Pierce's Work Will Be Shown All Over U.S." *Columbus Citizen-Journal* (November 17, 1981).

———. "Residing Downtown Gives Life a Big Plus." *Columbus Citizen-Journal* (September 7, 1983).

———. "At a Glance." *Columbus Citizen-Journal* (September 29, 1983).

———. "Elijah's Barbershop Now 'Historic Place.'" *Columbus Citizen-Journal* (October 4, 1983).

———. "Posthumous Honor for Elijah Pierce by Children at Douglas Alternative School." *Columbus Citizen-Journal* (May 9, 1984).

———. "Elijah Pierce Was Known for Sharp Wit." *Columbus Citizen-Journal* (May 11, 1984).

———. "Pierce Friends Aim to Keep Work Here." *Columbus Citizen-Journal* (June 27, 1984).

———. "City's Celebration of the Arts Dedicated to Elijah Pierce." *Columbus Citizen-Journal* (September 14, 1984).

———. "It's Time for Thanks to Some of Our Best." *Columbus Citizen-Journal* (November 22, 1984).

———. "Columbus Museum Purchases Pierce Carvings." *Columbus Citizen-Journal* (March 29, 1985).

Eichenberger, Bill. "Study of Pierce Offers Lesson in Art, Black History." *Columbus Dispatch Neighbor News, Central Metro* (January 29, 1986).

———. "Artist Carved Historic Niche." *Columbus Dispatch Neighbor News Central Metro* (February 5, 1986).

"80-Year-Old Stroudsburg Artist Exhibiting Work in Philadelphia." Easton, Pennsylvania: *Easton Express* (December 27, 1972).

"89 and Still Carving." *Columbus Citizen-Journal* (September 20, 1982).

Einhorn, Charles, and Pat Schmucki. "Museum of Art Director Budd H. Bishop." *Downtown Alive!* (November 20, 1986).

"Elijah Pierce." *ARTnews* (Summer 1972): 57.

"Elijah Pierce." *Columbus Citizen-Journal* (May 9, 1984).

"Elijah Pierce." *Key to Columbus* (1982).

"Elijah Pierce" (Obituary). *Columbus Dispatch* (May 9, 1984; May 10, 1984).

"Elijah Pierce" (Obituary). *New York Times* (May 10, 1984).

"Elijah Pierce" (Obituary). Toledo, Ohio: *Toledo Blade* (May 9, 1984).

"Elijah Pierce." *Ohioana Quarterly*, Annual Supplement (Autumn 1983): S12–S13.

"Elijah Pierce, Acclaimed Woodcarver Dies; Funeral Set for Friday." *Columbus Call and Post* (May 10, 1984).

"Elijah Pierce Art Exhibit to Continue in New Elijah Pierce Gallery, Part of Martin Luther King Jr. Center for Performing and Cultural Arts." *Columbus Dispatch* (January 14, 1990).

"Elijah Pierce, Artist." *Columbus Dispatch* (May 10, 1984).

"Elijah Pierce at Columbus (OH) Gallery of Fine Art through December 30." *Art Gallery Magazine* 17 (December 1973).

"Elijah Pierce at the Renwick Gallery." *Detroit News* (February 21, 1982).

"Elijah Pierce Awarded National Heritage Fellowship." *Dialogue: An Art Journal* (July–August 1982): 4.

"Elijah Pierce Carvings at Auction in San Francisco." *Ohio Antique Review* (December 1984): 43.

"Elijah Pierce Honored for Art Contributions." *Columbus Call and Post* (March 24, 1979).

"Elijah Pierce: *Joe Louis, World Champion, 1967.*" *Columbus Art* (Fall 1985): 19.

"Elijah Pierce: *Messages in Wood* Continues through Feb. 28." *Arts and Activities Monthly* (February 1982).

"Elijah Pierce Noted Folk Artist Receives University's First Honorary Degree." *Franklin University Beacon* (Summer 1980): 2.

"Elijah Pierce to Be Honored at Arts Council Reception." *Columbus Citizen-Journal* (September 13, 1982).

"Elijah Pierce to Get Heritage Award." *Columbus Citizen-Journal* (July 3, 1982).

"Elijah Pierce's Woodcarvings Displayed in Corcoran Gallery." *Columbus Citizen-Journal* (March 6, 1982).

"Elijah Pierce, Wood Carver." *Folk Art Finder* 13 (January–March 1992): 4–7.

"*Elijah Pierce: Woodcarver* Will Run through the End of the Year." *Columbus Museum of Art Newsletter* (August 1985).

"Elijah Pierce Woodcarvings." *Antique Review Preview* (December 1989): 12.

Ellis, Mark. "Famous Woodcarver Buried." *Columbus Dispatch* (May 12, 1984).

Ericson, Jack, ed. *Folk Art Painting, Sculpture, and Country Objects.* New York: Mayflower Books, 1979.

"Experts Visit Museum." *Columbus Museum of Art Monthly Calendar* (July–August 1991).

"Famed Ohio Woodcarver Dies." Elyria, Ohio: *Elyria Chronicle Telegram* (May 9, 1984).

Fennessy, Tom. "Carving Preserves a Fearsome July 4." *Columbus Dispatch* (July 4, 1980).

"Festival to Feature Local Artists' Works." *Columbus Call and Post* (April 11, 1981).

"15 Win Folk-Art Fellowships." *New York Times* (May 31, 1982).

"15 Winners of National Heritage Fellowships of National Arts Endowment Are Announced." *New York Times* (June 1, 1982).

"Folk Art." *Cleveland Plain Dealer Magazine* (November 11, 1979).

"Folk Art Exhibit." Oberlin, Ohio: *Oberlin News-Tribune* (October 6, 1983).

"Folk Artist at the Renwick Gallery in Washington." *Antiques and Arts Weekly* (December 12, 1981).

"Folk Artist Elijah Pierce Weeps as Mrs. Reagan Views His Work." *Columbus Citizen-Journal* (January 14, 1982).

"Folk Artist Pierce to Show 'Sermon.'" Oberlin, Ohio: *Oberlin News-Tribune* (September 22, 1983).

"Folk, Naive, and Outsider Art at Miami U." *Folk Art Finder* 11 (July–October 1990): 4.

Forman, Nessa. "Two Self-Taught Americans: Their Visions Clear, Their Colors Bright." *Philadelphia Sunday Bulletin* (December 31, 1972).

Foster, Kathy Gray. "Woodcarver Shapes a Legend." *Columbus Dispatch* (September 20, 1982).

Fryer-Kohles, Jeanne. "Tribute to Elijah Pierce." *Columbus Art* (Spring 1981): 6.

Franklin University Gallery, Columbus, Ohio. *Afro-American Art from the Collection of Ursel White Lewis* (exh. bro.). 1981.

"Gallery 200 Slates Tribute to Pierce." *Columbus Dispatch* (October 27, 1979).

"Gallery Will Display Pierce's Artistry." *Columbus Call and Post* (November 23, 1989).

Garrett, Betty. "Barber's Primitive Carvings Defy Words." *Columbus Citizen-Journal* (January 10, 1972).

———. "Elijah Pierce: 80-Year-Old Folk Artist Hauled from Obscurity." *Columbus Citizen-Journal* (February 8, 1973).

———. "Elijah Pierce: Sculptor, Preacher, Barber." *ARTnews* (March 1974): 114–115.

Garrett, Betty, and Edward R. Lentz. *Columbus: America's Crossroads.* Tulsa, Oklahoma: Continental Heritage Press, 1980.

Gilmore, Phyllis. "A Home for Elijah's People." *Ohio Antique Review Preview* (December 1980–January 1981): 1–3.

Gilson, Nancy. "Riffe Gallery Exhibit Will Buck Tradition of Folk Art." *Columbus Dispatch* (December 1, 1989).

———. "Elijah Pierce: A Graceful Life, An Amazing Artist." *Columbus Dispatch* (January 14, 1990).

"Golden Age Hobby Show Features Pierce." *Columbus Citizen-Journal* (May 4, 1983).

Gorisek, Sue. "Folk Art." *Ohio Magazine* (November 1980): 19–21.

Hall, Jacqueline. "Prolific Pierce Career on View." *Columbus Dispatch* (July 7, 1985).

———. "Elijah Pierce Show Viewed with Delight." *Columbus Dispatch* (November 10, 1985).

———. "Delightful 'Folk Art' Full of Surprises." *Columbus Dispatch* (December 10, 1989).

———. "Art in 30s, 40s Focus of Show." *Columbus Dispatch* (August 19, 1990).

Hall, Michael D. *American Folk Sculpture: The Personal and the Eccentric* (exh. cat.). Bloomfield Hills, Michigan: Cranbrook Academy of Art Galleries, 1971.

———. Transcription of audiotaped interview with Elijah Pierce, fall 1971. Archives, Columbus Museum of Art.

———. *Stereoscopic Perspective: Reflections on American Fine and Folk Art*. Ann Arbor and London: University Microfilms International Research Press, 1988.

Hamlet, Janice D. "The 'Gospel' According to the Primitive Art of Elijah Pierce." *Columbus Homes and Lifestyles* (July–August 1984): 12–16.

———. "Nationally Acclaimed Woodcarver Receives Tributes from Columbus." *Columbus Call and Post* (October 2, 1982).

———. "Noted Woodcarver Elijah Pierce Celebrates 91st Birthday with Friends." *Columbus Call and Post* (April 14, 1983).

Hartigan, Lynda Roscoe. *Made with Passion: The Hemphill Folk Art Collection in the National Museum of American Art* (exh. cat.). Washington, D.C., and London: National Museum of American Art, Smithsonian Institution Press, 1990.

Hayes, Ben. "Carver." *Columbus Citizen-Journal* (October 26, 1967).

———. "Downtown." *Columbus Citizen-Journal* (February 6, 1973).

———. "Horses." *Columbus Citizen-Journal* (April 20, 1973).

———. "Slave Times." *Columbus Citizen-Journal* (July 6, 1973).

———. "Canal Water." *Columbus Citizen-Journal* (November 19, 1973).

———. "In Chapel St." *Columbus Citizen-Journal* (February 23, 1974).

———. "Designers." *Columbus Citizen-Journal* (March 4, 1974).

———. "Buildings." *Columbus Citizen-Journal* (November 14, 1974).

Heinke, Ed. "Ace Woodcarver to Participate in Golden Age Show." *Columbus Citizen-Journal* (September 3 , 1979).

———. "Seniors' Show Features Carved Works." *Columbus Citizen-Journal* (April 1, 1980).

———. "Successes 'After 60' Give 14 a Berth in Ohio Hall of Fame for Senior Citizens." *Columbus Citizen-Journal* (October 21, 1980).

Hemphill, Herbert Waide, Jr. *Folk Art USA since 1900 from the Collection of Herbert Waide Hemphill, Jr.* (exh. cat.). Williamsburg, Virginia: Abby Aldrich Rockefeller Folk Art Center, 1980.

Hemphill, Herbert W., Jr., ed. *Folk Sculpture U.S.A.* (exh. cat.). New York: Brooklyn Museum, 1976.

Hemphill, Herbert W., Jr., and Robert Bishop et al. *The Herbert Waide Hemphill, Jr. Collection of 18th, 19th, and 20th Century Folk Art* (exh. cat.). Sandwich, Massachusetts: Heritage Plantation of Sandwich, 1974.

Hemphill, Herbert W., Jr., and Julia Weissman. *Twentieth-Century American Folk Art and Artists*. New York: E. P. Dutton, 1974.

Herban, Mathew, and Tricia Herban. "Billboards Can Be Artistic, but What's Solution to Problem?" *Columbus Citizen-Journal* (April 5, 1982).

———. "Museum Exhibits Pierce's Carvings." *Columbus Citizen-Journal* (September 16, 1985).

Hobbs, J. Kline, Jr., introduction to *American Black Art: The Known and the New* (exh. cat.). Battle Creek, Michigan: Battle Creek Civic Art Center, 1977.

Horwitz, Elinor Lander. *Contemporary American Folk Artists*. Philadelphia: J. B. Lippincott, 1975.

———. *The Bird, the Banner, and Uncle Sam*. Philadelphia and New York: J. B. Lippincott, 1976.

Hoster, Jay. "Elijah Pierce: An American Original. He Preaches Sermons in Wood." *Cleveland Plain Dealer Magazine* (November 11, 1979): 22–23, 29, 31, 33, 39–40.

Howard, Arnett. "Woodcarver Elijah Pierce Inducted in Hall of Fame." *Columbus Call and Post* (November 1, 1980).

———. "'AfroFair '82' Weekend Headliner at Mt. Vernon Plaza Focal Point." *Columbus Call and Post* (June 12, 1982).

Hufford, Mary, Marjorie Hunt, and Steven Zeitlin. *The Grand Generation: Memory, Mastery, and Legacy* (exh. cat.). Washington, D.C., and Seattle: Smithsonian Institution in association with University of Washington Press, 1987.

Hughes, Robert. "Finale for the Fantastical." *Time* (March 2, 1982): 70–71.

Hume, Rose. "Museum Buys Elijah Pierce's Woodcarvings." *Columbus Dispatch* (May 29, 1985).

Igoe, Lynn Moody, with James Igoe. *250 Years of Afro-American Art: An Annotated Bibliography*. New York and London: R. R. Bowker, 1981.

Important Americana (auction cat.). Sotheby's, New York, January 30–February 2, 1991.

In Memory of Elijah Pierce. Cincinnati, Ohio: Christ Episcopal Church Memorial Service Program (November 19, 1984).

Johnson, Jay, and William C. Ketchum, Jr. *American Folk Art of the Twentieth Century*. New York: Rizzoli, 1983.

Jones, Carolyn. Transcriptions of audiotaped interviews with Elijah Pierce, 1972. Archives, Columbus Museum of Art.

Jones, Carolyn, producer. *Elijah Pierce: Woodcarver*. Columbus, Ohio: Ohio State University (16mm, 20 minutes), 1974.

Jones, Carolyn, and Raymond Kook, producers. *Sermons in Wood*. Columbus, Ohio: Ohio State University and Center for Southern Folklore (16mm and videotape, 27 minutes), 1976. Distributed by the Center for Southern Folklore, Memphis, Tennessee.

Katonah Museum of Art. *Spirits: Selections from the Collection of Geofferey Holder and Carmen de Lavallade* (exh. cat.). Katonah, New York, 1991.

Kehres, Kevin. "Columbus Artist Elijah Pierce Dies." *Columbus Dispatch* (May 8, 1984).

Keny and Johnson Gallery. *Elijah Pierce* (exh. bro.). Essay, Maude Southwell Wahlman. Columbus, Ohio, 1985.

Kernan, Michael. "Piercing, Wondrous Woodcarvings." *Washington Post* (March 21, 1976).

Ketchum, William C., Jr. *All-American Folk Arts and Crafts*. New York: Rizzoli, 1986.

"King Center Needs Volunteers to Greet Art Exhibit Visitors." *Columbus Call and Post* (February 8, 1990).

"Kojo Studio Features Rare, Unique Gifts." *Columbus Call and Post* (December 20, 1980).

"Kojo Art Studio Grand Opening Sunday." *Columbus Call and Post* (June 3, 1978).

Lavitt, Wendy. *Animals in American Art*. New York: Alfred A. Knopf, 1990.

"Lecture, Art Show Set at Schumaker [*sic*] Gallery." *Columbus Call and Post* (February 24, 1979).

Lee, Lucien E. "Tribute for Elijah Pierce." *Columbus Call and Post* (May 10, 1980).

Livingston, Jane, and John Beardsley. *Black Folk Art in America 1930–1980* (exh. cat.). Jackson, Mississippi: University Press and Center for the Study of Southern Culture, for the Corcoran Gallery of Art, Washington, D.C., 1982.

Lubell, Ellen. "Elijah Pierce." *Arts Magazine* (December 1976): 34.

McLane, Roger, and Bill Barbour. *Visionary Constructions* (exh. bro.). Columbus: Ohio State University Gallery of Fine Art, 1985.

McMurray, Kelly. "Mainstreaming the Legacy of Elijah Pierce." *Columbus Monthly* (August 1984): 16.

McNeely, Shirley. "Museum Carves Out New Home for Woodcutter Elijah Pierce's Folk Art." *Columbus Dispatch* (July 3, 1985).

Marinoff, Scott. "Black Hall Praises Columbus Residents." *Ohio State University Lantern* (April 22, 1975).

Marsh, Betsa. "The Woodcarver of Long Street." *Columbus Monthly* (June 1975): 55–58.

Marty, Kathy. "Impressions of a Folk Artist: An Afternoon with Elijah Pierce." *Journal of the Ohio Folklore Society* (Spring 1972): 29–33.

Massillon Museum. "Elijah Pierce Woodcarvings." *Massillon Museum Newsletter* (November 1989–January 1990).

"Master Carver Meets Master: 'Preacher in Wood' Laid to Rest." *Columbus Call and Post* (May 17, 1984).

Meyer, George H., ed. *Folk Artists Biographical Index*. Detroit, Michigan: Gale Research Co., 1987.

Miami University Art Museum. *Contemporary American Folk, Naive, and Outsider Art: Into the Mainstream?* (exh. cat.). Essays, Eugene Metcalf and Gary Schwindler; entries, Bonnie Kelm. Oxford, Ohio, 1990.

Milwaukee Art Museum. *American Folk Art: The Herbert Waide Hemphill, Jr. Collection* (exh. cat.). Essays, Michael D. Hall, Herbert Hemphill, Jr., Russell Bowman, and Donald B. Kuspit. Milwaukee, Wisconsin, 1981.

"Ministers' Art Will Be Exhibited at Ohio State." *Columbus Call and Post* (May 30, 1985).

"Minority Arts Today." *Artspace* (September–October 1982): 3.

Moe, John F. "Folk Art and Society: A Material Folk Culture Perspective on Utilitarian/Aesthetic Artifacts," *Ohio Antique Review* (January 1984): H-12.

———. "Reflexivity and Autobiography: The Case of the Afro-American Artist Elijah Pierce." Paper given at the American Folklore Society Meeting, Baltimore, Maryland, October 1987.

———. *Amazing Grace: The Life and Art of Elijah Pierce* (exh. cat.). Columbus, Ohio: Martin Luther King Jr. Center for the Performing and Cultural Arts, 1990.

———. "Visioni del Sacro: Arte Afro-Americana Autobiografica." *La Ricerca Folklorica* 24 (1991).

———. *Elijah Pierce* (forthcoming).

Moore, Gaylen. "The Vision of Elijah." *New York Times Magazine* (August 26, 1979): 28–30, 34–35.

Morford, Martha. "Highlights of the Permanent Collection." *Columbus Museum of Fine Arts News* (July 1978).

Muller, Charles. "Columbus Ohio's Elijah Pierce: Seventy Eight Years of Carving—Seven Years of Fame." *Antique Review Preview* (August 1978): 8–11.

"National Festival to Honor Elijah Pierce." *Columbus Dispatch* (June 1, 1982).

"Nationally Acclaimed Woodcarver Elijah Pierce Receives Tributes from Columbus." *Columbus Call and Post* (October 2, 1982).

Neil, Louise. "A Tribute to an Artist—Elijah Pierce." *Artspace* (November–December 1982): 14.

New Epiphanies: Religious Contemporary Art (exh. cat.). Colorado Springs, Colorado, and Columbus, Ohio: Gallery of Contemporary Art, University of Colorado, and Ohio Foundation on the Arts, 1983.

"Oberlin College Hosts National Conference on the Education of Black Americans," *National Greater News* (October 8, 1983).

"Octogenarians Exhibit at Peale House." West Chester, Pennsylvania: *West Chester Daily Local News* (December 21, 1972).

"Ohio Arts Council to Honor Elijah Pierce at Reception." *Columbus Call and Post* (September 18, 1982).

Ohio Expositions Commission, Ohio State Fair. *American Folk Art from Ohio Collections* (exh. cat.). Columbus, Ohio, 1980.

———. *1988 Ohio State Fair Fine Arts Exhibition: Holidays* (exh. cat.). Columbus, Ohio, 1988.

"On Earth as It Is in Heaven: The Carvings of Elijah Pierce." *Exhibitions and Events—Akron Art Museum* (July–August 1987).

"On Earth as It Is in Heaven: The Carvings of Elijah Pierce." *Dialogue: An Art Journal* (May–June 1987): 68.

"Opening of 'Sermons in Wood,'" Oberlin, Ohio: *Oberlin College Observer* (September 29, 1983).

"Opens Gallery." *Columbus Call and Post* (January 5, 1980).

O'Regan, Marianne. "Elijah Pierce: Master Barber—and Master Woodcarver." Cincinnati, Ohio: *Cincinnati Post* (October 9, 1976).

Oshod, Ted. "Concerned Citizens Bring Community Center to Life." *Columbus Call and Post* (January 6, 1983).

"Outstanding Citizen Sought for United Black World Week." *Columbus Call and Post* (January 14, 1978).

"Part of Roman Johnson Is Sharing Artistic Rhythms." *Columbus Call and Post* (March 22, 1980).

Paulson, George, M.D. "Art of Columbus Man Displayed in Washington Corcoran Gallery." *Columbus Call and Post*, Letters to the Editor (March 20, 1982).

Peale House Galleries, Pennsylvania Academy of the Fine Arts. *Elijah Pierce* (exh. bro.). Philadelphia, Pennsylvania, 1972.

Peeples, Stephanie R. "Contemporary Folk Art." *Columbus Art Review* (July–August 1990): 5–6.

Perrone, Jeff. "Elijah Pierce, Phyllis Kind Gallery." *Artforum* (January 1977): 60–61.

Philadelphia College of Art. *Transmitters: The Isolated Artist in America* (exh. cat.). Philadelphia, Pennsylvania, 1981.

Phillips, Debra. "Proxmire Tells Franklin Grads It's Their Job to Fight Inflation." *Columbus Citizen-Journal* (April 21, 1980).

"Pierce." *Columbus Dispatch* (May 9, 1984).

"Pierce Carving Given to Branch." *Columbus Call and Post* (June 24, 1978).

"The Pierce Collection at Columbus Museum of Art." *Columbus Dispatch* (June 1, 1985).

"Pierce, Four Others, Are Honored by Ohioana Library Association." *Columbus Citizen-Journal* (October 17, 1983).

"Pierce Sculpture Draws High Bid at MSC Auction." *Columbus Call and Post* (January 14, 1978).

"Pierce Sculpture, Kojo Photos to Be Auctioned." *Columbus Call and Post* (December 6, 1980).

"Pierce Story on TV." *Columbus Call and Post* (November 24, 1973).

Pierce's Wood Carving Exhibit: Over 1000 Carvings (gallery bro.). Columbus: Elijah Pierce, n.d.

Piper, Frances W. "Small Galleries in Spotlight." *Columbus Dispatch* (October 17, 1971).

———. "OSU Sculptor Helps Pierce Show Carvings in New York." *Columbus Dispatch* (February 27, 1972).

———. "Three Columbus Artists Offer Original Show at Huntington." *Columbus Dispatch* (February 11, 1973).

———. "Elijah Pierce Is Recognized for His Outstanding Carvings." *Columbus Dispatch* (November 25, 1973).

Pounds, Stephen. "'Uncola Man' Geoffrey Holder Admires Elijah Pierce Artwork." *Columbus Citizen-Journal* (November 16, 1983).

"Primitive Folk Artist Works with Pocket Knife." Carrollton, Georgia: *Carrollton Times Georgian* (February 9, 1985).

"Rare Exhibition to Feature Works of Columbus Artists." *Columbus Call and Post* (January 3, 1981).

"Readying Pierce Exhibit at Columbus Museum of Art." *Columbus Citizen-Journal* (June 27, 1985).

Reilly, Robert. "Artist's Life Begins at 80 for These Two." *Philadelphia Inquirer*, date unknown (probably December 1972). Archives, Pennsylvania Academy of the Fine Arts.

"Rhodes, Pierce Will Be Honored." *Columbus Citizen-Journal* (October 9, 1982).

Ricco, Roger, and Frank Maresca, with Julia Weissman. *American Primitive: Discoveries in Folk Sculpture*. New York: Alfred A. Knopf, 1988.

Roberts, Norma J. "Focus on the Collection." *Columbus Museum of Art Calendar* (February 1986).

Rumford, Beatrix T., and Caroline J. Weekley. *Treasures of American Art from the Abby Aldrich Rockefeller Folk Art Center*. Boston, Toronto, and London: Little Brown & Co. in association with the Colonial Williamsburg Foundation, 1989.

Rosenak, Jan, and Chuck Rosenak. *Museum of American Folk Art Encyclopedia of Twentieth-Century American Folk Art and Artists*. New York: Abbeville Press, 1990.

Russell, John. "A Remarkable Exhibition of Black Folk Art in America." *New York Times* (February 14, 1982).

Schwindler, Gary. "Elijah Pierce (1892–1984)." *Dialogue: An Art Journal* (January–February 1986): 18–19.

———. "New Traditions/Non-Traditions: Contemporary Folk Art in Ohio." *Dialogue: An Art Journal* (March–April 1990): 27–28.

———. "Museum Profile: The Columbus Museum of Art." *Folk Art Messenger* (Spring 1991): 8–9.

Seibert, Margaret Armbrust. Transcriptions of selected audiotaped interviews with Elijah Pierce, 1980, 1981. Archives, Columbus Museum of Art.

———. Transcription of excerpt from audiotaped interview with Estelle Pierce, 1991. Archives, Columbus Museum of Art.

Severinghaus, J. Walter, Dorothy C. Miller, and Robert Rosenblum. *Art at Work: The Chase Manhattan Collection*. New York: E. P. Dutton, 1984.

Shonkweiler, Bonny. "City Mourns Loss of Many During 1984." *Columbus Citizen-Journal* (December 30, 1984).

Siporin, Steve. *American Folk Masters*. New York: Harry N. Abrams, 1992.

Smith, Starita. "OSU to Show Art of 7 Local Blacks." *Columbus Dispatch* (February 10, 1985).

————. "Museums, Collectors Preserve the Art Legacy of Elijah Pierce." *Columbus Dispatch Neighbor News Central* (February 10, 1988).

"Smithsonian Exhibits Pierce's Works." *Columbus Dispatch* (December 27, 1981).

Southern Ohio Museum and Cultural Center. *Touching Wood* (exh. cat.). Introduction, Jean Robertson McDaniel and Craig McDaniel. Portsmouth, Ohio, 1982.

Setagaya Art Museum. *Naivety in Art* (exh. cat.). Essays, Herbert Waide Hemphill, Jr., and Gail M. Mishkin. Tokyo, 1986.

Taylor, Michael. "Woodcarver Just Listens to Nancy." *Columbus Citizen-Journal* (January 25, 1982).

Thomas, Robert D., ed. "Columbus' Famous Woodcarver." *Columbus Unforgettables: A Collection of Columbus Yesterdays and Todays*. Columbus: Robert D. Thomas, 1983.

"3 Blacks Receive Governor's Awards." *Columbus Call and Post* (March 6, 1982).

"To Exhibit Carvings—Woodcarver Elijah Pierce." *Columbus Call and Post* (July 1, 1978).

Treadwell, David. "Sermons in Wood." *Ebony Magazine* (July 1974): 67–74.

Tully, Judd. "Black Folk Art in America." *Flash Art* (November 1983): 34.

UWM Art Museum. *Personal Intensity: Artists in Spite of the Mainstream* (exh. cat.). Essay, Frank C. Lewis. The University of Wisconsin, Milwaukee, 1991.

WCBE-FM, 90.5 Classic Radio Program Guide (January 1990): cover, p. 2.

Wessa, Pauline. "Franklin U. Exhibiting 43 Black Artists' Work from Lewis Collection." *Columbus Citizen-Journal* (January 13, 1981).

Williams, Mary Ann, producer, host. *Afromation*. Interviews with Elijah Pierce, Aminah Robinson, and Robert Stull, October 12, 1973. Columbus: WOSU-TV and Department of Black Studies, Ohio State University, 1973.

Williams, Mary Ann, producer. *Elijah Pierce, Woodcarver*. Columbus: Department of Black Studies, Ohio State University (film, 29 minutes), 1976.

Williams, Regina. "Woodcarver Content to Walk with God, Carve His Images." *Columbus Call and Post* (February 7, 1981).

Wilson, Judith. "Black Folk Art: A Vision Endures." *Museum* (March–April 1982): 39–41.

Wolf, Jeffrey. Transcription of selected portions of audiotaped interview with Elijah Pierce, 1974. Archives, Columbus Museum of Art.

"Woodcarver Elijah Pierce." *Winston-Salem Journal* (December 28, 1981).

"Woodcarver Elijah Pierce Shapes a Legend." *Columbus Dispatch* (September 20, 1982).

"Woodcarver Honored." *Columbus Dispatch* (April 13, 1980).

"Woodcarver Pierce to Be Featured at Crafts Fest." *Columbus Call and Post* (October 6, 1983).

"Woodcarver Wins National Fellowship." *Columbus Dispatch* (June 1, 1982).

"Work Admired." *Columbus Citizen-Journal* (June 15, 1974).

"Yule Art Fair Set at Beatty Center." *Columbus Call and Post* (December 30, 1972).

Zanesville Art Center. *The Painted Woodcarvings of Elijah Pierce* (exh. bro.). Zanesville, Ohio, 1981.

"Zoo Event Features Wood Art." *Columbus Dispatch* (September 21, 1978).

LENDERS TO THE EXHIBITION

ARIENT FAMILY COLLECTION

JERROLD A. BASOFIN

EDWARD V. BLANCHARD AND M. ANNE HILL

JILL AND SHELDON BONOVITZ

GENE BOUGHTON

ROGER BROWN

JOANNE BUZZETTA

HOWARD AND MIMI CHENFELD

ROSE CHENFELD

DEWELL DAVIS

SARAH AND JOHN FREEMAN

ESTELLE E. FRIEDMAN

LEE GARRETT

MR. AND MRS. WILLIAM GILMORE

GITTER-YELEN FOLK ART COLLECTION

ROBERT M. GREENBERG

MR. AND MRS. RICHARD E. GUGGENHEIM

JULIE HALL

MICHAEL D. HALL

DENNIS AND MARTHA HAYES

BRETT AND VICCI JAFFE

JANET FLEISHER GALLERY, PHILADELPHIA

ROGER MCLANE

DR. AND MRS. GERHARD E. MARTIN

GEORGE H. MEYER

MIAMI UNIVERSITY ART MUSEUM, OXFORD, OHIO

HARVEY S. SHIPLEY MILLER AND J. RANDALL PLUMMER

MILWAUKEE ART MUSEUM

MIKE AND CINDY NOLAND

DR. ALAN JAY OMINSKY

ALEXIS G. PIERCE

MR. AND MRS. MEYER P. POTAMKIN

MR. AND MRS. ANDRÉ PREVIN

AMINAH AND SYDNEY ROBINSON

THE SCHUMACHER GALLERY, CAPITAL UNIVERSITY,
    COLUMBUS, OHIO

GEORGE AND MIRIAM VAN WALLEGHEM

DR. SIRI VON REIS

WEXNER CENTER FOR THE ARTS,
    THE OHIO STATE UNIVERSITY, COLUMBUS, OHIO

LANFORD WILSON

JEFFREY WOLF AND JEANY NISENHOLZ-WOLF

MARGOT WOLF

PRIVATE COLLECTIONS